Leadership
and the
Bush Presidency

PRAEGER SERIES IN PRESIDENTIAL STUDIES

Robert E. Denton, Jr., General Editor

Leadership and the Bush Presidency

PRUDENCE OR DRIFT IN AN ERA OF CHANGE?

Edited by
RYAN J. BARILLEAUX
and
MARY E. STUCKEY

Praeger Series in Presidential Studies

Westport, Connecticut
London

Library of Congress Cataloging-in-Publication Data

Leadership and the Bush presidency : prudence or drift in an era of
  change? / edited by Ryan J. Barilleaux and Mary E. Stuckey.
      p.   cm. — (Praeger series in presidential studies, ISSN 1062–0931)
  Includes bibliographical references and index.
  ISBN 0–275–94418–2 (alk. paper)
    1. United States—Politics and government—1989– 2. Bush, George,
  1924– .   I. Barilleaux, Ryan J. II. Stuckey, Mary E.
  III. Series.
  E881.L43   1992
  973.928—dc20   92–12107

British Library Cataloguing in Publication Data is available.

Library of Congress Catalog Card Number: 92–12107
ISBN: 0–275–94418–2
ISSN: 1062–0931

First published in 1992

Praeger Publishers, 88 Post Road West, Westport, CT 06881
An imprint of Greenwood Publishing Group, Inc.

Printed in the United States of America

The paper used in this book complies with the
Permanent Paper Standard issued by the National
Information Standards Organization (Z39.48–1984).

10 9 8 7 6 5 4 3 2 1

To the faculty
and alumni
of
"Camp Dartmouth"

Contents

Tables

Preface

This book had its origins in a week-long conference held at Dartmouth College in the summer of 1988. That meeting, jointly sponsored by the American Political Science Association (APSA) and the Spoor Dialogues on Leadership, brought together over forty individuals, most of them from academia, to discuss recent research and teaching in the area of political leadership. The conference, which its participants affectionately began to call "Camp Dartmouth," was for many of us a rare opportunity to engage in extended discussions of similar interests among ourselves and with the distinguished group of lecturers assembled for the conference. Many of the participants at "Camp Dartmouth" shared an interest in presidential leadership and formed a continuing network for conversations and research on this topic. Over the past several years, these endeavors have included informal meetings at professional conferences, exchanges of ideas and research materials, a panel at the 1991 meetings of the APSA, and this book. Of course, we realized that our group did not exhaust expertise in the field, and we reached out for assistance from others, especially younger scholars, working in the area of presidential leadership.

We are indebted to many people and organizations for this book. First, we must thank the APSA and the Spoor Dialogues for making the original conference possible. We wish to thank as well Richard Winter and his staff at the Nelson Rockefeller Center of Dartmouth College, which organized and coordinated the event. We wish also to thank those who served as the faculty of "Camp Dartmouth": Fred I. Greenstein, Erwin Hargrove, William Riker, Evelyn Fink, Bernard Bass, Roger Masters, and Denis Sullivan. Of course, we cannot forget our fellow participants in the conference who made it especially enjoyable.

We also want to thank Bob Denton, the general editor of the Praeger Series in the Presidential Studies, Anne Kiefer, our editor, Stephen Hatem, production editor, and the entire staff at Praeger Publishers for their support and assistance. This is not the first book that either of the editors has done with Praeger; their professional and courteous handling of authors and books makes it easy to come back again.

Every edited volume is obviously a group effort, but we as editors take final responsibility for this book. While the analyses presented in the various chapters reflect the judgment of the individual contributors, as editors we have endeavored to make sure that each chapter is clear and to the point. If the reader should disagree with something that follows, that is a matter for the author in question. The organization, selection, and presentation of the book is the editors' fault or achievement, whichever the case may be.

Introduction

George Bush sought the presidency as the political heir of Ronald Reagan. He promised continuity with the president who had charted a "new direction in American politics," rather than proclaiming he would set out his own course for the nation. With Bush's election, it seemed that the United States would experience at least four more years of Reaganism, only now without Reagan. The new president represented himself as a "kinder, gentler" version of his former boss, and no great changes loomed on the horizon. Many observers predicted a caretaker presidency and expected an unexciting term for President Bush, who was expected to remain in his predecessor's shadow.

Four years later, however, the world seems a very different place. First, the Soviet Union withdrew from eastern Europe. By 1990, Germany was reunited and non-communist governments were installed in Hungary, Czechoslovakia, Poland, and other nations. In 1990 and 1991, the United States led a coalition of states, including the Soviet Union, that suppressed and ultimately overturned the invasion of Kuwait by Iraq. Finally, in 1991, the Soviet Union itself came apart in a heady three-week period that began with an unsuccessful coup against President Mikhail Gorbachev and ended with the dissolution of the centralized Soviet regime and independence for the Balkan republics. A loose (and perhaps ephemeral) Commonwealth of Independent States was created.

Through it all, there stood George Bush, sometimes participant, sometimes observer, sometimes shaper of the major events of the period. He was castigated as a bystander to the liberation of Eastern Europe, although his role in facilitating German unification was not insubstantial. In the war against Iraq, he appeared as the unbending apostle of Kuwait's sovereignty, commanding a major diplomatic and military effort to right an unforgivable wrong. In the days of upheaval in the Soviet Union, he played the calm statesman who could articulate finely nuanced policy positions and who announced to the world the return of Gorbachev from captivity and the failure of the coup. His performance in office during these unstable times gave him the image of a confident expert in foreign affairs. The president's popularity remained strong, and Democratic challengers for the 1992 election were hard to find.

But there is more to the story of the Bush presidency than this record of apparent foreign policy achievements. In domestic affairs, the president seems to have little or no agenda. He has offered few concrete proposals to Congress, he has had to concede much to the Democrats in framing a budget, and he repeatedly saw his plan for cuts in the capital gains tax frustrated on Capitol Hill. Even in foreign affairs, there were questions about the ultimate effect of the war against Iraq, with Saddam Hussein still in power well after the war's end. Others refuted the wisdom of the administration's maintenance of close relations with the People's Republic of China in the wake of the 1989 suppression of the pro-democracy demonstrators in Beijing's Tiananmen Square. Finally, although Mr. Bush derided concern with what he calls "the vision thing," a number of critics wondered aloud whether the president and his advisers had any real idea of where they were headed.

Clearly, much had happened during the Bush years, but how much of it was owing to presidential leadership and how much could be ascribed to the flow of events? As Mr. Bush headed for the 1992 election, the question that had dominated his accession to office and the first months of his tenure remained: Is George Bush a leader, or has he allowed the United States to drift toward disaster?

Pundits and politicians have given considerable attention to the issue of George Bush's leadership. The president's opponents charge him with paying undue attention to opinion polls, focusing on symbol rather than substance (e.g., his attention to the flag-burning issue), and allowing the nation to drift, especially in domestic matters, at a time that they argue so loudly demands leadership from the White House. In response, Mr. Bush's defenders applaud him for his prudence in the face of international instability, resolution in the face of Iraqi aggression, realistic approach to dealing with the nation's problems in a time of tight resources, and strong public support. These points, they argue, are evidence of the president's abilities.

The issue of leadership and the Bush presidency is one that has relevance both now and for the future. The world faces the prospect of building a post–Cold War and post-Soviet international order, while at home the nation may soon face a time of reckoning on budgetary and domestic affairs. President Bush's conduct of office and his approach to leadership matter today, but they will also affect his successors as well as the larger American political system.

LEADERSHIP AND THE AMERICAN PRESIDENCY

Leadership is a subject of enduring interest to those who study American politics, perhaps because our political system seems designed to inhibit its exercise. In a system of "separated institutions sharing powers" (Neustadt, 1990, 29), it is difficult for anyone to give clear and consistent direction to national policy. The American republic works well to prevent the tyranny its founders feared, but in the process it appears to leave no officer or organ of government truly in charge. When circumstances demand leadership, however, attention usually turns to the presidency.

At crucial moments in the history of the republic (e.g., the Civil War), and especially in the twentieth century, calls for national direction have tended to focus on the presidency. In Congress, the very term "leadership" calls to mind not grand statesmanship, but the not-too-powerful officials who head party caucuses and committees. One of the most famous books on the national legislature touts "courage" rather than leadership as the chief virtue in a member of Congress (Kennedy, 1960). There has been attention to leadership by those in appointed executive positions, such as Alexander Hamilton or George Marshall, but these officials are always on a leash that leads back to the Oval Office. There is little sustained discussion of national leadership in the judiciary, because the courts provide such infertile ground for those who would exercise national leadership. Judges have no constituency, spend all their time in the somewhat obscure world of lawyers, and are ultimately passive because they are bound to cases and have little opportunity for initiative. Even when the Supreme Court attempts to take the lead in shaping policy, as it did in the realm of civil liberties during the years of the Warren Court, it is generally confined to a narrow band of issues and problems.

The presidency, however, is where many hopes rest when we speak of leadership. Whether because they wish to do so or because no one else really can, presidents face substantial pressures to provide direction in setting national goals and policies, marshalling whatever efforts and coalitions are necessary to achieve these ends, and moving the nation toward some well-defined purpose. As James David Barber put it: "What all this means is that the President's *main* responsibilities reach far beyond administering the Executive Branch or commanding the armed forces. The White House is first and foremost a place of public leadership" (1977, 5).

Just what is presidential leadership, and how do we know it when we see it? The answer is not obvious, for leadership is a concept that has at least two meanings. The first is an instrumental one. One of the leading textbooks available on the presidency at this time has as its title *Presidential Leadership*

(Edwards and Wayne, 1990), although it has difficulty defining its subject. As the authors state in their introduction, "We want to know whether the president can influence the actions and attitudes of others and affect the output of government" (p. 13). Influence, then, is what many observers mean when they speak of leadership—charting a course, doing what it takes to get there, and then succeeding or failing in doing so.

But does influence exhaust the subject? For many analysts it does not. Is not the particular direction in which a president wants to move the nation, and even the methods he uses to effect that move, also relevant? Richard Neustadt believes that to be the case. He, like many who comment on leadership, also imbues the term with a normative meaning. In his reflections on evaluating presidential leadership, Neustadt poses the following as his primary question: "What were [the president's] purposes and did these run with or against the grain of history; how relevant were they to what would happen in his time?" (1990, 167). Barber, in his assessment of presidents, asks whether an incumbent's actions correspond to the "climate of expectations" of the time (1977, 9).

Bert Rockman, in *The Leadership Question*, defines the issue of direction in a slightly different way. He sees a dilemma for presidents in their need to balance governability and legitimacy (1985, 2). The chief executive must not only lead, he contends, but do so toward ends and by means that are consistent with American constitutional democracy. In other words, the issue of leadership is not merely one of whether the president has clear goals and can get to them, but more importantly, whether the chief executive is taking the nation in the right direction ("with or against the grain of history" and relevant to the times) and by the right route (legitimacy).

To assess whether George Bush or any other chief executive has exercised leadership, it is necessary to examine both the influence and the direction toward which that influence is applied. Certainly, there will be disagreements about how much influence President Bush or any other incumbent has had in any situation. There will also be controversy over whether the president's goals were appropriate ones. But these problems should inform rather than paralyze those interested in the subject of leadership. In the pages that follow, there will be a number of divergent views about influence, purpose, and means. Such variety is a strength rather than a flaw of this collection, because it contributes to a better understanding of George Bush, his conduct of office, and the institution of the presidency. Presidential leadership is complex, and our studies of it should reflect that fact, rather than try to ignore it.

THE BUSH PRESIDENCY

While every presidency is fraught with surprises, the coming of the Bush presidency in 1989 certainly did not portend what was ahead: that the new incumbent would be witness to historic change in the international arena; that the candidate given to speaking in a mixture of preppie slang and bureaucratic jargon would become pastmaster of the clear, informative press conference; that the man derided as a "lap dog" and a "wimp" would go to war so aggressively and so successfully; or that the rather bland successor to the Great Communicator would himself achieve impressive public support in opinion polls. Despite this surface success, however, the four years of Mr. Bush's term have raised a number of questions about his leadership abilities, about the office that he occupies, and about the role of the presidency in the American political system. Moreover, there is the question of the legacy of the Bush presidency for the future of the office and for government in the United States.

The chapters in this book address these questions and the surprises of the Bush years. Each chapter has its own particular angle and focus, but all are united by a core of driving questions: Has George Bush exercised presidential leadership? In what ways? To what ends? What will be the legacy of his actions for future presidents, and for the larger national and international political systems?

To address these issues, we have divided the book into five sections. Part 1 provides a sense of perspective for the chapters that follow. It contains two chapters that look at leadership, at Mr. Bush's style of conducting his presidency, and at the context in which he is operating. Part 2 examines questions of whether and how George Bush has provided leadership within the institutions of the American political system. We give specific attention to the executive branch, Congress, and American federalism. In Part 3, we move out to the larger political system. Here, the contributors turn their attention to the president's relations with public opinion, with his own Republican Party, and with conservatives. Part 4 takes up the president as policy leader in three areas: domestic affairs, foreign policy, and civil rights. The last part of the book turns directly to the future. In Chapter 11, Norman Thomas addresses issues of accountability that are present in this administration and that will continue to be important to future presidents. It provides a forward-looking end to the series of chapters on President Bush and the future of the office and the American political system.

The book concludes with a chapter in which the editors draw together the points made by the various authors and speculate on a more comprehensive answer to the questions posed here. As the presidency progresses through its third century, it is important that we develop a better understanding of this office on which we have so often pinned our hopes. For better or worse, the chief executive is our foremost political leader, and President Bush occupies that position at a significant time in American and world history. We owe ourselves a careful examination of leadership and the Bush presidency.

REFERENCES

Barber, James David. 1977. *The Presidential Character*, rev. edn. New York: Prentice Hall.

Edwards, George C., and Stephen J. Wayne. 1990. *Presidential Leadership*, rev. edn. New York: St. Martin's Press.

Kennedy, John F. 1960. *Profiles in Courage*. New York: Harper.

Neustadt, Richard. 1990. *Presidential Power and the Modern Presidents*. New York: Free Press.

Rockman, Bert. 1985. *The Leadership Question*. New York: Praeger.

*Leadership
and the
Bush Presidency*

PART 1

IS PRESIDENT BUSH A LEADER?

Chapter 1

George Bush and the Changing Context of Presidential Leadership

RYAN J. BARILLEAUX

What kind of leader is George Bush? Is he a leader at all? These questions are asked of every chief executive. They strike at the heart of the contemporary presidency, which, as Franklin Roosevelt once asserted, is "primarily a place of moral leadership." Americans expect their presidents to be leaders. "Great" presidents are those believed to have been so, and aspirants for the office routinely promise to offer the virtues necessary to guide the nation through the difficult years ahead.

Just as candidates offer themselves as the individuals best suited to the times in which they run for office, so are incumbent presidents assessed according to whether they provided the kind of leadership necessary for their years in power. To that extent, presidential leadership is bound up with the circumstances of an administration rather than by some universal standard for all chief executives at all times. As Barbara Kellerman has described the task, "Good leadership is said to be the result of good fit between leaders and followers and between leaders and the tasks at hand" (1986, 349). In the same regard, Richard Neustadt asks of each president he would appraise, "What were his purposes and did these run with or against the grain of history; how relevant were they to what would happen in his time?" (1990, 167).

Evaluating a president's putative leadership requires that we make reference to the particular time in which the incumbent lives and works. George Bush's tenure in office has not taken place in a vacuum, and it cannot be assessed as such. At the same time, however, we cannot allow context to overwhelm us and conclude that each officeholder is merely a victim of circumstances. The presidency is a malleable office that clearly allows chief executives to make of it what they will.

The circumstances of George Bush's presidency have been peculiar, perhaps unique in modern history. The Bush years have seen the concurrence of more significant transitions than have taken place most eras. The end of the Cold War and the collapse of the Soviet Union presented President Bush with opportunities and challenges of world-historic proportions. At home, an environment of competing and seemingly entrenched coalitions in the White House and on Capitol Hill has made domestic governance all the more difficult.

How does George Bush's leadership style fit these times? That question is crucial to assessing his effectiveness as a leader. To answer it, we must measure the "fit" among the three elements of leadership. To do so requires a good sense of each. For all the difficulties involved in taking stock of the personality, worldview, and mind of an individual, or of getting a fix on why followers follow, it seems easier to get a sense of a leader and followers than to describe the situation in which attempts at leadership take place.

But what aspects of the situation should we consider in measuring the fit of leadership? That issue is the focus of this chapter, which will attempt to shed light on the issue of George Bush's leadership by outlining the context of his presidency. Context in turn will better enable us to "place" a president and assess the goals and means of leadership in the White House. Then it can offer some preliminary conclusions on the fit between Mr. Bush and the tasks at hand.

The environment in which a president operates is complex but not incomprehensible. Several analysts have offered snapshots of presidential context, but there have been few attempts to develop a rounded and usable sketch of the chief executive's working world. Constitutional analysts such as E. S. Corwin (1984), Richard Pious (1979), and Harold Hongju Koh (1990) have attempted to place the president in the American constitutional–legal order. Institutional analysts such as Fred Greenstein (1978; 1988) and this author (Barilleaux, 1988a) have focused on the development and institutionalization of the presidential office. Political analysts such as Richard Neustadt (1990) and Stephen Skowronek (1990) have attempted to describe the political situation of the chief executive, while Erwin Hargrove and Michael Nelson (1984) have discerned a cyclical pattern that has marked the environment of presidential policy making in the twentieth century. Comparative analysts such as Bert Rockman (1985, 1990) have attempted to employ a transnational perspective, although their work has tended to concentrate on structural constants (the tripartite system of American government, an anti-statist political culture, etc.) that offer little real help in taking stock of the leadership context of any individual president. Richard Rose (1991) looks outward to the president's international context, but his analysis is driven by an overwhelming message that "the international system is stronger than the president." His analysis is thus of limited value to those who do not share his assumptions and his agenda. In sum, we have no general model of presidential context to assist our assessment of the tasks at hand faced by a president.

Building on the work of these scholars, however, we can sketch a model of presidential context that is relevant to evaluating leadership in the White House. What we need is a sense of the chief executive's environment that is coherent but sophisticated enough to distinguish between contextual factors that change and those that endure.

An effective approach is one that sees the chief executive at the center of a series of concentric circles, with immediate and shifting short-term environmental factors (which usually seem most pressing to those in the White House and those watching presidents) near the center. More fundamental and more enduring factors are farther out, forming the background of the president's environment.

An appropriate metaphor for presidential context, then, is the Ptolemaic model of the universe. In many ways, the old geocentric image of the heavens, familiar to Aristotle and Shakespeare (see Craig and Bevington, 1973; Tillyard, 1942), gives us a coherent view of the presidential world picture. Our Ptolemaic model of presidential context consists of three spheres: the constants of the presidential environment (farthest from the center); several long-term dynamics of context; and a number of short-term dynamics shaping the tasks at hand (closest to the center). Every president works at the center of this environment, although the precise context varies from one incumbent to another.

THE PRESIDENTIAL WORLD PICTURE

The Constants

Times and circumstances differ, but certain constants shape the working world of chief executives in the most profound and most subtle ways. They are the firmament of leadership context. Chief among these constants is the international state system in which the United States plays a part. The system operates under a condition of anarchy because there is no overarching world government, and it is dominated by territorial states that jealously guard their legal sovereignty and political independence (Kellerman and Barilleaux, 1991). The primary principle governing state action is that of self-help. As the chief architects and supervisors of foreign policy, presidents direct U.S. relations with the other components of this system.

In the domestic realm, the most enduring aspect of the president's environment is the American constitutional system. "The constitutional separation of powers . . . links presidents past and present in a timeless and constant struggle over the definition of their institutional prerogatives," observes Skowronek (1990, 117), because "the basic structure of presidential action has remained essentially the same." Executive power in this system is significant but limited. Nevertheless, presidents often struggle against the strictures of the system because the Constitution creates a set of roles—commander-in-chief, chief diplomat, and others—that encourage officeholders to try to expand their power. In the end, however, while the power that goes with the Oval Office is much greater today than it was a century ago, the structural outlines of American government remain unchanged.

Formal structure is complemented by American political culture, which shapes the way the nation thinks about and behaves in political affairs (see Devine, 1972; Hargrove and Nelson, 1984; Kellerman and Barilleaux, 1991; Lipset, 1979; Rockman, 1985). American political culture is characterized by an emphasis on liberty and political equality, the rule of law, a sense of political efficacy, and a general belief in the exceptional nature of the American system. Furthermore, as an extension of the core belief in liberty, citizens generally accept market-oriented approaches to settling questions of economics (capitalism), politics (e.g., the heavy use of polls), and even culture (e.g., good taste and manners defined by what is popular). While not determining the complete shape of presidential action, this culture frames what policies and initiatives are acceptable on the part of the chief executive.

Long-Term Dynamics

The intermediate sphere of presidential context consists of three long-term dynamics: institutional context, domestic political context, and international political context. These elements change over decades and thus influence the tasks at hand for each incumbent.

Institutional Context

The presidency has undergone considerable evolution since 1789, moving through three phases: traditional, modern, and postmodern (Barilleaux, 1988a). The traditional presidency encompassed most of the history of the office, lasting from its creation through the Hoover administration. It was marked by the presidency as an office that took second place behind a powerful Congress, although American history was often punctuated with flashes of presidential aggressiveness and even dominance (the Jacksonian era, the Civil War).

The modern presidency, the legacy of Franklin Delano Roosevelt, was marked by a growing presidentialism in American government: Political power and public expectations increasingly focused on the White House, and the president employed broad foreign-policy powers and an aggressive legislative agenda to steer national policy. Many of our conceptions of presidential power and the workings of the tripartite system, such as Neustadt's analysis, are based in this stage of the office's evolution.

The modern presidency gradually gave way to a postmodern office in the years after the fall of Richard Nixon (an institutional interregnum occurred in the Ford-Carter years), with Ronald Reagan giving final shape to the revised institution. Six major characteristics mark the newest phase in the life of the presidency:

1. *The revival of presidential prerogative power*—includes expanded unilateral executive power over war-making and arms-control negotiations (the weakness of the War Powers Resolution, the use of parallel unilateral policy declarations to make arms-control policy), new budgetary prerogatives (the institution of "top-down" budgeting and Office of Management and Budget [OMB] dominance within the executive branch), and greater White House control over administrative rulemaking (through the administrative clearance process).

2. *Governing through public politics*—chief executives attempting to govern by direct communication with the public and control of their image, as in Ronald Reagan's frequent televised addresses to the nation or George Bush's almost unceasing news conferences.

3. *The rise of a presidential general secretariat*—the executive office has become a big and bureaucratic central staff through which the chief executive directs and supervises the work of the executive branch, with the concomitant requirement that presidents increasingly focus on White House management in order to successfully run the larger government.

4. *Vicarious policy making*—the president's influence is now often felt through the actions and decisions of his appointees, especially those in the judiciary and on regulatory commissions, an influence that was always important but has grown even more so in this period of the "regulatory state" (Seidman and Gilmour, 1986) and effectively permanent judicial activism.

5. *The president as chief whip in Congress*—a postmodern president must act in the fashion of a legislative whip in order to build coalitions in a Congress marked by decentralization and fragmentation of power.

6. *The new vice presidency*—since the 1970s, vice presidents have played a larger role in the White House, backed by a large and sometimes influential staff, than did their predecessors in the nation's second office.

Domestic Political Context

The domestic political context in which a president operates is complex, but it can be characterized by two long-term dynamics: the rise and fall of domestic political coalitions, and cyclical patterns in domestic policy making. Each of these variables affects the exercise of presidential leadership.

Long-term domestic coalitions ("regimes"). Stephen Skowronek argues that a central feature of the president's political context is "the changing shape of the political regimes that have organized state-society relations for broad periods of American history, and it links presidents past and present at parallel junctures of 'political time' " (1990, 117–18). He discusses the rise of new and dominant political coalitions (regimes), their maintenance, and eventual decline. He examines presidential leadership tasks and strategies through this lens, allowing him to compare those engaged in regime construction (Andrew Jackson, Franklin Roosevelt, and, implicitly, Ronald Reagan), managers of ongoing regimes (Polk and Kennedy), and those attempting to govern in enervated regimes (Pierce and Carter).

According to Skowronek, regime builders are thrust into office because of upheaval in governmental control (essentially a failure of the old coalition to maintain authority). They are then faced with the "fundamentals of political regeneration—institutional reconstruction and party building" (1990, 122). Franklin Roosevelt's institutional legacy was the establishment of the executive office of the president, which gave the chief executive greater policy-making capacity. His "Grand Coalition" of labor, ethnic groups, and the "Solid South" made the Democratic Party dominant in national politics for much of the twentieth century.

Regime managers face a very different task.

In an established regime, the majority party president comes to power as a representative of the dominant political alliance and is expected to offer a representative's service in delegate style. . . . The leader is challenged . . . to complete the unfinished business, adapt the agenda to changing times, and defuse the potentially explosive choices among competing obligations. (1990, 130–31)

Presidents in an enervated regime face "the truly impossible leadership situation . . . that of the affiliated leader in a vulnerable regime" (1990, 158). The prospective leader in such a context attempts to govern without "any clear warrant for action." If the president tries to affirm the commitments of the regime (as did Pierce), he appears to be a symptom of the old order's problems. If he attempts to distance himself (as did Carter), he is left without a political base. Skowronek concludes: "Either way the president becomes the foil for another great repudiator" who can build a new regime (1990, 158).

This approach is appealing because it allows leadership analysts to make sense of the domestic tasks at hand in a way that is not only coherent but allows for comparison within parallel situations (e.g., regime managers against one another) and across different periods of "political time" (e.g., the problems and opportunities of regime builders versus those in enervated regimes). But it is not without problems.

One flaw is that Skowronek does not really deal with changes in other parts of the president's environment beyond "regime" status—institutional development, changes in the international arena, and so on—that affect leadership responsibilities and opportunities. An even bigger problem is that Skowronek seems to assume that a single dominant regime is the norm in

American politics. Indeed, writing about the 1980 election in an early version of his analysis, Skowronek (1984, 130) characterized the Republicans' capture of the White House and the Senate as an interregnum between regimes (although in later versions he tends to portray Ronald Reagan as a regime builder). This point reveals an underlying assumption about the nature of American government that may be anachronistic. We live in an age of divided government and need explanations of our politics that can do more than speak of how things are supposed to work.

Divided government means that we may have to alter the way Skowronek characterizes presidents. He distinguishes presidents who are "regime insiders" (e.g., Kennedy) from "regime outsiders" (e.g., Eisenhower), based on their status in the dominant coalition. But who is an insider or an outsider in an era of apparently permanently divided government?

In order to deal with this confusion, we must refine the concept of political time. Divided government can be best understood as a situation of competing regimes or coalitions. In our age, the Democratic coalition has established a firm grip on Congress (at least the House), while the Republicans appear to have changed the locks on the White House. The idea of competing regimes means that two political coalitions are vying for control of national politics, with each having achieved partial victory by securing dominance in one branch of our separated institutions. In a situation such as this one, there is little relevance to a distinction between regime "insiders" and "outsiders"—every president belongs to one of the competing coalitions.

Political scientists and other commentators have generally had a hard time coming to terms with the fact of divided government and describe it almost universally in negative terms. It is said to induce "gridlock," "paralysis," and other ills. But all of these complaints are based on the assumption that the constitutional system did not intend for governmental power to be divided. Skowronek seems to believe that the constitutional framers really did not mean it when they spoke of separation of powers.

The framers did indeed mean what they said. Divided government certainly makes programmatic and efficient policy making nearly impossible, but there is nothing unnatural about it. Indeed, it is consistent with Willmoore Kendall's characterization of the constitutional system as tapping "two majorities" in the nation (1960). When he wrote over three decades ago, Kendall responded to those critics of Congress who castigated the legislature for failing to support the only representative of the whole nation, the president. His answer was that the U.S. Constitution created a government of two majorities (legislative and executive), each of which was a legitimate expression of popular will.

Consistent with Kendall's analysis, we can see divided government as a manifestation of the two majorities, that is, of two regimes competing for dominance in American politics. Some observers may wish to regard this as a temporary situation that will be corrected when one coalition is finally able to assert its control across the board, but such an attitude will not help us to understand contemporary politics. Divided government has become too common a feature of our system to continue treating it as an aberration.

What does all this mean for the concept of political time? It means that the leadership analyst must determine whether the president is part of an environment characterized by competing regimes (e.g., Reagan, Bush) or by the existence of a monopoly regime (e.g., Franklin Roosevelt, Kennedy). Under a monopoly regime, Skowronek's analysis of regimes remains useful as it stands. But in the context of divided government, the situations of maintenance and enervation may be merged for presidents of either regime. Leaders from either party will be faced with the task of serving the coalition, adapting to change, and trying to balance between identification with their regime's problems and keeping too much distance from their coalition. For example, a regime-manager president who faces a Congress controlled by the other coalition (e.g., George Bush) must come to terms with his opposition without losing his own base. A regime-manager whose party controls Congress (e.g., a Democratic successor to Bush) still cannot take much for granted, for his coalition has only a tentative hold on the White House and his regime's congressional party is relatively free of presidential control.

Cycles of domestic policy making. Where does an individual president fit into the ebb and flow of public policy? Some presidents, such as Franklin Roosevelt, Lyndon Johnson, and Ronald Reagan, are associated with significant domestic policy change. Other administrations, such as those of Dwight Eisenhower and Jimmy Carter, are noted for stability and even frustration in policy. But is the president alone responsible for the record of his years in office? Or is the policy context something that influences White House leadership?

Hargrove and Nelson have discerned a cyclical pattern that has marked the succession of presidents since the time of Theodore Roosevelt. Domestic policy, they argue, "can be understood in terms of recurring cycles of electoral political competition and public policy making within the bounds of American political culture. The focus of these cycles has been the presidency" (1984, 67). The heart of each of these cycles has been a "presidency of achievement . . . in which great bursts of creative legislative activity occurred that altered the role of government in society in the service of some combination of purpose values of liberty and equality and process values of higher law and popular sovereignty" (1984, 67). These included parts of the administrations of Wilson, Franklin Roosevelt, Johnson, and Reagan.

Presidencies of achievement are bracketed by two other kinds of administrations. Before achievement, there is the "presidency of preparation" (perhaps more than one), in which the groundwork for change is laid but the incumbent lacks the political base that enables him to see it to fruition (Teddy Roosevelt and Kennedy). After achievement, there is the "presidency of consolidation" (again, perhaps more than one) "in which reform

[is] not rejected but rationalized, slowed down, and in effect legitimized" (1984, 67) for previous opponents (Harding, Coolidge, Eisenhower, and Nixon). The cycle is occasionally punctuated by the "presidency of stalemate" (Taft, Truman) in which the president's agenda bears little relation to what the public expects and is willing to accept.

Hargrove and Nelson do not see it as deterministic of White House behavior or accomplishment, but the cycles do suggest that executive leadership is heavily influenced by the "policy time" in which an incumbent operates. Presidents who attempt to act "out of turn," such as in Truman's push for the Fair Deal when the country wanted consolidation, tend to fail. Others, who have an appealing agenda but not the political support to win its passage (Kennedy, Carter), serve as presidents of preparation but cannot claim to be ones of achievement.

International Political Context

Just as no presidency takes place in a vacuum, neither does the United States exist in one. The world impinges on American government, and the president is the pivotal figure on whom U.S. foreign policy depends. Two dynamics shape the international political context of the presidency: long-term international alignments and ruling paradigms for American foreign policy.

Long-term international alignments. For a good portion of American history, this facet of the president's environment was not tremendously important. Isolationism meant that the United States remained an inward-looking nation and domestic matters took priority. But the emergence of a bipolar world in the period of the Cold War certainly altered the context of leadership, as well as the president's responsibilities and opportunities to act.

The international facet of the president's environment is now in flux. The last few years have seen the end of the Soviet empire in eastern Europe and of the monolithic Soviet Union itself, a significant improvement in relations between Washington and Moscow, and a general breakdown in the bipolar military order that prevailed for most of the post-World War II period. Depending on the events of the next few years, the United States may emerge as the only military superpower of any consequence or may retreat into isolationism. Whatever the world's political and military future, the international economy has already become a multipolar system. The United States, once dominant, is now one rich nation among many, including Japan and Germany.

No one can predict the exact shape of the "new world order" or, at this point, America's role in that future. Therefore, there is no easy way to assess the president's leadership tasks in its international context, except to focus on the chief executive's responsibility for molding an American role in the post-Cold War world and directing foreign policy toward that end.

Foreign-policy paradigms. American foreign policy has not been static. Hargrove and Nelson suggest that their cycles of domestic policy have relevance in this area, although they are vague about stating a clear pattern. They also tend to draw conclusions about a president's foreign policy from his domestic "policy time," such as in underplaying Truman's importance to postwar American foreign policy because of domestic stalemate. But the foreign-affairs presidency often works according to a different rhythm than that of domestic politics because of greater executive autonomy and the behavior of other actors in the international arena. We need a better means of accounting for the foreign policy context.

A better approach would be to recognize that to a great extent, American foreign policy has been guided by ruling paradigms that shaped policy for several decades. These paradigms define the United States' role in the world, provide perspective on the long-term international interests of the nation, and frame the national debate on the course of foreign policy.

Isolationism was the paradigm until well into the twentieth century. Theodore Roosevelt modified the overall structure by asserting the need to develop and occasionally use military power in the Americas, but he did not alter the basic approach. Wilson attempted to replace isolationism with internationalism but was defeated. Franklin Roosevelt was ultimately able to accomplish what Wilson had attempted; Truman then fundamentally altered the new paradigm by anchoring it on the doctrine of the containment of communism (Gaddis, 1982). In our time, it is not clear what the new paradigm will be. Depending on what the president is able to make of the "new world order" that appears to be emerging, it may be isolationism, a kind of internationalism, or a time of drift.

As the chief architects of American foreign policy, presidents work in the context of policy paradigms. A few presidents create new paradigms (Truman). Some attempt to modify an existing paradigm to suit new conditions or accommodate additional goals (Nixon and detente). Most live within the existing paradigm, even if they adopt different strategies and tactics for carrying it out: Eisenhower, Kennedy, and Johnson shared assumptions about the bipolar world and America's place in it; Reagan, reflecting the amended paradigm, stressed containment but also pursued detente. The chief executive's ultimate achievements or frustration are framed by these conditions and presidential responses to them.

Short-Term Dynamics

The sphere of presidential context closest to the center is made up of those short-term dynamics that are often the focus of so much attention and punditry: electoral cycles and election outcomes, indicators of the president's political support, and short-term events and circumstances. Because these factors receive probably excessive attention during a president's time in office, and even afterward, they shall be reviewed only briefly below.

Election Outcomes and Electoral Cycles

While the underlying political alignments (i.e., regimes or coalitions) of American politics wax and wane over decades, elections come and go at a much more rapid pace. The margin by which a president is elected or re-elected affects perceptions (in Congress, the bureaucracy, and even in other nations) about that incumbent's mandate to achieve his goals. Similarly, the relative success of the president's party in congressional elections affects his ability to win support for his proposals on Capitol Hill. Ronald Reagan's 1980 victory and accompanying election of a Republican-dominated Senate certainly contributed to a sense among Democrats that they had to take the new president and his agenda seriously.

Elections also shape the president's environment in another way. Congress is tied to a two-year cycle and the White House to a four-year one. These facts produce a rhythm to Washington politics that chief executives must face. As Harry McPherson recalls, Lyndon Johnson's summary assessment of the situation was that "you've only got one year" in which to achieve anything (Kernell and Popkin, 1986, 96–97). While not all presidents share Johnson's pessimism, elections affect what they can and cannot do, as well as when they are able to act.

Short-Term Political Support for the President

Indicators of short-term support for the chief executive receive considerable attention in both the media and the White House. Votes in Congress, especially the question of whether the latest action represents a victory or defeat for the president, get considerable attention in the headlines. So do the volatile and often mercurial movements in public support for the incumbent. Ours in age in which there is effectively continuous polling of presidential popularity, a fact not lost on any player in national politics. Indeed, some presidents, such as George Bush, are accused by their critics of watching the polls too closely, but public support for the chief executive is taken as a sign of and a factor in the incumbent's ability to influence events. Other omens of short-term support, including the stock market, also condition the exercise of leadership.

Short-Term Events and Circumstances

While long-term factors powerfully shape the demands and opportunities for presidential leadership, so do the fast-breaking events and circumstances that loudly call for attention. Crises, natural disasters, shifts in the economy, and various political and economic upheavals at home and abroad often dominate the headlines and White House deliberations. The president must respond to these "fires in the in-basket" as well as offer leadership that transcends the daily press of events.

But how much credit should a chief executive receive for responding to short-term problems and how much should we demand a more-forward look-ing approach to the Oval Office? In other words, how do we weigh a president putting out fires against his responsibility to build more firehouses?

A partial answer is suggested by our Ptolemaic model itself. If we under-stand that the president's environment is a complex one, we can achieve a sense of perspective on how much to expect of a chief executive. We can see presidential evaluation as a subtle exercise, not merely an easy summary judgment on greatness, near-greatness, and so on. Evaluation requires that we weigh short-term factors against less immediate but more fundamental forces swirling beyond the closest elements of the presidential world picture. As other work on evaluation has demonstrated (Barilleaux, 1985; 1988b), measuring the fit between a chief executive and the tasks at hand requires sensitivity to the conflicts and tradeoffs involved in the conduct of office as well as the fact that all things are not equal in public affairs.

Our Ptolemaic model of context is applied to individual officeholders in Table 1.1. Used with caution, it suggests how environmental factors affect evaluations of presidential leadership. For example, we can turn to the case of Harry Truman. According to the model of presidential context, he was a modern president, a regime manager, domestically a president of stalemate, and in foreign policy the Cold War architect whose reputation was tarnished by the frustrations of the Korean War. But considering the relative importance of the tasks at hand, constructing a paradigm for postwar American policy takes precedence over everything else. To that extent, Truman may not get high marks for the Fair Deal or the "forgotten war," but he deserves the impressive reputation he has acquired in recent years.

GEORGE BUSH IN PRESIDENTIAL CONTEXT

We can now return to the question of the fit between George Bush and the tasks at hand. The record of his 1988–1992 term indicates that certain elements of his leadership style are effective but that his conduct of office bears several risks.

The Bush Leadership Style

Like any other president, George Bush has brought to the Oval Office his own particular operating style (compare Jones, 1983; Kellerman and Baril-leaux, 1991). It is a complex and sometimes self-contradictory approach to leadership that consists of seven characteristics:

1. Concentration on foreign policy. The hallmark of the Bush presidency is the chief executive's overriding concern for foreign affairs. Most of his time, energy, and enthusiasm are spent on international issues. This fact is not surprising, given the president's career (at the United Nations, as U.S. representative to China, as CIA director), but certainly it is unmistakable.

Table 1.1
Presidents in Context

	HOOVER	FDR	TRUMAN	EISENHOWER	JFK	LBJ	NIXON	FORD	CARTER	REAGAN
I. CONSTANTS										
International System		--								
Constitutional System		--								
American Political Culture		--								
II. LONG-TERM DYNAMICS										
Institutional:	Traditional Presidency	Modern Presidency--------							Interregnum----------	Post-Modern Presidency
Domestic:										
Coalitions: (monopoly)	Enervated	Builder	Manager	(Outsider)	Manager	Manager	(Outsider)	(Outsider)	Enervated	
(competing)										Builder
Policy:	Consolidation	Achievement	Stalemate	Consolidation	Preparation	Achievement	Consolidation	Stalemate	Preparation	Achievement
International:										
Alignments:	Multipolar	War	bipolar----------							
Paradigm:	Isolation	International--------	Containment/1 (coexistence phase)				Containment/2 (detente phase)			
III. SHORT-TERM DYNAMICS										
Elections:	---------variable---------									
Political Support:	----------variable----------									
Events:	relevant events and circumstances identifiable for each incumbent									

Bush's most important policy initiatives (the Persian Gulf war, arms reductions, etc.) and most talented subordinates (Secretary of State James Baker, National Security Adviser Brent Scowcroft) are in this area. Concomitant with this concentration has been an extremely modest domestic policy agenda.

2. Seeking consensus, but being prepared for confrontation. Profiles of George Bush before and shortly after he assumed office emphasized his devotion to leadership through consensus. His approach to the Persian Gulf crisis in 1990 and 1991 was centered on building an almost universal coalition of nations and broad national support for his resistance to Iraq's invasion of Kuwait. Similarly, he has invoked consensus for the purpose of settling budget controversies and other domestic issues. Yet, when consensus is unachievable, the president uses confrontation to take on those who resist him. He has repeatedly confronted Democrats in Congress over such issues as civil rights, judicial appointments, and even budgeting. Moreover, he has tended to stretch his autonomous executive power to get his way, as in his threat to wage war against Iraq without Congress if the legislature would not lend its support to his policy.

3. Proceeding cautiously, but being prepared to act boldly. The president is generally portrayed as possessing an "instinctive caution." When Mr. Bush seemed to let his first 100 days in office pass without advancing any real agenda, his inaction was taken as confirmation of his unwillingness to move in haste. His response to the collapse of the Soviet empire in 1989 led several observers to urge him to "do something" to respond to the momentous changes underway, but the administration moved carefully and at its own pace.

Yet the president can be bold when he so chooses. In the Persian Gulf, he marshaled the opposition to Iraq's invasion, pushed the United Nations to a new unity, and waged a ferocious war. In the wake of the failed 1991 Soviet coup attempt, he announced major unilateral cuts in the American nuclear defense structure. Bold strokes punctuate an otherwise careful approach to governing.

4. Use of secrecy and surprise. One consistent element of the Bush leadership style has been the president's proclivity for secrecy and surprise. Planning for his 1989 summit-at-sea with Soviet President Mikhail Gorbachev was withheld from most of the president's subordinates, including Secretary of Defense Dick Cheney, until shortly before the meeting was publicly announced. The president's 1991 reduction of nuclear forces was also developed in nearly complete secrecy. Indeed, President Bush was frustrated that his planned announcement of the cut was leaked a few hours before he would speak to the nation: he wanted it to be a complete surprise to his audience.

5. Reliance on personal contacts. George Bush is famous for his devotion to cultivating personal contacts with other political leaders. In international affairs, his style of "Rolodex diplomacy" enabled the president to forge the

broad anti-Iraq coalition at the U.N., to hold NATO together during the difficult period of 1989–90, when West Germany wanted desperately to reunite with its eastern counterpart, and to participate in resistance to the 1991 Soviet coup by communicating directly with Russian President Boris Yeltsin. At home, he has employed phone calls, frequent meetings, friendly visits, and private notes to cultivate and maintain good relations with Capitol Hill, even in the midst of confrontations. As *National Journal* described his early contacts with legislators, "he invited members of Congress, who were used to presidential standoffishness, to bounce on beds upstairs in the White House" (1990, 7). This method has not, however, always brought President Bush the results he wanted.

6. A hands-on approach to policy making. Unlike his predecessor, President Bush is interested in the details of government. He is heavily involved in the policy development processes of the White House, intervenes with congressional leaders when he believes this action will help, and stays in almost continual touch with a wide range of foreign leaders. In consequence, the successes and failures of his administration bear the marks of his involvement.

7. Guarding his image. George Bush and his advisers have been attentive to the president's image in two respects. First, the White House has engaged in a strategy of watching public opinion polls. Many of the administration's critics have charged that the president has been unwilling to make initiatives in domestic policy or take the blame for the state of the economy because of an obsessive desire to maintain popular support. But there is more to these charges than mere politics: Even senior officials admit as much. In 1989, when the president was under pressure to come forward with a grand design for a post–Cold War order, Secretary of State Baker suggested that George Bush's high public support scores insulated him from such criticisms.

Second, President Bush has tended to use public politics in order to build support for his policies, as well as to distinguish himself from his predecessor in office. Weak where Mr. Reagan was strong, in delivering a speech from prepared text, the president has tended to "go public" by holding frequent impromptu news conferences. These events, in which Mr. Bush can show off his command of facts and his ease in fielding reporters' questions, allow him to communicate directly with the voters who see him so often on the evening news. Impromptu news conferences are also an example of the Bush White House's subtle approach to image manipulation: Unannounced news conferences reduce reporters' preparation time and generally keep them behind the camera. What the public sees is a confident, informed president who knows how to answer faceless journalists.

George Bush and the Dynamics of Context

Using the Ptolemaic model outlined above, Table 1.2 "places" George Bush in a presidential context. The results suggest how the dynamic elements of his environment affect his performance in the Oval Office.

Table 1.2
George Bush and the Dynamics of Context

Long-term Dynamics

Institutional Context:	post-modern presidency
Domestic Political Context:	
Coalitions:	(competing) regime manager
Policy Context:	presidency of consolidation
International Political Context:	
International Alignments:	post-Cold War
Foreign-Policy Paradigm:	??

Short-term Dynamics

Elections:	big win in 1988 election, but no "coattails;" Republican losses in 1990 congressional midterm
Political Support:	public opinion supported Bush in 1989 and 1990, but dropped after 1990 budget summit failure; support rose during and after the Persian Gulf crisis and war (high of 91 % approval at end of war), but slipped badly in fall of 1991
Events, Circumstances:	collapse of Soviet empire, 1989; budget summit failure, 1990; Persian Gulf crisis and war, 1990-91; abortive Soviet coup, 1991; recession, 1991-92; Mideast peace conference, 1991; presidential campaign gets underway, 1992.

Institutional Context

The conduct of the Bush presidency demonstrates that the office has moved into a new phase of its institutional evolution. Mr. Bush has shown an eagerness to make use of presidential prerogatives. In Panama and in the buildup of American forces in Saudi Arabia in 1990, the president carried on in the tradition of assertive executive military actions. Just as significantly, he and Budget Director Richard Darman continued the trend of centralizing executive budget-making in the White House. Mr. Bush has also maintained the administrative clearance process finalized during the Reagan years, demonstrating a determination to keep White House control over rulemaking in the departments. Recent reports have indicated the role of the White House Council on Competitiveness (chaired by Vice President Dan Quayle) in shaping or killing new regulations that its members believe threaten American trade board.

President Bush has also confirmed the tendency of recent incumbents to "go public," to behave as "chief whip" in Congress, and to use high-level appointments (e.g., Clarence Thomas) to advance his agenda. It is clear that the Bush administration bears the stamp of the postmodern presidency.

Domestic Political Coalitions

As a regime builder, Ronald Reagan changed the terms of political debate in the nation, altered the direction of public policy, and left an institutional legacy (the postmodern presidency and an institutionalized deficit that prevents new social programs). As his successor, George Bush is a regime manager in an environment of competing coalitions. His task is a demanding one. His coalition, like that of the Democrats, is always in an somewhat enervated state. Thus, the president has at times gone to great lengths to promote bipartisanship. His inaugural address invoked it; he worked hard to build good relations with Democratic leaders and members of Congress; and he has undercut aides who are unduly critical of his partisan opponents. However, he has on other occasions attacked Congress and its Democratic leaders for intransigence and undermining his goals, whether after the failure of the 1990 budget summit or in the wake of the battle over Clarence Thomas's nomination to the Supreme Court. This Jekyll-and-Hyde approach appears to be an awkward attempt to cope with the conflicting pressures of his political time.

Domestic Policy Context

Mr. Bush has exhibited conflicting tendencies. Overall, he appears to be acting as a president of consolidation, offering few policy initiatives and concentrating on softening some of the harder edges of the Reagan administration: offering more funding for programs Reagan wanted to eliminate; dropping some of Reagan's confrontational rhetoric on the issues of racism, AIDS, the role of government, and so on; and appointing moderates in many positions (e.g., the Environmental Protection Agency [EPA]), where the previous administration had chosen an ideological approach.

At the same time, however, Mr. Bush has behaved as a president of achievement when he lacked the political base to do so. Despite repeated rebuffs from the Democrats and evidence that the public has not accepted his argument, the president has persisted in his efforts to win a cut in the tax on capital gains. Like Harry Truman's Fair Deal, this is a case of the president misreading his mandate.

Indeed, Mr. Bush has not made much progress on the budget, one issue in which the public has expected leadership. Some of his problems certainly arise from his awkward place in political time, but clearly there is more to the president's difficulties than that. Ever uneasy with the "vision thing," he has never articulated a sense of direction for national policy. He bears the blame for his own failings here, even if he can share some of it with circumstances.

Foreign Policy Paradigm

The president's own outlook on foreign policy is best characterized as "conservative internationalism." The Wilsonian tradition of internationalism among most American foreign-policy elites has two main branches: a liberal one, which emphasizes the nation's role in leading the world to a more progressive, democratic future (the view of Kennedy and Johnson), and a conservative branch that emphasizes American intervention in world affairs to maintain stability in the international system and protect national interests (the Nixon-Kissinger view). Each offshoot accepts the values of the other; the difference is in emphasis. George Bush's conservative internationalism has become the temporary paradigm for American policy. The president has attempted to provide a vision for the future, proclaiming that "we need to build a new, enduring peace—based not on arms races and confrontations, but on shared principles and the rule of law" (*New York Times*, 1991, A8). But no one can yet say whether he will be able to translate a general outlook on foreign affairs to an enduring paradigm for policy.

Short-Term Dynamics

For most of his time in office, short-term factors have allowed and even encouraged the president to indulge his preference for foreign policy. But the turn of events has also revealed the risks of doing so. George Bush came to office after a strong win in the 1988 election. He wore essentially no coattails, with many Republicans in Congress running ahead of him in their own districts. His party suffered further setbacks in the 1990 midterm congressional elections, so he has never had a strong partisan base on Capitol Hill like Ronald Reagan's Republican Senate in the years 1981–87.

Political support for the president has waxed and waned. He enjoyed good approval scores in 1989 and 1990 but slipped badly after the failure of the 1990 budget summit. The Persian Gulf crisis and war made President Bush a national hero, sending his approval rating as high as 91 percent at the end of the war. This sort of endorsement did not last, but support remained strong in the wake of upheavals in Moscow in August 1991. The recession of 1991–92 damaged the president's public standing as a majority of voters concluded he was spending too much time on foreign affairs.

Assessing George Bush as Leader

In a once-famous send-up of dry historical tomes, *1066 and All That* raced through British history, delivering pithy summaries of entire centuries and dispatching most of England's monarchs with the epithets "good" or "bad." In the United States, we have often felt the urge to do the same with our presidents. We look for short-cut ways to render final judgment on them, whether in lists of great and not-so-great presidents, or in two-by-two tables that force all chief executives into boxes that Garry Wills (1983) compared with "I'm okay, you're okay" pop psychology.

The preceding discussion has demonstrated, however, that such shorthand approaches to evaluating leadership are misleading. Sensitivity to context can inform our assessments of presidents, even if it complicates them. So, the question asked in the beginning—Is George Bush an effective leader?— has no single answer. But some conclusions are apparent.

First, the president's emphasis on foreign policy, while aligned with his personal interests, is to some extent a rational response to his environment. As a regime manager in an era of competing coalitions, following a president of achievement in domestic policy, George Bush is not well placed in political time or policy time to win support for any major domestic initiatives. Moreover, the international political context of his tenure has demanded presidential attention for extended periods.

But Mr. Bush cannot afford to ignore domestic affairs. While he has been seriously constrained by the context of his times, the president has not made the most of his situation. He essentially mishandled budget negotiations with Congress, including members of his own party, in 1990. He refrained from offering any substantive program in education, one of his central campaign issues. And he waited far too long in 1991 to turn his attention to the economy. These actions left him vulnerable to opponents' charges of inattentiveness to matters at home and ultimately to the vicissitudes of public opinion.

Short-term events and circumstances have generally supported Mr. Bush's inclinations and have also shown the risks of his approach to leadership. Even within the frame of the president's own leadership style, however, we can see that context affects our evaluation. George Bush cannot merely "handle" international affairs during his time in office and call that leadership; he must lead in a way that fits the tasks at hand. The clear task for this president is to develop and articulate a new paradigm for American foreign policy. The rapid changes in the world that have occurred since Mr. Bush took office place a premium on his doing so, especially since he has chosen to put almost all of his eggs in this basket. If he can meet this obligation, he will have done much and could rank with Truman in his contribution to foreign policy. If, however, he cannot produce a new paradigm, whatever individual achievements he can claim (e.g., nuclear force reductions in 1992) will tend to pale beside the overwhelming importance of his missed opportunity. This task should be the chief goal of a second Bush term.

The future needs more attention from the Bush White House in a second administration. If the president wants a Republican successor, he will have to develop a more visible domestic agenda and a set of principles for foreign policy. President Bush will also need to find a less awkward way to deal with the fact of competing coalitions than his Jekyll-and-Hyde behavior of the first term. A clearer sense of purpose for his presidency and for national policy, something less than the "vision thing" but more than a set of discrete positions, is definitely in order. If he is able to meet this challenge, George Bush will have set the stage for future presidents to proceed effectively through a post-Cold War and postmodern political world. If not, he will come to be seen much like Jimmy Carter: an executive who presided unsuccessfully during a time of transition.

Are these conclusions all that different from what even casual observers have already discerned? Yes, in this respect: an understanding of context goes far beyond just saying, "Well, he's much better in foreign affairs than in domestic policy." Context, as examined in the model outlined above, helps us to appreciate why that is so and how the different pieces of the Bush presidency and its environment fit together. While a preliminary sense of the fit between the president and the tasks at hand may be relatively easy, a more sophisticated and therefore more accurate appraisal takes hard work.

REFERENCES

Barilleaux, Ryan J. 1988a. *The Post-Modern Presidency*. New York: Praeger.

———. 1988b. "Presidential Conduct of Foreign Policy." *Congress and the Presidency* 15 (Spring): 1–23.

———. 1985. *The President and Foreign Affairs*. New York: Praeger.

Corwin, E. S. 1984. *The President: Office and Powers, 1787–1984*, 5th edn. Edited by Randall Bland, Theodore Hinson, and Jack W. Peltason. New York: New York University Press.

Craig, Hardin, and David Bevington, eds. 1973. *The Complete Works of Shakespeare*, rev. ed. Glenview, Ill.: Scott, Foresman.

Devine, Donald J. 1972. *The Political Culture of the United States*. Boston: Little, Brown.

Gaddis, John Lewis. 1982. *Strategies of Containment*. New York: Oxford University Press.

Greenstein, Fred. 1988. *Leadership and the Modern Presidency*. Cambridge, Mass.: Harvard University Press.

———. 1978. "Change and Continuity in the Modern Presidency." In *The New American Political System*. Edited by Anthony King. Washington: American Enterprise Institute, pp. 45–86.

Hargrove, Erwin, and Michael Nelson. 1984. *Presidents, Politics, and Policy*. New York: Knopf.

Jones, Charles. 1983. "Presidential Negotiation with Congress." In *Both Ends of the Avenue*. Edited by Anthony King. Washington: American Enterprise Institute, pp. 96–130.

Kellerman, Barbara. 1986. *Political Leadership: A Source Book*. Pittsburgh: University of Pittsburgh Press.

———, and Ryan J. Barilleaux. 1991. *The President as World Leader*. New York: St. Martin's Press.

Kendall, Willmoore. 1960. "The Two Majorities." *Midwest Journal of Political Science* 4 (November): 317–45.

Kernell, Samuel, and Samuel Popkin, eds. 1986. *Chief of Staff*. Berkeley: University of California Press.

Koh, Harold Hongju. 1990. *The National Security Constitution*. New Haven, Conn.: Yale University Press.

Lipset, Seymour Martin. 1979. *The First New Nation*, rev. edn. New York: Norton.

National Journal. 1990. 6 January: 6–10.

Neustadt, Richard. 1990. *Presidential Power and the Modern Presidents*. New York: Free Press.

New York Times. 1991. 30 January: A8.

Pious, Richard. 1979. *The American Presidency*. New York: Basic Books.

Rockman, Bert. 1990. "The American Presidency in Comparative Perspective." In *The Presidency and the Political System*, 3rd edn. Edited by Michael Nelson. Washington: Congressional Quarterly Press, pp. 57–82.

———. 1985. The Leadership Question. New York: Praeger.

Rose, Richard. 1991. *The Postmodern President*, 2nd edn. Chatham, N.J.: Chatham House.

———. 1984. *The Leadership Question*. New York: Praeger.

Seidman, Harold, and Robert Gilmour. 1986. *Politics, Positions, and Power*, 4th edn. New York: Oxford University Press.

Skowronek, Stephen. 1990. "Presidential Leadership in Political Time." In *The Presidency and the Political System*, 3rd edn. Edited by Michael Nelson. Washington: Congressional Quarterly Press, pp. 117–62.

———. 1984. "Presidential Leadership in Political Time." In *The Presidency and the Political System*. Edited by Michael Nelson. Washington: Congressional Quarterly Press, pp. 87–132.

Tillyard, E.M.W. 1942. *The Elizabethan World Picture*. New York: Vintage.

Wills, Garry. 1983. *The Kennedy Imprisonment*. New York: Bantam.

Chapter 2

Governance as Political Theater: George Bush and the MTV Presidency

MARY E. STUCKEY AND FREDERICK J. ANTCZAK

Theater and politics have always been closely entwined. There is much about the theater arts that can be understood as explicitly political; politics can also be helpfully understood as containing elements of the explicitly theatrical (Edelman, 1988). This is particularly true of the politics surrounding the American presidency, especially as that institution has developed into the distinctively personalistic and rhetorical office it is today (Ceasar, Thurow, Tulis, and Bessette, 1981; Lowi, 1985; Kernell, 1986; Tulis, 1987; Windt, 1986). In the modern world, the theater of politics is staged on television.

As the world of entertainment television has become increasingly influenced by technology, so have political television and the political leadership that increasingly governs publicly through television. The intersection between television technology and stylistic adaptations to that technology in the last decade has indisputably occurred most clearly on MTV. Just as entertainment television has been influenced by the unconnected imagery, uncontexted, fragmented, and visually privileged style of MTV, political television, and, by extension, political leadership, has also assimilated large measures of the MTV style. This style, according to a recent issue of *TV Guide*, involves "quick-cut editing and slick, flashy imagery," a "visual style [that] has become just another part of the entertainment landscape" (Polskin, 1991, 7).

At first blush, words like "slick" and "flashy" seem to have little to do with politicians like George Bush. But understanding recent politics as MTV-style political theater is notably useful for analyzing Bush's leadership as it reflects and furthers the process of public governance in a media age. Since the extraordinarily television-dependent presidency of Ronald Reagan, scholars have struggled to come to terms with the role of communication, theater, and television in the political life of the nation (Blumenthal, 1990; Parenti, 1992). A similar struggle is going on to understand and interpret the policies, actions, and behaviors of George Bush. In adapting his style to the expectations and culture of television, Bush has assimilated much of the fragmented, disconnected style of MTV. Bush acts to accommodate not a constituency, but an electorate mediated by polls. He is accountable not to the public, but to public opinion. Like MTV, Bush is subject to the variety of whims, inconsistencies, and short attention spans that increasingly characterizes the viewing audience, and thus the voting public.

The pressures involved in appealing to this audience engender a new kind of leadership, one that is made possible by the technologies of modern communication and polling, and one that is made viable by our national acceptance of a specific kind of politics. To observe George Bush is to observe how this kind of leadership is played out in the context of the American presidency. This chapter addresses the questions of what this new kind of leadership means instrumentally for George Bush, institutionally for our understanding of the presidency, and ethically for the moral life of the nation.

ACT 1: SETTING THE STAGE
FOR PRESIDENTIAL LEADERSHIP

Presidents have always adapted to fit their conception of the office to the prevailing political climate, public expectations, and the technology of communication (Stuckey, 1991). These adaptations have affected the institution of the presidency in striking and important ways. Rhetoric has become increasingly important to modern presidents, who spend more and more of their time on their public speech (Ceasar, Thurow, Tulis, and Bessette, 1981; Hart, 1987; Tulis, 1987). Consequently, scholars focus attention on the nature of the "plebiscitary presidency" (Lowi, 1985) and the various strategies involved in "going public" (Kernell, 1986).

Sidney Blumenthal argued that one result of the new technology in the age of information is the "permanent campaign" (1980). This is a new kind of politics in which "issues, polls, and media are not neatly separate categories. They are unified by a strategic imperative. . . . The elements of the permanent campaign are not tangential to politics: they are the political process itself" (1980, 10). With the decline of party structure, discipline, and workers, television commercials and media appearances not only serve to mobilize voters but also to govern the nation once the election is over. While the permanent campaign is a recognizable and dominant aspect of presidential politics, Blumenthal contends that the "permanent campaign will permeate politics down to the most remote legislative district as politicians feel the need to retain consultants to give them the advantage" (1980, 26).

Presidents and other politicians can no longer rely on traditional means of garnering and maintaining public support. The political parties are weak, and the formal institutional links between the leaders and the governed have largely broken down. But as the sources of such support have eroded, the need for such support has increased. As Congress increasingly ceded power and responsibility to the president, the office came to dominate the federal government. Congress can act less responsibly now than in the past because Congress is, in fact, less responsible for policy than in the past. The president is now responsible for developing national policy.

The president is also responsible for communicating the content and implications of policy. In an increasingly media-dominated society, the communications process affects both the institutions that develop policy and the policies that are developed by those institutions (Altheide and Snow, 1979; Arterton, 1987). Both the increased prevalence of media and technological advances are responsible for this phenomenon.

With radio, a more personalized brand of political leadership developed. The president could become present in the homes of the electorate, his voice part of the family circle.* He became an intimate. Television heightens this intimacy, bringing the presidential face as well as the presidential voice into the living room and reducing the formal distance between speaker and audience. Because presidential communication increasingly means televised communication, presidents have adapted their message and style to fit the medium. This means shorter speeches, speeches whose language supports visual images, speeches where argument is reduced and assertion expanded, and speeches that heighten emotional content and reduce rational, developed appeals (Jamieson, 1988; Noonan, 1990). These speeches, in other words, have considerable stylistic commonalities with an MTV video.

Ronald Reagan, of course, epitomized the adaptation of politics to television, a fact that many thought would create problems of comparison for his successor. But Bush has translated his personal style into a different style of communication—a style that is remarkably successful on television. An MTV-style approach, visually privileged, fragmented, and image-dominated is a logical next step in the evolution of political television as it has been in entertainment television. The remainder of this chapter explores the reasons behind the success of Bush's approach and analyzes its implications for the present administration as well as for the presidency as an institution.

---

*The use of the male pronoun is a matter of some controversy, for the presidency is clearly an all-male club, and it would be foolish indeed to pretend otherwise. Yet it is not a matter of necessity that it remain so indefinitely; accordingly, the male pronoun is used when discussing the past office; when appropriate, gender-neutral terms are used.

ACT 2: BUSH'S PUBLIC SPEECH AND
THE MTV STYLE

All presidents, like all politicians, adapt to their political cultures and make use of the prevailing modes of communication to capture and maintain public support. As president, Bush is constrained by the tactics and behaviors of his predecessors in office as well as by his own style and preferences. Even more, Bush is constrained by his audiences. Daniel Webster and Henry Clay could speak for days, and their audience would remain with them. Thomas Jefferson and Calvin Coolidge could eschew speaking almost completely, and their audiences would not object. But George Bush, in order to be perceived as "leading," must also be seen speaking. Both the fact of the speech and the visual impact of the president seen to be talking are important elements of the MTV style.

In MTV, the music is not enough; if there is no video, there will be no recognition of the song. The presidency is increasingly subjected to a similar dynamic. If the president talks and it doesn't make the nightly news, is it "real" speech? Does it matter? Many scholars have noted that the act of speaking is becoming as important—if not more important—than the content of speech (Hart, 1987). And George Bush is a president who puts enormous weight on the act of speaking.

Bush speaks to the press more frequently than most modern presidents. He favors the impromptu press conference above formal televised speeches (Edwards, 1991), and during the frequent crisis periods since he took office (the Panama invasion, fall of the Berlin wall, Persian Gulf conflict, the attempted coup and its aftermath in the Soviet Union) Bush has held press conferences almost daily. This gives Bush the appearance of openness; the electorate sees him, and sees him often, responding to questions from the media. Bush uses these opportunities to allow the story of his presidency to be told without appearing manipulative, pedantic, or overbearing. The rhetoric surrounding the Panama invasion illustrates this point.

The removal of Noriega from power in Panama was closely tied to Bush's need for a dramatic success in the war on drugs. Even the code name of the invasion, "Operation Just Cause," was related to Bush's drug rhetoric: "Victory, victory over drugs is our cause, a just cause" (Bush, 1989b). Noriega, who initially was portrayed by Bush as a "dictator" (Bush, 1989a), later became an "indicted drug trafficker" and a "thug" (Bush, 1989c), as American hostility and the likelihood of intervention increased. The president assumed the role of hero to counter the depiction of Noriega-as-villain, and the American people assumed the role of audience in the televised melodrama of the invasion and Noriega's eventual capture. The same sort of appeal resurfaced as tensions in the Persian Gulf escalated.

In both Panama and the Persian Gulf, Bush represented the united forces of morality against a recurrence of Nazi-style oppression (Stuckey, in progress). Within days of the Iraqi invasion of Kuwait, for example, Bush compared Iraq to Germany ("Iraq's tanks stormed in blitzkrieg fashion") and indicated that the situations were similar:

We succeeded in the struggle for freedom in Europe because we and our allies remained stalwart. Keeping the peace in the Mideast will require no less. . . . If history teaches us anything, it is that we must resist aggression or it will destroy our freedoms. Appeasement does not work. As was the case in the 1930s, we see in Saddam Hussein an aggressive dictator threatening his neighbors. (Bush, 1991a)

Later, he used the theme again and again: "The world is now called upon to confront another aggressor, another threat made by a person who has no values when it comes to respecting international law, a man of evil standing against human life itself" (1990b).

He referred to the "Kuwaiti underground" (1990c), the "Kuwaiti resistance" (1990d), and the "Kuwaiti theater of war" (1991b). He also compared Iraq's attack on Kuwait to Germany's invasion of Poland: "Hitler . . . marched into Poland. . . . The Death's Head regiments of the SS . . . their role was to go in and dissemble the country. . . . We're dealing with Hitler revisited, a totalitarianism and a brutality that is naked and unprecedented in modern times" (1990e).

If the role of Adolf Hitler was assigned to Saddam Hussein, Franklin Roosevelt's role clearly belonged to George Bush. Bush was the leader who had seen war, who hated war, who could quote Roosevelt, and who understood how Roosevelt as war leader had felt. Bush spoke to troops at Pearl Harbor (1990f), gave a speech on the fiftieth anniversary of the "Four Freedoms" speech (1991b), and told a national audience, "I've seen the hideous face of war and counted the costs of conflict in friends lost" (1991a).

Bush was Rooseveltian in many of his public appearances, relying on news conferences, refusing to answer questions that related to troop movements, deflecting other questions to administration officials. In many ways, it was a masterful performance.

In his Gulf War speech, Bush relied on Rooseveltian rhetorical appeals to make the case that this was "not another Vietnam." But as the examples indicate, Bush used those appeals in a fragmentary fashion, as subtexts in speeches rather than as a developed argument that was itself the theme of a speech. In this, Bush is following a pattern laid out by political speakers since at least the nineteenth century. Yet as speeches lose more and more of their argumentative quality, and increasingly depend on emotional associations between otherwise unconnected elements for their persuasive force, viewing political speech is rendered indistinguishable from viewing other kinds of television, and the viewer is left with the same dulled sensibilities and minimal attention span that MTV provides.

In addition to his predilection for speaking publicly, Bush also frequently speaks about speaking. He is fond of reciting facts about other conversations, especially about his conversations with other world leaders (1990f; 1991b; 1991c). Bush's frequent contacts and close personal relations can produce some remarkable successes on the world scene, as the 1989 NATO summit and the multinational response to the recent Middle East crisis illustrate. It appears, however, that this consultative form of leadership is best suited to foreign affairs, where the American president is increasingly viewed as one leader among many.

In domestic affairs, however, the president is expected to dominate, to "lead." It is not surprising that it is in domestic politics that Bush's leadership is often questioned. This questioning creates pressure on Bush to provide, at the very least, the appearance of domestic leadership. The MTV style, attuned to appearance above all else, allows Bush to respond to that pressure, while adapting little of his actual conduct of the presidency to focus his attention on the problems and issues of domestic policy making.

Television presents complex realities in a simplified form, which is becoming increasingly simplified as even the brief television images are becoming briefer, and the images become sharper although less distinct. On television, if a president does not appear to control events, this is not treated as part of a complex world (events cannot be controlled by a single person all of the time) but as a simple truth (the president is not in control). This in turn is viewed as evidence of that particular president's weakness (this president is incapable of controlling events). Thus, the appearance of lacking mastery is perceived as due to a personal lack of ability rather than part of a situation that is not amenable to presidential control.

It is this dynamic that induces presidents to define situations in ways that they can appear to control. For Lyndon Johnson, for example, declaring "war on poverty" put him in a position of command at a time that he needed to buttress his authority. Gerald Ford's WIN (Whip Inflation Now) campaign was a similar but much less effective technique. To appear in control, a president must be able to react to unexpected events, to place them in an ongoing context.

In some senses, presidents tell the nation stories. Unexpected occurrences that produce anxiety must be integrated into the story, and the anxiety must be removed (Cassirer, 1955). The more integrated the story, the more reassuring it will be, and the stronger the president will appear. Televised communication encourages our presidents to be good storytellers. They are increasingly judged by the quality of their narrative line. As the narrative lines associated with entertainment television become less stable, linear, and predictable, the pressures exerted on the president-as-narrator change. As audiences become less accustomed to filling in the blanks of entertainment television plots, presidents become more able to leave gaps in their plots. This does not mean that their role as interpreter is less important, or that they are any less storytellers than before. It does mean that they face different constraints and different possibilities in their storytelling, that they tell different sorts of stories to different sorts of audiences.

George Bush is a good example of how the change in storytelling conventions can work to a president's advantage. Bush may lack a single, unified narrative vision, such as the one that characterized Ronald Reagan (apparent in his incapacity to explain what's new about the "New World Order" beyond a collapsing Soviet Union). But he is still distinctively "in charge" of that new world order, a concept that is usefully vague, dimly associated with "freedom and democracy," "self-determination," and "adherence to international law" (Bush, 1991d).

Like all communicative elements of the presidency, this approach is not without its limitations. In the context of domestic politics, for instance, the image-laden, purposefully vague ethos is less persuasive. Where Reagan assumed the role of both the narrator and the hero in his story of America (Lewis, 1987), Bush allows himself to be bit player in the background of stories, and appears hopeful that in complicated times, the role of hero will fall to him by a kind of default. Or perhaps he is not "hero" so much as "genial omnipresence," directing and ordering events that he has no part in constructing; he is increasingly America's VJ.

And he is good in the role. Bush, as a television moderator, avoids grating; he is neither harsh nor contentious. He avoids the use of confrontational or disunifying rhetoric and public personality clashes, thus limiting the target and strategies of potential opponents. Bush rarely if ever espouses unpopular causes or bucks the trends of public opinion. His staff conducts polls regularly, and the president does not hesitate to act on the findings of those polls (Gergen and Walsh, 1989). The Bush administration, however, does not tend toward the unified "theme of the day" understanding that typified the Reagan years; the Bush who appears in his public character is not a unified construct. It is therefore difficult to come to grips with his public image. He presents no clear profile that can be lauded or attacked. Instead, he is an amalgam of the constructs created by his staff, by himself in his press conferences, by the media, and by the public as they interpret and react to the interpretations offered to them by others.

While the United States, and indeed the world, are increasingly part of Marshall McLuhan's "global village," the polity is also increasingly fragmented internally, and there are many discrete publics, rather than one generic "public" (Windt, 1990; xiii). Knowing this, Bush can tailor specific appeals to specific publics, generate images that are ambiguous enough to be read differently by different constituencies, and fear little overlap between groups. Like an MTV audience, people can find a little something for everyone, and it is wrapped up in a package that owes more to diversified labeling than any generic differences.

Bush thus uses press conferences as an opportunity to "go public" on international issues, and keeps domestic issues as smaller, discrete subtexts that run through the background of his speech without ever intruding into the perceptual foreground. In this, he has certainly been assisted by international events. This tendency to rely on foreign rather than domestic policy is not new with Bush; neither is the disposition to foreground image. Bush is representative of a trend in televised politics, one that he inherited, and one that he will undoubtedly pass on in its extended form to his successor in the office. An analysis of the implications of that trend is presented in the concluding section.

THE DENOUEMENT: IMPLICATIONS AND DISCUSSION

The inauguration of an MTV-style fragmentation of presidential image-making has implications for three main areas of concern: there are instrumental implications for Bush as president, institutional implications for the presidency as a political office, and ethical implications for the polity as a whole.

Bush's tendency to focus on international issues and to base his presidency in foreign policy to the exclusion of domestic concerns renders him potentially vulnerable. This vulnerability has less to do with his (almost certain) re-election than with the equally certain problems of governing in the second term. Because he does not seek public support for specific, well-defined issues, there is no perceptible punishment for legislators who vote against White House-sponsored initiatives:

Bush's style is to make a deal. He negotiates quietly, outside the glare of publicity and with as little rancor as possible. He then announces a compromise, shifts his position to accommodate the outcome, and invites the country to applaud the spirit of bi-partisanship and cooperation. (Schneider, 1990)

Bush's refusal to take political risks, to stand for a clearly defined position, generates an equally risk-free, positionally vague strategy for his opponents. Further, his tendency to compromise and to make deals provides an incentive for those who disagree with him to maintain their opposition and to force a deal.

As MTV sacrifices context in its video presentations, in failing to provide a national vision, Bush also sacrifices the context through which he can interpret events. His only context is the remnant of Reaganism, which, given events in Europe and the Soviet Union, is fast becoming passé. Every action, every event in the Bush administration must be explained from scratch. There is no ongoing understanding of the president and the world he inhabits to serve as a reference point. In this, George Bush risks resembling Jimmy Carter, as an in-basket president, dealing with the issues that cross his desk in a competent manner, but failing to appear in control of events (Barnes,

1990). This is particularly true in the setting of new issues or unexpected occurrences, and it is likely to gain relevance as Bush drifts—or risks appearing to drift—into a second term.

The MTV style is not a characteristic of merely a particular president or pair of presidents but of the presidency as an institution. George Bush, it is true,

did not by himself hollow out the government. It was empty when he got to the White House, though his subsequent policies have ensured that it stay empty, ineffectual, symbolic only. His distinctive contribution to the time is his own lack of purpose and agenda. (Myerson, 1990, 140)

But whether Bush is responsible for "hollowing out the office" or is merely continuing a process no one person can be held responsible for, the institution does appear to be increasingly hollow. Just as MTV, never a medium of onerous substance or depth, has become increasingly shallow, monotonous, and vacuous, the presidency under George Bush seems to be becoming ever more ceremonial and symbolic. Just as MTV lacks a continuing frame of reference, George Bush lacks an overarching context by which to interpret events. Instead, as president, Bush appears ever more like an MTV VJ, introducing events without interpreting or controlling them. Neither MTV nor Bush has any apparent reason for being. They are; that is enough. They require no commitment, no real engagement.

The changes in the communicative aspects of the presidency that we label here the "MTV style" are not necessarily indicative of the erosion of democratic discourse. As the nation has fragmented into a series of disconnected publics, perhaps a fragmented approach to communications and leadership is the most appropriate style. It is hard to construct a culture out of a variety of unrelated elements. Presidents increasingly resort to a fragmented, visually landscaped communications style in response to the fact of an increasingly inchoate polity. On an instrumental—and perhaps on a constitutive level—this makes sense.

We do, however, suspect that despite this, democratically responsible narratives are those that are better sustained and more coherent than those influenced and produced by the MTV style. We are not arguing for a more issue-based, rational discourse, but for a discourse that is enriched and drawn together by the quality of its stories, not reduced and divided by them.

In a sense, we are arguing for a discourse that explicitly recognizes the role of narrative in public life, and for attention to be paid to that narrative. The alternative may well be a polity that mindlessly echoes, "I want my MTV," and settles for public discourse that will further erode any sense of national community.

REFERENCES

Altheide, D., and R. Snow. 1979. *Media Logic*. Beverly Hills, Calif.: Sage.
Arterton, C. 1987. *Teledemocracy: Can Television Protect Democracy?* Beverly Hills, Calif.: Sage.
Barnes, F. 1990. "Teflon II." *The New Republic*. February 12.
Blumenthal, S. 1990. *Pledging Allegiance: The Last Campaign of the Cold War*. New York: Harper/Collins.
————. 1980. *The Permanent Campaign*. New York: Touchstone.
Bush, George. 1991a. "Radio Address to the Nation on the Persian Gulf." *Weekly Compilation of Presidential Documents*. January 5.
————. 1991b. "Address before a Joint Session of Congress on the State of the Union." *Weekly Compilation of Presidential Documents*. January 29.
————. 1991c. "Press Conference on the Persian Gulf Conflict." *Weekly Compilation of Presidential Documents*. March 1.
————. 1991d. "The President's Press Conference." *CBS News*. September 2.
————. 1990a. "Remarks on the United States Military Action in Panama." *Weekly Compilation of Presidential Documents*. Dec. 22.
————. 1990b. "Remarks at a Republican Party Fund-Raising Luncheon in North Kingstown, R.I." *Weekly Compilation of Presidential Documents*. August 20.
————. 1990c. "The President's News Conference on the Persian Gulf Crisis." *Weekly Compilation of Presidential Documents*. August 28.
————. 1990d. "Remarks Following Discussions with Amir Jabir al-Ahmed al-Jabir Al Sabah of Kuwait." *Weekly Compilation of Presidential Documents*. September 28.
————. 1990e. "Remarks at a Fund-Raising Dinner for Gubernatorial Candidate John Rowland in Stamford, Conn." *Weekly Compilation of Presidential Documents*. October 23.
————. 1990f. "Remarks to Officers and Troops at Hickham Air Force Base in Pearl Harbor, Hawaii." *Weekly Compilation of Presidential Documents*. October 28.
————. 1989a. "Remarks to the Council of the Americas." *Weekly Compilation of Presidential Documents*. May 2.
————. 1989b. "Address to the Nation on Drug Control Strategy." *Weekly Compilation of Presidential Documents*. Sept. 5.
————. 1989c. "Address to the Nation Announcing the United States Military Action in Panama." *Weekly Compilation of Presidential Documents*. Dec. 20.
Cassirer, E. 1955. *The Myth of the State*. Garden City, N.Y.: Doubleday.
Ceasar, J., G. Thurow, J. Tulis, and J. Bessette. 1981. "The Rise of the Rhetorical Presidency." *Presidential Studies Quarterly* 11 (Spring): 233–51.
Edelman, M. 1988. *Constructing the Political Spectacle*. Chicago: University of Chicago Press.
Edwards, G. 1991. "The Public Presidency: The Politics of Inclusion." In *The Bush Presidency: First Appraisals*. Edited by C. Campbell and B. A. Rockman. Chatham, N.J.: Chatham House, pp. 129–55.
Gergen, D., and Walsh, K. 1989. "The Rise and Rise of George Bush." *U.S. News and World Report* 107: 25, 28.
Hart, R. P. 1987. *The Sound of Leadership: Presidential Communication in the Modern Age*. Chicago: University of Chicago Press.

Jamieson, K. H. 1988. *Eloquence in an Electronic Age: The Transformation of American Political Speechmaking*. New York: Oxford University Press.

Kernell, S. 1986. *Going Public: New Strategies of Presidential Leadership*. Washington, D.C.: Congressional Quarterly Press.

Lewis, W. F. 1987. "Telling America's Story: Narrative Form and the Reagan Presidency." *Quarterly Journal of Speech* 73: 280–302.

Lowi, T. 1985. *The Personal President: Power Invested, Promise Unfulfilled*. Ithaca, N.Y.: Cornell University Press.

Myerson, H. 1990. "George Bush and 'the Vision Thing.' " *Dissent* (Spring): 137–40.

Noonan, P. 1990. *What I Saw at the Revolution: A Political Life in the Reagan Era*. New York: Random House.

Parenti, M. 1992. *Make-Believe Media: The Politics of Entertainment*. New York: St. Martin's Press.

Polskin, H. 1991. "MTV at 10: The Beat Goes On." *TV Guide*. August 3–9: 4–9.

Schneider, W. 1990. "The In-Box President." *The Atlantic*. January: 34.

Stuckey, M. 1991. *The President as Interpreter-in-Chief*. Chatham, N.J.: Chatham House.

———. In progress. "Remembering the Future: Rhetorical Echoes of World War II and Vietnam in George Bush's Speech on the Gulf War." In *Virtual War: Video Knowledge and Public Consciousness*. Edited by Bethami A. Dobkin.

Tulis, J. 1987. *The Rhetorical Presidency*. Princeton: Princeton University Press.

U.S. News and World Report. 1990. "How to Rule Without a Big Schtick." February 5.

Windt, T. 1990. *Presidents and Protestors: Political Rhetoric in the 1960s*. Tuscaloosa, Ala.: University of Alabama Press.

———. 1986. "Presidential Rhetoric: Definition of a Field of Study." *Presidential Studies Quarterly* 16 (1): 102–16.

PART 2

THE BUSH PRESIDENCY IN THE GOVERNMENT

Chapter 3

George Bush and
the Executive Branch

JANET M. MARTIN

In recent years, the bashing of the federal bureaucracy has been a favorite sport and strategy of presidents. In part, this hostile stance comes from contemporary presidents' desire to maintain a perpetual "outsider" image for public relations purposes. But it probably also arises from real frustration, for the president must attempt to control the bureaucracy to govern effectively, and the bureaucracy can be a very cumbersome creature to control. A statement in the Volcker Commission Report[1] emphasized the importance of this relationship:

No president can be effective alone. He or she must rely upon a sizeable number of top officials . . . to ensure the quality and effectiveness of government. These men and women—presidential appointees, senior career executives, and personal and confidential assistants—implement the President's agenda, hire and promote the key staff, draft the budget, enforce the laws, try to anticipate problems and get the facts, and motivate the civil service. . . . A President sets a powerful example for a 2.2 million non-postal civilian work force, and for the nation as a whole. To the extent presidential and career executives are committed to the highest levels of integrity and performance, and work in full partnership to secure faithful execution of the laws, public respect will also follow. (Volcker, 1990, 11–12)

Thus, in assessing the leadership of a president, one critical criterion is the relationship between the president and the administration, and the resulting "leadership for governance."[2]

While there is a separation of powers system in the United States, leadership is required, and the president, by nature of this singular office heading a government of millions, can centralize power.

A newly elected president comes into office with a perceived mandate to govern, a result in part of an exaggerated margin of victory due to the mechanics of the electoral college. The president is expected to present an agenda, and lead the Congress and move the bureaucracy to carry out that agenda. This perception is enhanced by the attention given to a president's inaugural address and first State of the Union message, in which a president is expected to set forth an agenda for both the coming year and the remainder of his or her term. There is even talk of a "honeymoon" with the press, Congress, and the public in the first six months in which the president is traditionally given the benefit of the doubt on judgments and decisions.

During this period, a great deal of attention is focused on a president's structuring of the government. While the Cabinet as a collectivity is generally not perceived as being of much importance in the governing of the nation, the symbolic importance of the Cabinet is emphasized, with attention focused on its demographic composition. Is there a balance of interests represented in terms of geography, gender, racial, ethnic, and religious groupings? The appointment of individual secretaries receives a great deal of attention.[3] In subsequent weeks, the announcement of appointments of men and women to head agencies, fill vacancies on boards and regulatory commissions, and fill hundreds of positions requiring Senate confirmation will also be duly reported by the media.

The expectation of a "new administration" is so embedded in the American political psyche that during the 1988 campaign, candidate George Bush was pledging a year before the election that he "would bring in a lot of new people" in order "to present a fresh outlook for his Administration" (Boyd, 1987, B12). This was said by a candidate who was a part of the incumbent administration, and holding the number two position in that administration!

However, a president's ability to gain control over his or her administration remains problematic. While several thousand partisan officials are brought in to head departments and agencies, programs will still be managed and run by career bureaucrats who remain in their posts from administration to administration. Aberbach and Rockman's pioneering study of the nature of conflict between the bureaucracy and the president clearly presents the problems of a president in managing a bureaucracy filled with careerists, not necessarily of a partisan or ideological compatibility with the president, and appointees *not* as ideologically committed to the president's ideals (Aberbach and Rockman, 1976). In a preliminary study of the Reagan administration, these authors vividly demonstrate that even in the case of a two-term administration, with the same party in control of the Senate for over half the duration of the administration, and a clear sense of the desired ideological leanings of appointees, there is still a tension inherent in the structure of the administration (Aberbach, Rockman and Copeland, 1990). They note:

Although career civil servants may reflect changes in the political climate . . . they are generally a more cautious and skeptical lot than the types a zealous administration is likely to appoint. This is evident in our data in the differences between the beliefs of Republican political appointees and Republican careerists. (p. 191)

In addition, while a president "can force the rate of turnover in personnel up at the career level," this process takes time, often longer than the term of office of a president (p. 192). Finally, administrators also have "congressional committees and program constituencies with which to contend" and may face a problem of divided loyalties and interests (p. 192). According to the Volcker Commission Report, presidents may find that:

Political appointees, especially at lower levels, may not be the best qualified, and they may be appointed because of support from Members of Congress or interest groups. Thus their loyalty may be split between the President and others. A number of Presidential appointees have even argued that political appointees, because of their divided loyalties, are less responsive than career civil servants. (Volcker, 1990, 223–24)

As presidents have sought to increase control over the bureaucracy, there has been an increase in the number of top presidential appointments to fill the highest posts in each department and agency (Ingraham, 1987). The number of Senate-confirmed appointments a president is allowed to make has increased from seventy-one in 1933 to 152 in 1965 (Pfiffner, 1987, 58) to over 400 (Mitchell, 1989) at the start of the Bush administration. However, there has long been a tension in the president's ability to manage the bureaucracy—the equivalent to a manager of a company's control over employees. Over 100 years ago, an assault was made on the president's ability to control the bureaucracy through patronage appointments by the passage of the Pendleton Act in 1883, which set up the Civil Service system, allowing a president today to appoint but "one seventh of one percent of the 3 million civilian employees in the federal civil service" (Meisler, 1988, 44a).[4]

As if the task of forming an administration through which to govern is not difficult enough, George Bush faced a situation not seen by any modern president. Not since 1928 had a president been elected to the highest office in the nation of the same party as his predecessor without being elevated from the vice president to the president due to resignation or death.

Thus, a new problem in administration and management faced President Bush. How does the party fit in with an administration? If a Republican administration is succeeding another Republican administration, and the support for the newly elected president was drawn in part from those who voted for the president on the basis of satisfaction with the last administration, can the new president change those individuals in the top administrative and management posts?

Another difficulty testing the leadership skills of the new president was the economic situation: "When President Bush entered office, the 1989 budget, with a deficit of $152 billion, was already in effect. Bush also inherited the Gramm-Rudman-Hollings Act, which required proposals for a balanced budget in the foreseeable future" (Rose, 1991, 319). What does it mean to lead a department or agency in an era of fiscal austerity? Are policy and program decisions being made by OMB? Are agency and department heads finding themselves limited to a reactive role to budget guidelines coming from the White House?

A SEARCH FOR "NEW" FACES

To assess the leadership strategies of President Bush in forming his administration, a useful starting point is an examination of the search for personnel to head the departments and agencies. Chase G. Untermeyer, who served in the transition, was named director of personnel and employed a staff of 29 paid and 198 volunteer workers to pore over 16,000 resumes, both solicited and unsolicited, that arrived by the time of the inauguration (Solomon, 1989e, 140). By June, files for more than 45,000 individuals had been received (Pfiffner, 1990, 68). It was not expected that their responsibilities would lessen until the fall.

The fact that the transition to a Bush administration was a "friendly takeover" was a mixed blessing. . . . On the one hand, there was no rush, as there would be with a party-turnover transition, to ensure that the opposition political party was out of office as soon as possible. . . . On the other hand, since they were loyal Republicans and had supported George Bush, many hoped and expected to stay on into a Bush Administration. (Pfiffner, 1990, 67–68)

The selection process to fill the top 400 Senate confirmed positions in the executive branch seemed to take longer than was the case for preceding administrations (Davidson and Oleszek, 1990, 230). While ethics and financial disclosure requirements have been in place for a number of years, new burdens faced the head-hunters of the Bush administration. The FBI was required to go back to a nominee's high school years for background checks (Waidmann, 1990). A new condition of employment in the Bush administration was an agreement to submit to drug testing as part of the "drugfree workplace plan that President Ronald Reagan announced in 1986" (Devroy, 1990, 14).

In December, it became clear the president-elect and top transition officials were dissatisfied with the number of minorities and women being

Table 3.1
Number of Weeks for Confirmation of Appointments, 1964–90

	Mean	Median
	(in weeks)	
Johnson	6.8	4.0
Nixon	8.5	7.0
Ford	11.0	8.0
Carter	11.8	10.0
Reagan, 1st term	14.6	14.0
Bush	8.4	6.3

Sources: Data for the Johnson-Reagan years are from Christopher J. Deering, "Damned If You Do and Damned If You Don't: The Senate's Role in the Appointment Process," in G. Calvin Mackenzie, ed. *The In-and-Outers* (Baltimore: Johns Hopkins University Press, 1987). Data for the Bush years are taken from CRS Reports for Congress on Presidential Nominations.

suggested for appointive posts (Devroy, 1988). Bush responded by adding the following individuals to his transition team: Betty Heitman, a former president of the National Federation of Republican Women, to help with the recruitment of women; Jose Martinez, a former Air Force officer and aide to former Senator Tower, to assist in the recruitment of Hispanics; and Constance Newman, a former official in the Department of Housing and Urban Development (HUD), to help identify blacks for top posts (Weinraub, 1988, 42). In addition, time was taken to call a meeting of state campaign chairs in order to broaden the pool of job candidates (Seib, 1988). But perhaps the biggest challenge was in deciding who would remain from the Reagan administration.

While it did take awhile for the president to name appointees to fill the posts at the highest levels, he could not complain about any unwillingness on the part of the Congress to confirm his appointments. The president received the cooperation of the U.S. Senate in spite of its Democratic majority. Having a president who himself had served in Congress and had pledged in his inaugural address, a willingness to work with Congress resulted in the Senate's moving quickly to confirm his choices. As Table 3.1 indicates, the Bush nominees, facing a Democratic Senate, were confirmed far more rapidly than were the first-term appointments of Reagan, who had a Republican Senate.

In the cabinet, Attorney General Richard L. Thornburgh, Treasury Secretary Nicholas F. Brady, and Education Secretary Lauro Cavazos had been appointed in the final months of the Reagan administration, with the approval of then-Vice President George Bush, with the full understanding and expectation that these individuals would continue on in the Bush administration.

While the Bush Cabinet rarely met, individual secretaries became more prominent in ways that suggested a revival of the Cabinet vis-à-vis the president's advisers in the executive office of the president. The basis for this enhanced role lay in the nature of the relationship between the president and his cabinet secretaries: A number of the secretaries had known Bush for years.

Bush "put a high premium on the 'comfort factor' and . . . [chose] Cabinet members that he would feel free to pick up the telephone and call" (Hoffman, 1988b). Dick Cheney, at the time a Republican leader in Congress, commented on the lack of new faces promised by Bush: "This is one of the few countries in the world where we place a premium on new faces. . . . There's a professionalism in the business of politics and government that Bush has tapped. . . . You're not trying to put together a cast for a new soap opera on television" (Hoffman, 1988b). None of the members of the Cabinet were strangers. They came from "the campaign, his friends and people he knew and served with under Presidents Reagan, Ford, and Nixon" (Hoffman, 1988b). This suggested that the Cabinet members would play a more prominent role in the Bush administration than is typical in most administrations, in which a president selects his closest friends for the White House staff, but not the Cabinet (Solomon, 1989c, 1704).

However, the problem still remained for the new administration: Was the new administration to be a continuation of the Reagan-Bush administration, or was it to move forward in a new direction? There would inevitably be tension within the administration in its formative stages due to the nature of the same party being re-elected to the White House.

A case in point is the Department of the Interior. While the president had pledged during the campaign to be the "environment president," Manuel Lujan, the new secretary of the Interior Department, while generally supportive of pro-development policy, also tried to balance the conservationists' positions with pro-development interests. Aides who had followed Lujan, a former member of Congress, from Capitol Hill, decided not "to challenge the status quo" in the department and the policies of hold-overs of the Reagan administration, some of whom still had ties to the former and controversial Secretary of the Interior James Watt (Lancaster, 1990). Thus, it would be difficult for the "environment president" to move quickly in this regard. While it was not urgent that all positions be filled quickly with Bush appointees (because Republicans were serving in these posts), the longer the Reagan appointees remained, the more difficult it would be for the Bush administration to present a clear agenda and identifiable program for governing the nation. While the president was of the same party as his predecessor, he still needed an agenda, people to help set the agenda and carry it out. Carl Brauer, a historian at Harvard University's John F. Kennedy

School of Government, has said, "You don't have policy until you have people" (Solomon, 1989f, 143).

DEMOGRAPHIC CHARACTERISTICS OF THE BUSH APPOINTEES

Demographically, the Bush appointees are not unlike those of previous administrations, as can be seen by looking at the demographic characteristics of those appointed in the first one and one-half years. However, the influence of the longtime Washington experience of President Bush is reflected in those selected for his first round of appointments.[5] Richard Viguerie, a conservative fund-raiser, went so far as to announce, "The real winner in the 1988 election is the Washington establishment" (Allen, 1989).

For the first time since the 1974 elevation of Gerald Ford to the presidency upon the resignation of Richard Nixon, there is a Washington insider in the White House. Earlier studies have shown that an "administration tends to turn to the greater Washington community for recruitment of political appointees as a term progresses" (Martin, 1991, 175). As the president and administration work with those in the Washington community—careerists in the departments and agencies, members of Congress, and interest group lobbyists—there is an increased sense of trust and enhanced respect for the members of the Washington community. Moreover, once an administration has been in office for a year or two, there grows a pool of individuals who have gained experience in lower-level appointed posts—for example, as assistant agency heads—who may be tapped for advancement to a higher post. This is the pattern observed in Table 3.2 for the Reagan administration. President Reagan, who campaigned as a Washington outsider, tended to recruit more men and women from the Washington area in his second term than in his first term. President Bush, who since the late 1960s has served as a member of the House of Representatives, ambassador to the United Nations and China, chairman of the Republican National Committee, director of the CIA, and vice president, was the consummate Washington insider, and his recruitment of administration personnel reflected a difference in professional background and experience from his predecessors. While Presidents Carter and Reagan had to gain confidence in the Washington community before turning to those individuals to join the administration, these individuals already had the trust of President Bush.

Occupation and Past Experience

As would be expected from the first administration elected to succeed an administration of the same party in the modern era, the Bush presidency retained a greater percentage (12.5%) of the appointees of the preceding administration than did all other administrations since Kennedy. Earlier stud-

Table 3.2
Geographical Background of Presidential Appointments, 1981–90

Percentage living and working in Washington, D.C.,
Virginia, or Maryland, at time of appointment:

	Women	Men
Reagan, 1st term	64.7% (N=34)	47.8% (N=318)
Reagan, 2nd term	82.2 (N=74)	70.2 (N=386)
Bush, 1989-June, 1990	78.5 (N=79)	63.8 (N=320)

Sources: Data for the Reagan years are from Christopher J. Deering, "Damned If You Do and Damned If You Don't: The Senate's Role in the Appointment Process," in G. Calvin Mackenzie, ed. *The In-and-Outers* (Baltimore: Johns Hopkins University Press, 1987). Data for the Bush years are taken from the CRS Reports for Congress on Presidential Nominations.

ies have suggested that the nature of same-party succession to the White House may influence recruitment patterns for an administration.[6] That is, when a president of the same party moves into the White House, there is a greater tendency to draw on those individuals already serving in executive branch posts for appointed positions, because they have experience and would also be likely to support the new president's program. In the last 60 years, until the Bush presidency, administrations with a same-party succession pattern came about due to the president's death or resignation and elevation of the vice president to the presidency.[7] In looking at Table 3.3, there is continuing evidence to support the theory that presidents in a same-party succession pattern draw more heavily from the executive branch in making appointments than do administrations coming in with a party change in the White House. Presidents Johnson, Ford, and Bush all drew more heavily from executive departments (same department, another department, or reappointment) than did Presidents Kennedy, Nixon, Carter, and Reagan in their first terms. Even though a president may not feel that control over the bureaucracy and structure of government can be achieved, there at least is a difference in perception of the federal executive sector on the part of presidents who come into the White House having witnessed their party in control of the bureaucracy. Whereas President Reagan exhibited hostility toward the bureaucracy throughout his two terms, and "remained the self-styled outsider in his valedictory speech on domestic policy decrying 'the Washington colony' for being out of touch with the nation," President-elect Bush sent different signals to the bureaucracy (Hoffman, 1988a). For example, while recent presidents had used the post of ambassador to the United Nations for political patronage purposes, President-elect Bush turned to a career Foreign Service officer—Thomas Pickering—to fill this sensitive post.[8] Similarly, one observer noted that the people the new president "wants to

Table 3.3
Occupation Immediately Prior to Appointment by Administration

	Kennedy	Johnson	Nixon	Ford	Carter	Reagan	Bush
Public Service:							
Reappointment	4.8%	9.2%	7.9%	6.2%	2.0%	6.3%	12.5%
State, local	7.6	4.1	6.3	3.4	10.1	3.0	5.1
Member of Congress	2.4	0.4	1.3	2.1	1.2	0.9	0.7
Congressional staff	5.4	1.5	1.0	2.7	5.2	4.6	4.6
Same department	16.3	29.9	20.5	27.4	16.1	24.1	15.1
Another department	13.0	21.8	19.2	26.0	17.0	20.3	21.2
Other government	2.1	1.5	0.3	0.7	1.2	1.3	1.0
Total:	51.5	68.4	56.5	68.5	52.8	60.5	60.2
Private Sector:							
Business/ banking	16.0	10.7	16.6	13.0	10.1	15.5	11.3
Private law	10.3	7.0	11.3	7.5	12.7	8.9	12.0
Educ./Research	12.1	10.3	10.3	6.2	14.4	7.7	7.4
Other	9.9	3.6	5.1	4.9	10.1	6.9	9.0
Total:	48.3	31.0	43.3	31.6	47.3	39.0	39.7
n=	331	271	302	146	347	821	391

	Reagan's 1st Term	Reagan's 2nd Term
Public Service:		
Reappointment	1.4%	10.0%
State, local	5.3	1.3
Member of Congress	1.4	0.4
Congressional staff	6.2	3.5
Same department	16.6	30.2
Another department	16.6	23.3
Other government	0.9	2.4
Total:	48.4	71.1
Private Sector:		
Business/banking	20.8	10.9
Private law	12.6	6.1
Educ./Research	10.1	5.9
Other	8.1	6.1
Total:	51.6	29.0
n=	356	460

Source: CRS Reports to Congress.

see first thing in the morning are career government workers: the analysts from the CIA" (Hoffman, 1988a).

Education

As expected, the Bush appointees are highly educated—a pattern found in previous studies of presidential appointees.[9] Some 75.1 percent ($N = 393$) have advanced degrees, giving the appointees of his administration a slightly higher rank than the Reagan appointees (74.7%, $N = 806$), and fourth rank of the last seven administrations. Almost a third of the Bush appointees have a law degree (32.8%), ranking the Bush administration last, down from a high of 48.6 percent ($N = 251$) in the Johnson years. About 18.6 percent of the Bush appointees have doctoral degrees, more than the Reagan administration (17%), but ranking only fourth of the last seven administrations.

Age

The median age of the appointees is forty-eight ($N = 389$). There is a noticeable difference in the median age of men and women appointees, with women averaging forty-two years of age ($N = 76$), and men forty-nine ($N = 313$). This was also true in the Reagan administration, and in part reflects the difference in the nature of posts to which men and women are appointed, with fewer women at the rank of, for example, Cabinet secretary, where average ages are higher. The next section will explore this further.

Gender

Before the election, candidates George Bush and Michael Dukakis had both made commitments that they would appoint more women in their administration than had been done before (Havemann, 1988). The Bush administration received praise from a number of sources early on for the percentage of appointments going to women, including the National Women's Political Caucus, which has coordinated a bipartisan Coalition for Women's Appointments. The coalition worked with the Bush transition team to identify and recommend women for top administrative posts.[10] Some 19.7 percent ($N = 402$) of all top-level Senate-confirmed appointments made in the first year and a half of his administration went to women. This is a sizeable increase from the appointments going to women in both President Reagan's first term (9.5%, $N = 357$) and second term (15.9%, $N = 464$). As Table 3.4 illustrates, if the Bush administration continues to recruit women to fill vacant positions at the same rate as was done early in the administration, we will see a return to the pattern observed since the 1970s whereby succeeding administrations increased the percentage of women ap-

Table 3.4
Women as a Percentage of Total Appointments, 1969–90

Nixon	3.0% (N=301)
Ford	6.0 (N=151)
Carter	15.0 (N=360)
Reagan	13.2 (N=826)
Bush	19.7 (N=402)

Source: CRS Reports to Congress.

Note: These figures exclude ambassadors, but include Cabinet secretaries, regulatory, commissioners, sub-cabinet appointments, heads of most of the large independent agencies and other key Senator-confirmed appointees of the President.

pointed. The only aberration will then be during the Reagan years, where there was a drop in the percentage of women appointed from the level of the preceding Carter administration.

However, in looking at the top-level appointments in President Bush's initial Cabinet, only one appointment went to a woman.[11]

While this is better than the record of President Reagan, who did not appoint a woman to head a Cabinet department until 1983, as of June 1991, Bush had only appointed two women to do so. (By the end of his term, Carter had made four Cabinet appointments to women, and Reagan had made three appointments to women.)

In looking at initial appointments made to sub-Cabinet posts, the Bush administration appointed women to nine departments, equaling the record number of departments to which women were appointed under President Carter (see Table 3.5).[12] By the end of one and a half years, the Bush administration had appointed women to sub-Cabinet posts in all departments, except the newly created Department of Veterans Affairs. Only one president, Jimmy Carter, had appointed women to sub-Cabinet posts in all departments.

Federal Administrative Experience

Presidents have long been suspicious of the loyalty of the bureaucracy. When Eisenhower brought in a Republican administration for the first time in twenty years, the new administration was "determined to weed out large numbers of Democratic bureaucrats and to reclassify a number of administrative positions from civil service status to Schedule 'C' or policy-appointive status" (Aberbach and Rockman, 1976, 456). Similarly, the next Republican administration to succeed a Democratic administration had the same perception of a career civil service hostile to the Nixon agenda and administration.

Table 3.5
Appointment of Women to Sub-Cabinet Posts in the Departments

Women appointed to departments as initial appointments:

Kennedy: None
Johnson: Agriculture
Nixon: Defense, HHS (formerly HEW)
Ford: State
Carter: Agriculture, Commerce, HHS, HUD, Interior, Justice,
Labor, State, Treasury
Reagan: Agriculture, Commerce, HHS, HUD, Justice,
Transportation, Treasury
Bush: Agriculture, Commerce, Education, Energy, HHS, Justice,
Labor, State, Transportation

Women appointed to departments as midterm replacements:

Kennedy: Labor
Johnson: HHS (formerly HEW)
Nixon: none
Ford: Defense, HHS, HUD
Carter: Defense, Education, Energy, Justice, State,
Transportation
Reagan: Agriculture, Commerce, Defense, Education, Energy,
HHS, HUD, Interior, Justice, State,
Transportation, Treasury
Bush: Agriculture, Commerce, Defense, Education, Energy,
HHS, HUD, Interior, Labor, State, Treasury

Source: CRS Reports to Congress.
Note: Initial appointments are those made during the first six months of an administration,
except in the case of Lyndon Johnson, who inherited an administration and retained most
of the Kennedy appointments until November 1964. For Johnson, the initial appointments
are those made before November 1964.

In a study of the attitudes and party affiliation of political executives in eighteen federal agencies in Washington in 1970, Aberbach and Rockman demonstrated that the career bureaucracy in the domestic policy arena had "very little Republican representation" and was "dominated by administrators ideologically hostile to many of the directions pursued by the Nixon administration in the realm of social policy" (Aberbach and Rockman, 1976, 467).

The question thus becomes one of leadership and governance. The nature of the bureaucracy is such that it lacks any constitutional basis for support, yet is dependent on Congress, courts, and the president for direction. The system of separate but shared powers inevitably will contribute to tension as the president attempts to gain control over the government. Given the dependence of bureaucrats on Congress for program support, while a partisan shift may occur in the White House, it is not inevitable that a partisan and ideological shift will follow in the bureaucracy, since programs can continue with congressional support (and recent patterns suggest it is likely to find the White House controlled by the Republicans and Congress controlled by the Democrats).

The president is usually portrayed as facing a bureaucracy that cannot be managed. However, presidents have been successful in increasing the numbers of political appointees throughout the bureaucracy, including the movement of political appointees into more management and line positions. But, while highly educated, many of the appointees lack the management and policy skills necessary for the post (Ingraham, 1987).

However, in re-examining the federal executive in 1986–87, a partisan shift "among career executives, especially among the top category of SES career executives (CA-I)" was detected (Aberbach, Rockman, and Copeland, 1990, 181). A comparison of career executives from 1970 with those serving in 1986–87 reveals that more of the 1986–87 identify with the Republican Party. It could be that as the length of time one party controls the White House increases, the composition of the careerists in the civil service, especially in the Senior Executive Service, undergoes some change. Those ideologically opposed to the president and his top appointees may voluntarily leave government service, especially as they are passed over for top posts. In addition, others who may be attracted to government service by the platform of the party in control of the government or the ideological leanings of the president may be brought into government. There may also be a growing "bureaucratic accommodation to a president's specific programs and goals" (Cole and Caputo, 1979, 412).

It is interesting to read a passage written in 1976, in which Aberbach and Rockman hypothesize that:

further expansion of governmental activities in the social service areas will expand the bureaucracies and activities that seem to attract administrators with the most liberal viewpoints. Unless a conservative Republican President does act sharply to curtail the activities of administrators in these agencies or to politicize the agencies through extensive changes in personnel, he can expect many of his social policies to be received coldly by administrators there. (Aberbach and Rockman, 1976, 467–68)

It would appear as if the efforts of the Reagan administration to structure an administration more favorably inclined to support his policy agenda were successful to a certain extent. In part, this may have been assisted by the necessity to face a contraction of governmental services as Gramm-Rudman-Hollings (GRH) Act and successive budget agreements in the late 1980s provided a need to live with program reductions.

Table 3.6
Past Federal Administrative Experience by President

	Percentage of those having any federal administrative experience
Kennedy	61.3% (n=331)
Johnson	68.3 (n=271)
Nixon	59.9 (n=302)
Ford	64.2 (n=151)
Carter	54.4 (n=364)
Reagan	69.8 (n=827)
Reagan, 1st term	59.5 (n=358)
Reagan, 2nd term	77.8 (n=464)
Bush	74.4 (n=407)

Source: CRS Reports to Congress.

This shift in composition of the bureaucracy from 1970 to the mid-1980s may reflect the influence of the president. It also suggests that the party in control of the White House may have a greater role in affecting the governing of the departments and agencies than is usually acknowledged. One problem has always been the limited number of cases by which to test the effects of different administrations and partisan influence.

One interesting pattern to note in looking at the individuals recruited to fill appointed posts in the Bush administration is that a large proportion of these Bush appointees have had some type of federal administrative experience. The administrations with the greatest percentage of appointees with experience in the federal executive sector have all succeeded an administration of the same party (Johnson, Ford, Bush; see Table 3.6). The dramatic effect of same-party succession can be seen when comparing Reagan's first and second term (Reagan being the only president to successfully complete two terms of office since Eisenhower).

In spite of the Reagan-Bush same-party control of the White House, there continues to be a decline in the number of individuals who have multiple appointments (see Table 3.7), continuing the pattern of "in-and-outers."[13] Yet with same-party succession, there is an increase in the percentage of appointees with federal administrative experience. While it may be difficult for presidents to "control" the bureaucracy, the task may not be as formidable to those presidents fortunate enough to follow their own party to the White House. And the bureaucracy appears to provide a pool of candidates for appointive posts. Perhaps if one party were to continue control over the presidency, there might not be the tension often perceived between the president and the bureaucracy and presidential leadership and governance would be enhanced.

Table 3.7
Number of Appointments per Person by Administration

President	One Appointment	More than One Appointment
Kennedy	71.9%	28.0% (N=331)
Johnson	55.7	44.3 (N=271)
Nixon	58.3	41.7 (N=302)
Ford	64.9	35.2 (N=151)
Carter	77.2	22.7 (N=364)
Reagan	72.2	27.6 (N=827)
Bush	78.4	21.7 (N=407)

Source: CRS Reports to Congress.

AN ASSESSMENT OF LEADERSHIP

With the same-party continuity, President Bush assembled an administrative structure on paper that offered great promise and potential. A competent and highly regarded team, in the White House and in the top posts throughout the Cabinet departments and agencies, was put in place throughout 1989. Not surprisingly, given the president's stated preference for people he feels comfortable with and policy makers who have worked together in previous Republican administrations, there has been little visible feuding. "The President doesn't want policy made by conflict but by reasoned discussion," said one White House aide (Solomon, 1989c, 1705).

The president made overtures to the bureaucracy, which was not the traditional approach of most presidents, but was not unexpected of a man who had been employed in the federal government for the last twenty years.

George Bush ran as an insider, as someone who had "learned firsthand many of the intricate and sometimes obscure ways of government, from the workings of the Foreign Service to congressional staffs" (Hoffman, 1988a). Initially, in the first several months of the new administration, it appeared as though Bush were lagging behind his predecessors in filling top-level spots, and there was concern over lost opportunities to shape policy. By February 27, 1989, Bush had submitted only half of the number of names Reagan had submitted by the same point in his administration (McQueen, 1989, 1). Reasons for the delays were attributed to difficulties in identifying Bush loyalists for posts, the search for women and minorities, the meeting of ethics regulations, the "salary gap" between the public and private sectors, and "increased scrutiny of public officials' private lives and the time it takes the F.B.I. to do background checks" (Rosenthal, 1989, 4E).[14]

But perhaps more significantly, some speculated that since Bush, after a friendly takeover, had no clear mission, it became more difficult to attract individuals to join the administration (McQueen, 1989). As one observer noted, "Bush got through the 1988 campaign on symbols and values, . . . criminal furloughs, the Pledge of Allegiance, the American Civil Liberties Union, the death penalty and the menace of liberalism" (Schneider, 1989, 262). As a result, he had "no special agenda for the first hundred days." Instead, he used "the thematic approach, defining himself in terms of symbols and values rather than programs" (Schneider, 1989). This is not an approach designed to inspire people to enter government service, people who will be faced with the likelihood of giving up high-paying jobs and well-developed careers, as well as being subjected to ethics regulations, intensive background checks, and perhaps lost earnings, in exchange for vague exhortations to serve no clear agenda.

The result was a Cabinet dominated by individuals who are loyal to the president and have been friends with the president for many years: "In most cases, the Bush approach . . . has produced one big happy family in power: rarely does a Cabinet exude such unanimity and eschew back-stabbing" (Safire, 1990, 31). Bush has striven for a happy medium between the detached approach of his predecessor, and the too-intimately involved approach of Carter. Bush tries to be "neither too involved nor too remote" (Safire, 1990, 31). However, "the absence of creative tension has generated little excitement or innovation: no stewing, all stewarding" (Safire, 1990, 32). It has been observed that while "some skirmishing goes on, . . . as a result of the Bush emphasis on calm seas, internal order and at least the appearance of unanimity, . . . we miss the Rooseveltian turbulence that often leads to original thinking" (Safire, 1990, 32).

There have been few departures from the Cabinet. In December 1990, Rep. Lynn Martin (R-Ill.) was named Secretary of Labor, replacing Elizabeth Dole, and former Tennessee Governor Lamar Alexander replaced Lauro Cavazos as Secretary of Education. Clayton Yeutter also left the Cabinet to head the Republican National Committee, and Rep. Edward Madigan (R-Ill.), the ranking Republican on the Agriculture Committee, was named Secretary of Agriculture. In 1991, Richard Thornburgh left his post as attorney general in an unsuccessful bid to fill the remainder of the U.S. Senate term of the late Pennsylvania Senator John Heinz. William P. Barr, deputy attorney general, moved up to the post of attorney general. Overall, the Bush appointees were viewed quite favorably "for the depth of their experience and their competence" (Seib, 1988).

Yet the leadership at the top has been missing. While the focus has been on foreign policy, on the domestic front, the administration could either be said to be driven by or excused by the budget. The lack of an agenda is reflected in the data in Table 3.8. Data from the Center for Media and Public Affairs, which tracks press coverage of the president and the administration, demonstrates a lack of activity in the administration and, therefore, a lack of interest on the part of the press in covering the administration, when

Table 3.8
Major Network News Coverage of Each Administration during the First
Sixty Days

Coverage of:

	President	Administration
Carter	520	832
Reagan	399	1030
Bush	265	505

Source: Center for Media and Public Affairs, reported in "Hardship Post," by Fred Barnes, *The New Republic*, May 8, 1989, p. 8.

coverage of the Bush administration is compared with coverage given to either Carter or Reagan during an equivalent period of time.

No one, including the president, took on the role of overall architect of policy. The president, with wide breadth of federal service, lacked depth in any one area (except, perhaps, in the area of foreign policy, which he has repeatedly admitted is his favorite). Perhaps the best symbolic indication of the difficulty in setting an agenda and priorities is that in 1989, "for the first time since 1933, there was technically no State of the Union message" (Solomon, 1990, 140). Reagan gave a farewell address, and Bush gave an "address by the President to the joint session of Congress" on February 9.

While there has been little movement on domestic policy in the Bush administration, we can conclude on a positive note with regard to Bush's relationship with the cumbersome career bureaucracy discussed at the beginning of this chapter. Compared with recent administrations, the president has done much to enhance the working relationship between the career bureaucracy and the White House.

The first executive order signed by the president established the President's Commission on Federal Ethics Law Reform, and the first group addressed by President Bush outside of the White House were members of the Senior Executive Service.[15] He told them, "You're one of the most important groups I will ever speak to." He invited them to work with his political appointees and praised them for their "knowledge, ability, and integrity" (Bush, Jan. 26, 1989). The president probably did much to enhance the respect for public service through his words to the public servants:

I'm coming to you as president and offering my hand in partnership. I'm asking you to join me as full members of our team. I promise to lead and to listen, and I promise to serve beside you as we work together to carry out the will of the American people. . . . I want to make sure that public service is valued and respected, because I want to encourage America's young to pursue careers in government. (Bush, Jan. 26, 1989)

This perhaps will be the most important legacy of the Bush presidency in terms of the executive branch.

ACKNOWLEDGMENTS

I would like to thank John Winship and the editors for their helpful comments. Data for the years 1964–84 are taken from the National Academy of Public Administration's (NAPA) Presidential Appointee Project. I am appreciative of the assistance provided by Cal Mackenzie, Linda Fisher, and Paul Light in making that data set available. I am also most grateful for the assistance of three student research assistants at Bowdoin College—John Dougherty, Marty Malague, and Michelle Chaffee—for their help in compiling data for the years 1961–64, and 1984 to the present. John Dougherty held a Bowdoin College Surdna Undergraduate Fellowship for 1990–91, which enabled him to assist in this project.

NOTES

1. In 1987, the National Commission on the Public Service (referred to as the Volcker Commission, after Paul A. Volcker, chairman of the commission) was formed to address a "quiet crisis" in government and make recommendations to the president and Congress. The crisis was, and remains, the "erosion in the attractiveness of public service." While representing a "broad spectrum of political views," the members of the commission shared "a conviction that rebuilding an effective, principled, and energetic public service must rank high on the nation's agenda" (Volcker, 1990, xiii). The 1989 Report of the National Commission on the Public Service, the Volcker Commission Report, has been published in Paul A. Volcker, *Leadership for America*, Lexington, Mass.: Lexington Books, 1990.

2. "Leadership for Governance" is the title of one of the chapters in the Volcker Report.

3. For example, Richard Nixon "took an unprecedented step, going on national television to introduce the Cabinet *en bloc*" (Nathan, 1975, 37).

4. In 1990, the Supreme Court ruled in *Rutan v. Republican Party of Illinois*, in a 5–4 decision, "that federal state and local governments cannot refuse to hire, promote or transfer most employees because of their political affiliations or party activities" (Marcus, 1990, A1).

5. Presidential appointees to Senate-confirmed posts in executive departments, independent agencies, and regulatory boards and commissions are included in this analysis (which excludes ambassadors, U.S. marshals, U.S. attorneys, and appointments to legislative or judicial agencies). The appointments and confirmations of individuals have been identified using the series of CRS reports for Congress on Presidential Nominations to full-time positions, the *Congressional Record*, and *Weekly Compilation of Presidential Documents*, and communication with the White House Office of Personnel. All individuals appointed by June 1990, and confirmed by March 1991, have been included in the analysis of appointments made by President Bush.

6. For example, see Martin (1991), "An Examination of Executive Branch Appointments in the Reagan Administration by Background and Gender."

7. Truman, Johnson, and Ford.

8. For example, Reagan's appointment of Jeane Kirkpatrick, Carter's appointment of Andrew Young.

9. See David J. Stanley, Dean E. Mann, and Jameson W. Doig, *Men Who Govern* (Washington, D.C.: Brookings, 1967); Linda Fisher, "Fifty Years of Presidential Appointments," in G. Calvin Mackenzie, ed., *The In-and-Outers* (Baltimore: Johns Hopkins University Press, 1987).

10. The Coalition for Women's Appointments was made from eighty-eight groups representing a broad coalition, from the American Association of University Women (AAUW) to the YWCA (Havemann, 1988). The Coalition for Women's Appointments had helped the Carter White House identify women, and those supportive of women's issues, for consideration to appointive posts, but it had been "shut out entirely during the Reagan years" (Simpson, 1989).

11. Elizabeth Dole was appointed Secretary of Labor.

12. Initial appointments are those made in the president's first six months in office.

13. See Mackenzie, *The In-and-Outers*, 1987.

14. By December 1989, 75 percent of sub-Cabinet appointments were in place (Solomon, 1989a, 2952).

15. This is a bipartisan commission to develop ethics reform proposals for executive, legislative, and judicial posts. In setting up the commission, the president emphasized four key principles:

One, ethical standards for public servants must be exacting enough to ensure that the officials act with the utmost integrity and live up to the public's confidence in them. Two, standards must be fair. They must be objective and consistent with common sense. Three, the standards must be equitable all across the three branches of the Federal Government. And the fourth one—we cannot afford to have unreasonably restrictive requirements that discourage able citizens from entering public service. (Bush, *Public Papers*, Jan. 25, 1989)

REFERENCES

Aberbach, Joel D., and Bert A. Rockman. 1976. "Clashing Beliefs Within the Executive Branch: The Nixon Administration Bureaucracy." *The American Political Science Review* 70: 456–68.

Aberbach, Joel D., and Bert A. Rockman, with Robert M. Copeland. 1990. "From Nixon's Problem to Reagan's Achievement: The Federal Executive Reexamined." In *Looking Back on the Reagan Presidency*, edited by Larry Berman. Baltimore: Johns Hopkins University Press.

Allen, Henry. 1989. "The Return of the Insiders." *Washington Post*. January 18: D1.

Barnes, Fred. 1989. "Hardship Post." *The New Republic*. May 8: 7–9.

Barnes, James A. 1991. "Still Missing Reagan." *National Journal*. March 2: 510–13.

Berman, Larry, ed. 1990. *Looking Back on the Reagan Presidency*. Baltimore: Johns Hopkins University Press.

Bonafede, Dom. 1989. "Rating Bush." *National Journal*. April 8: 890.

Boyd, Gerald M. 1989. "The Bush Style of Management: After Reagan, It's Back to Details." *New York Times*. March 19: 1.

———. 1987. "Bush Envisions Hands-On Presidency." *New York Times*. November 23: B12.

Broder, David. 1988. "Bush—The Good News and the Bad." *Washington Post.* November 2: 21.

Bush, George. 1990. "Transcript of Bush's State of the Union Message to the Nation." *New York Times.* February 5.

———. 1989. January 26: "Remarks to Members of the Senior Executive Service." January 25: "Remarks on Signing the Executive Order Establishing the President's Commission on Federal Ethics Law Reform." *Public Papers of the Presidents of the United States.* Washington, D.C.: U.S. Government Printing Office.

Cole, Richard L., and David A. Caputo. 1979. "Presidential Control of the Senior Civil Service: Assessing the Strategies of the Nixon Years." *The American Political Science Review* 73: 399–413.

Cronin, Thomas. 1975. *The State of the Presidency.* Boston: Little, Brown.

Davidson, Roger H., and Walter J. Oleszek. 1990. *Congress and Its Members*, 3rd edn. Washington, D.C.: CQ Press.

Deering, Christopher J. 1987. "Damned If You Do and Damned If You Don't: The Senate's Role in the Appointments Process." In *The In-and-Outers.* Edited by G. Calvin Mackenzie. Baltimore: Johns Hopkins University Press.

Devroy, Ann. 1990. "For Appointees, a Job Condition." *Washington Post.* January 23: A14.

———. 1988. "Bush Likely to Tap Black for Cabinet." *Washington Post.* December 10: A4.

Fisher, Linda. 1987. "Fifty Years of Presidential Appointments." In *The In-and-Outers.* Edited by G. Calvin Mackenzie. Baltimore: Johns Hopkins University Press.

Havemann, Judith. 1989a. "Federal Vacancies Becoming Drag on Policymaking." *Washington Post.* March 18: A10.

———. 1989b. "Lacking Top Appointees, U.S. Agencies Face Growing Backlogs." *Washington Post.* May 1 (LEGI-SLATE Story No. 84241).

———. 1988. "Bush to Get 2,500 Conservative Resumes." *Washington Post.* November 15: A17.

Hoffman, David. 1988a. "At Last, a President Who Ran as an Insider, Not an Outsider." *Washington Post Weekly Edition.* December 26 to January 1, 1989: 31.

———. 1988b. "Familiar Faces Chosen to Fill Cabinet Room." *Washington Post.* December 25: 1.

Ingraham, Patricia W. 1987. "Building Bridges or Burning Them? The President, the Appointees, and the Bureaucracy." *Public Administration Review* 47: 425–35.

Kirschten, Dick. 1988. "Cabinet Power Won't Be the Same If President Bush Has His Way." *National Journal.* November 26: 3020–21.

Lancaster, John. 1990. "New Look, Old Mission at Lujan's Department." *Washington Post.* January 19: A1.

Mackenzie, G. Calvin, ed. 1987. *The In-and-Outers.* Baltimore: Johns Hopkins University Press.

Marcus, Ruth. 1990. "Job Patronage Barred by High Court Ruling." *Washington Post.* June 22: A1.

Martin, Janet M. 1991. "An Examination of Executive Branch Appointments in the

Reagan Administration by Background and Gender." *Western Political Quarterly*. 44: 173–84.

McAllister, Bill, and Judith Havemann. 1988. "Appointments Will Continue 'At My Own Pace,' Bush Says." *Washington Post*. November 24: A21.

McQueen, Michel. 1989. "Bush's Lag in Filling Top Posts Risks a Loss of Crucial Momentum." *Wall Street Journal*. February 28: 1.

Meisler, Stanley. 1988. "Washington Job Hunting Frenzy Has Roots That Go Deep." *Maine Sunday Telegram*. December 18: 44A.

Mitchell, George. 1989. *Congressional Record*. September 6: S10605.

Nathan, Richard P. 1975. *The Plot That Failed: Nixon and the Administrative Presidency*. New York: John Wiley and Sons.

Pfiffner, James P. 1990. "Establishing the Bush Presidency." *Public Administration Review* (January/February): 64–72.

———. 1987. "Political Appointees and Career Executives: The Democracy-Bureaucracy Nexus in the Third Century." *Public Administration Review* (January/February): 57–65.

Plano, Jack C., and Milton Greenberg. 1985. *The American Political Dictionary*, 7th edn. New York: Holt, Rinehart and Winston.

Rose, Richard. 1991. *The Postmodern President*, 2nd edn. Chatham, N.J.: Chatham House Publishers.

Rosenthal, Andrew. 1989. "It's Loneliest at the Top of the Bureaucracy." *New York Times*. July 23: 4E.

Safire, William. 1990. "Bush's Cabinet, Who's Up, Who's Down." *New York Times Magazine*. March 25: Section 6.

Schneider, William. 1989. "Symbols, Values May Not Be Enough." *National Journal*. January 28: 262.

Schwartz, Maralee, and Frank Swoboda. 1989. "Bush Assistant Describes Trouble Recruiting Women." *Washington Post*. January 12: A17.

Seib, Gerald F. 1988. "Bush's Appointments Mark Him as a Man of the Establishment." *Wall Street Journal*. December 14: 1.

Simpson, Peggy. 1989. "Bush: A Ladies' Man?" *Ms*. October: 67–69.

Solomon, Burt. 1990. "Influence Is Getting a Few Lines into Bush's State of the Union Speech." *National Journal*. January 20: 140–41.

———. 1989a. "Bush's Laggard Appointment Pace May Not Matter All That Much." *National Journal*. December 2: 2952–53.

———. 1989b. "At School Summit, Will Governors Ask Bush, 'Where's the Money?' " *National Journal*. September 23: 2354–55.

———. 1989c. "When the Bush Cabinet Convenes It's a Gathering of Presidential Pals." *National Journal*. July 1: 1704–5.

———. 1989d. "Bush's Disdain for Image Making May Come to Plague His Tenure." *National Journal*. March 11: 602–3.

———. 1989e. "A Longtime Bush Aide Takes Charge of Peopling." *National Journal*. January 21: 140.

———. 1989f. "Bush Promised Fresh Faces But He's Hiring Old Friends." *National Journal*. January 21: 142–43.

Stanley, David J., Dean E. Mann, and Jameson W. Doig. 1967. *Men Who Govern*. Washington, D.C.: Brookings.

Swoboda, Frank, and Judith Havemann. 1988. "Bush Transition Team Embarking on Search for New Talent, Diversity." *Washington Post*. December 3: A9.

U.S. Congress. 1973. Senate. Select Committee on Presidential Campaign Activities. *Executive Session Hearings*. "Watergate and Related Activities—Use of Incumbency—Responsiveness Program." 93rd Congress, 2nd Session. Washington, D.C. Exhibit 35, V. 19, p. 9006. Cited in Aberbach, Joel D., and Bert A. Rockman, "Clashing Beliefs Within the Executive Branch: The Nixon Administration Bureaucracy." *The American Political Science Review* 70: 457.

Volcker, Paul A. 1990. *Leadership for America* (The 1989 Report of the National Commission on the Public Service and the Task Force Reports to the National Commission on the Public Service). Lexington, Mass.: Lexington Books.

Waidmann, Brian. 1990. Special Assistant to the President. Interview with author. Washington, D.C.

Weinraub, Bernard. 1988. "Bush Plans a Drive to Recruit Minorities." *Washington Post*. December 4: 42.

Chapter 4

George Bush and Congress: The Question of Leadership

GARY LEE MALECHA AND
DANIEL J. REAGAN

Conservatives and liberals alike criticize President Bush as a cynical, opportunistic politician. George Will, for instance, has referred to him as a "weather vane" (1989, 78). Michael Kinsley (1991, 4) has declared that Bush has no principles worth abandoning. Many Republicans now openly question the depth of his ideological convictions, while most Democrats express contempt for his professed concern for the hardships confronting many Americans. References to Bush as being Janus-faced abound. Gary Trudeau lampooned apparent discrepancies in the president's behavior in his comic strip "Doonesbury" by inventing a new character, "Bush's evil twin, Skippy." *Time* awarded Bush its "Men of the Year" award, indicating that there are two presidents, a domestic one and a foreign one, and that the "domestic President Bush" is profoundly different from the "foreign President Bush" (1991). A veteran Washington political analyst offered a similar assessment in a recent interview, saying, "It seems to be that Bush is two personalities" (quoted in Jones, 1991a, 59). Finally, all indications are that in the election of 1992, Democrats will concede the achievements of the "foreign President Bush" while they simultaneously accentuate the lack of initiatives on the part of the "domestic President Bush."

Enlisting insights afforded by Richard Ellis and Aaron Wildavsky (1989) in their study of presidential leadership, we offer an analysis that modifies these conventional accounts. We will ultimately argue that Bush, in domestic affairs and foreign affairs, has approached relations with Congress in a predictable way.

Our chapter is divided into several parts. First, we sketch and apply the theoretical concepts that inform our analysis. Next, we examine Bush's approach to interbranch relations. To elaborate our argument, we then provide two detailed case studies of relations between Bush and Congress over issues in foreign affairs. Throughout the course of our chapter, we will show that Bush has adhered to what Ellis and Wildavsky have referred to as a "hierarchical" perspective in his dealings with Congress. Of equal importance, we will contend that in both domestic affairs and foreign affairs Bush, while attempting to convey an image of strength to obscure the weakness of his position, has consistently endeavored to shore up presidential authority to redress what he sees as an unfavorable and illegitimate structural balance that favors Congress in interbranch relations.

THE BUSH PRESIDENCY: STYLE AND CHALLENGES

Building on concepts developed in the anthropology of Mary Douglas (1970; 1982), Ellis and Wildavsky (1989; see also Wildavsky, 1989) postulate the existence of three contending types of political cultures: hierarchical, individualistic, and egalitarian.[1] From these they elaborate a conceptual framework designed to facilitate the study of political leadership.

Cultural Types

Hierarchies, according to cultural theory, institutionalize relations of authority. Followers are expected to defer to better informed and more qualified leaders. Inequalities in hierarchies are justified as the unavoidable effects of the specialization of function and division of labor that are accepted as the most expeditious and effective way to live together. Hierarchies are sustained by a "sacrificial ethic": The interests of the parts are subordinated to the pursuit of the collective good (Wildavsky, 1987, 6–7). Hierarchs, then, can be identified by the emphasis they place on "themes of social order, stability, harmony, and solidarity." Another "telltale sign" of a hierarchical bias is a belief in "structured inequality" (Ellis and Wildavsky, 1989, 6–7). Adherents of the other two cultures have a bias against authority and the exercise of leadership. Individualists value "self-regulation." To minimize the need for authority, they support a decentralized system of voluntary exchange. Valuing equality of opportunity "to compete," they can be identified by the extent to which they extol the virtues of markets (Ellis and Wildavsky, 1989, 7).

Egalitarians, meanwhile, "reject authority" and support a life of "voluntary association." Since communal life without relations of authority can only prevail in an environment populated by equals, they commit themselves to the ideal of greater social equality (Wildavsky, 1987, 6–7). They are therefore recognized by the emphasis they place on "the need to diminish differences" between individuals (Ellis and Wildavsky, 1989, 7).

Using this typology, it is possible to develop a classification of presidents and their cultural context. What is important is the manner in which presidents of varying "cultural propensities" relate to the contending cultures within the historical setting in which they operate. Since representatives of these three "ways of life" view and respond to authority differently, an understanding of this relationship requires comprehension of both a president's cultural affinities and the corresponding cultural and historical environments.

Bush as Hierarchal Leader

Bush's rhetoric suggests a commitment to hierarchy (see also Mullins and Wildavsky, 1991). Frequently invoking the "idea of community" (*New York Times*, 9 August, 1988, A14), he admonishes citizens, as he did in his inaugural address, to remember that "we are all part of a continuum, inescapably connected by the ties that bind" (*Congressional Quarterly Almanac*, 1989, 7-C). He qualifies his celebration of individual freedom and markets, asking the American people to bear in mind that "we are not the sum of our possessions. They are not the measure of our lives" (*Congressional Quarterly Almanac*, 1989, 8-C). "Prosperity," he avers, imposes obligations on the fortunate by affording them an opportunity to pursue "the better angels" (*New York Times*, 19 August, 1988). Committed to an ethic of sacrifice and service, he avows concern for both posterity and a "kinder and gentler" America.

In keeping with his cultural bias, Bush envisages America as a harmonious collection of smaller, public-spirited "communities." He deprecates those who mistake provincial, competing interests "locked in odd conformity" for "community" (*New York Times*, 19 August, 1988, A14). For him, the "state of the union" is instead "the sum of our friendships, marriages, families and communities" (*Congressional Quarterly Weekly Reports*, 2 February, 1991, 308). In that vein, he praises various groups and associations for their distinctive contributions to the nation's welfare (*Congressional Quarterly Almanac*, 1989, 13-C; *New York Times*, 19 August, 1988, A14; 28 November, 1991, A9). Unlike his predecessor, Ronald Reagan, he openly admits that even government, as "part of the nation of communities," has an important, albeit clearly defined, role to play. As he explains it, the realization of the public good presupposes a government that is both sufficiently empowered and limited: "Transforming America requires not only the power of the free market but also a dynamic government. . . . I believe in this kind of government, a government of compassion and competence. And I believe in backing it up" (*Congressional Quarterly Weekly Reports*, 12 June 1991, 1619).

For Bush, even political leadership is conceived in hierarchical terms: "Some see leadership as high drama, and the sound of trumpets calling. And sometimes it is that. But I see history as a book with many pages—and each day we fill a page with acts of hopefulness and meaning" (*Congressional Quarterly Almanac*, 1989, 9-C). Accordingly, he construes his role as president as one of maintaining stability and continuity. Preferring incremental policy adjustments designed to maintain the system, he has no need for a comprehensive vision for change. Thus he admits: "I respect old-fashioned common sense and have no great love for the imaginings of the social planners. You see, I like what's been tested and found to be true" (*New York Times*, 19 August 1988, A14).

The Context of the Bush Presidency

Recent literature on legislative–executive relations underscores sociopolitical variables that condition presidential leadership of Congress. Primary among these are the problems and agenda that a newly elected president inherits (Jones, 1990; 1991b; Pfiffner, 1988; Rose, 1991) and the partisan composition of a Congress with which the president must deal (Edwards, 1989; Bond and Fleisher, 1990).

There is little doubt that the legacy bequeathed by the Reagan administration has restricted Bush's policy options. For instance, Bush had little choice but to respond to the financial crisis in the savings and loan industry that Congress and the previous administration had left unresolved. Then, too, his maneuverability in offering initiatives to realize a "kinder and gentler" America has been circumscribed by past decisions and policies. Indeed, any initiative that Bush has wanted to pursue has had to be reconciled with efforts to bring the nation's large budget deficits under control.

Constraints like the foregoing were compounded by the peculiar road Bush traveled to reach the White House. As a sitting vice president, he was implicitly linked to an existing policy agenda. He reinforced this perception by conducting a campaign that purposely eschewed a discussion of issues and programmatic reforms (see Solomon, 1988, 2838). Instead of articulating a prospective legislative agenda, he opted to engage in negative attacks on Michael Dukakis while simultaneously promising, in rather nebulous rhetoric, to guard and build incrementally on Reagan's accomplishments (Weko and Aldrich, 1990). The result, concluded *National Journal* correspondent Jonathan Rauch (1989, 119), was that Bush "was elected with a mandate to change things, but not very much."

Not only was Bush encumbered by the problems and agenda that he inherited, but the partisan composition of 101st and 102nd Congresses put him at a disadvantage in interbranch relations. Although "coalition government" (Sundquist, 1988) has been the norm since the election of 1956, Bush's elevation to the presidency in 1988 was especially distinctive, for his party actually lost ground in Congress. Continuing a trend that has been underway since the 1960s (Fiorina, 1990), many of those who voted for Bush in 1988 split their ticket and voted for Democratic congressional candidates. In fact, Bush's impact on congressional races was so negligible that he ran behind the winning candidate in about 85 percent of the House districts (Cohen, 1989, 1048). Conditions for Bush, moreover, did not improve in the 1990 off-year election, when his party, already down by 85 seats in the House and 10 in the Senate, lost additional seats. As a result, in the 102nd Congress, Bush has been on even weaker footing.

Because Republicans have had only a working minority in Congress, Bush has been compelled to rely on Democrats to support his initiatives. The trouble with this is that the number of conservative southern Democrats, who in the past were amenable to forging an alliance with a Republican president on issues like defense, civil rights and fiscal policy, has eroded appreciably in recent years. Yearly analyses of legislative voting patterns conducted by *Congressional Quarterly* have pointed to a secular decline in the frequency with which the "conservative coalition" appears on votes taken. For the most part, this coalition has been moribund during the Bush years (see *Congressional Quarterly Weekly Reports*, 30 December, 1989, 3551–55; 22 December, 1990, 4192–95; 28 December 1991, 3759–60). This demise of the "conservative coalition" is emblematic of an ideological transformation that has occurred within the congressional parties. The decline in the number of conservative southern Democrats and northern liberal Republicans has rendered each party in Congress more ideologically homogenous and polarized (Wilson, 1986). With a few exceptions, *Congressional Quarterly*'s measure of partisan voting, its party unity index, has shown that moderate increases in partisanship have emerged over the last few years (*Congressional Quarterly Weekly Reports*, 30 December 1989, 3546–50; 22 December 1990, 4188–91; 28 December 1991, 3755–58). *National Journal*'s recent analyses of voting patterns (Cohen and Schneider, 27 January 1990; 19 January 1991) reveal similar results. Its data also indicate that Democrats are more inclined to support liberal policies, while Republicans are more likely to back conservative causes.

Duane Oldfield and Aaron Wildavsky (1991) suggest that today congressional Democrats consistently support policies that promote greater equality while congressional Republicans, though they are a bit more difficult to characterize, are usually arrayed on two different dimensions, corresponding roughly to social and economic conservatism, that is, hierarchy and competitive individualism. Further reinforcing this ideological division in Congress has been what Benjamin Ginsberg and Martin Shefter (1990) have shown to be the Republican Party's recent success in reorganizing under its "auspices" some of the major political forces that traditionally supported Democrats. They contend that under Reagan and Bush, the Republican

Party has been able to manufacture electoral coalitions comprising the business community, young and fiscally conservative upper-middle-class suburbanites, and conservative blue-collar ethnics and southern evangelicals. Consequently, as the Democratic Party has become more egalitarian, the Republican Party has come to be dominated by an admixture of hierarchical and individualist elements (see also Dionne, 1991).

As the above suggests, the environment in which Bush has operated has not been conducive to dramatic presidential leadership. Unresolved problems, an extremely large deficit, and a policy agenda inherited from the previous administration converged to make bold presidential initiatives unlikely. Working within a constitutional structure that diffuses power, Bush, moreover, has found his task complicated by the cultural predispositions of members in Congress. The ideological transformation of congressional parties in the last decade has culminated in a Congress that is generally less amenable to the exercise of authority that inheres in active presidential leadership. Thus, Bush has had to confront the problem of maintaining coalitions of the competing cultures of hierarchy and individualism that make up his party. To advance his objectives, he has also been compelled to appeal to or neutralize a growing egalitarian opposition. In such an environment, presidential success has been problematic.[2]

BUSH: HIERARCH AS PRESIDENT

Bush embarked on a journey to restore comity between Congress and the executive branch as soon as he took the oath of office. Invoking "old ideas" and hierarchical values like "duty, sacrifice, commitment, and a patriotism that finds its expression in taking part and pitching in," he called for a "new engagement" between the Congress and the presidency. Turning to the leaders of Congress during his inaugural address, he said: "To my friends— and yes, I do mean friends—in the loyal opposition—and yes, I mean loyal: I put out my hand." What he sought was a relationship in which the members of the different branches of government subordinated partisan and institutional interests to the good of the whole: "We need compromise; we've had dissension. We need harmony; we've had a chorus of discordant voices. . . . A new breeze is blowing—and the old bipartisanship must be made new again" (*Congressional Quarterly Almanac*, 1989, 7-C, 8-C, 9-C).

Initially, members of Congress welcomed Bush's approach. "The style," observed Senator Thad Cochran (R-Miss.), "is refreshing to members who thought the last administration was a little confrontational" (*Congressional Quarterly Weekly Reports*, 6 May 1989, 1018). Yet even though Bush has repeatedly expressed a desire to work with Congress in a spirit of cooperation and trust, it is common today to hear of the disappointment and acrimony that mark his dealings with the legislative branch.

Although he is conciliatory, Bush has never misunderstood cooperation with Congress as acceding to what he understands to be the legislature's usurpation of executive powers. Instead, he has indicated his interest in preserving constitutional forms and proper interbranch relations. On matters like the budget, for example, he has stressed the primacy of the constitutional roles and responsibilities of Congress (*Congressional Quarterly Weekly Reports*, 26 May 1990, 1685). At the same time, with many in his administration emphasizing the deleterious effects of congressional encroachment on executive power, Bush has signaled his intention to "draw the line" between the two branches. "The president," as Secretary of Defense Dick Cheney put it, "genuinely respects the role of Congress, but he also has decided to stand up forthrightly to preserve the powers of his own office" (*Congressional Quarterly Weekly Reports*, 3 February 1990, 291). But to Bush this has meant more than simply holding ground at the level realized during the Iran-Contra scandal; for him it has also entailed the assertion of presidential authority to regain powers lost to Congress. Thus, once he assumed office he charged John Sununu, his former chief of staff, C. Boyden Gray, his White House counsel, and Dick Thornburgh, his former attorney general, with the task of restoring and safeguarding executive powers.

To realize and protect his programmatic objectives, Bush, in hierarchical fashion, has relied on the constitutional prerogative of the veto. Although most scholars of the presidency concede that reliance on veto power signifies weakness rather than strength, Bush has managed to earn respect for the "savvy" and "mastery" with which he has wielded that power (*Congressional Quarterly Weekly Reports*, 23 June 1990, 1934; 27 July 1991, 2041). Through it he has, as Woodrow Wilson envisaged, transformed the executive office into "a third branch of the legislature" (Wilson, 1956, 177). As Senator Dale Bumpers (D-Ark.) lamented: "The president is ruling the country by the rule of 33 plus one" (*Congressional Quarterly Weekly Reports*, 27 July 1991, 2044).

Bush's success in using the veto can be traced to his ability to cultivate an illusion of strength. Building on Victor Thompson's concept of "dramaturgy," Ellis and Wildavsky (1989) write that hierarchical leaders situated in an anti-authority context can create and manage impressions of influence and power. Something like this appears to be a strategy of the Bush administration. Bush, as James Sundquist surmised, "has been careful in selecting his targets. . . . When he knows he's going to lose, he goes ahead and signs the bill" (*Congressional Quarterly Weekly Reports*, 27 July 1991, 2044).

Enlisting the veto more than any president other than Gerald Ford in the last 30 years, he still has not been overridden. This has created an appearance of strength. Indeed, Senator Richard Lugar (R-Ind.) has observed that this "extraordinary batting average" has given the president's "threats" greater "credibility" (*Congressional Quarterly Weekly Reports*, 23 June 1990, 1934; CQW, 22 September 1990, 2991). As a result, even though Speaker Foley has asserted that "we don't fall over dead every time a president says that he's inclined to veto something" (*Congressional Quarterly Weekly Reports*, 31 March 1991, 1000), others, like Representative Vic Fazio (D-Calif.), have conceded that even the threat of using the veto has many Democrats frustrated and disillusioned. "We have," he admitted, "fallen into the trap of thinking that if we don't have a two-thirds vote we should do nothing" (*Congressional Quarterly Weekly Reports*, 27 July 1991, 2041; 22 September 1990, 2991–94).

This perception has allowed Bush to shape major pieces of legislation. Through the use of the veto, he has determined major provisions in legislation pertaining to child care, the minimum wage, civil rights, clean air, the extension of unemployment benefits, transportation and a host of other measures (see Sinclair, 1991; *Congressional Quarterly Weekly Reports*, 27 July 1991, 2041–45). He has also used it to kill several pieces of legislation, including measures pertaining to abortion, medical and family leave, and foreign affairs.

Bush has also endeavored to advance his ends by shoring up the authority of his office. For example, Bush and members of his administration have sought to enhance the position of the president's control over expenditures by contesting the earmarking of funds put into spending bills by Congress (*Congressional Quarterly Weekly Reports*, 3 February 1990, 293). He also set out to expand the executive's constitutional control over legislation by attempting to "pocket" veto bills sent to him during temporary adjournments within a congressional session (*Congressional Quarterly Weekly Reports*, 2 December 1989, 3285). Moreover, recent evidence suggests that the Bush administration has selectively used its power to exempt items in supplemental spending bills from budget ceilings on discretionary programs by declaring an emergency, thus giving to the executive the power to exercise what is tantamount to a line-item veto (*Congressional Quarterly Weekly Reports*, 6 July 1991, 1820–21).

THE HIERARCH IN ACTION: FOREIGN AFFAIRS

The most far-reaching efforts by Bush to shore up authority by managing the constitutional roles of the office, however, have come in foreign affairs. In what follows we give careful attention to U.S. relations with China and Panama. These two cases illustrate the way Bush has sought to reclaim powers that he believes Congress has usurped, including the decision to commence armed conflict on executive authority alone; to control covert operations, trade policy, and immigration affairs; to impound funds; and to employ a line-item veto.[3]

China

On 3 June 1989, the Chinese government attacked a pro-democracy movement. Government tanks rolled over unarmed protestors camped in Tiananmen Square, while soldiers shot others dead. Fleeing demonstrators were tracked down and beaten, jailed or killed. The brutality of this confrontation shocked many in the United States. It also touched off a policy dispute between the Bush administration and the Congress that has yet to be resolved. Tracing the contours of this dispute highlights Bush's hierarchical propensity to exploit constitutional prerogatives to build up presidential authority.

The thrust of Bush's initial response to the crackdown was to suspend a number of commercial and military contacts (*Congressional Quarterly Weekly Reports*, 10 June 1989, 1425; 1 July 1989, 1642). Congress immediately called on the president to impose more severe sanctions and, over the administration's objections, proposed retaliatory responses of its own (*Congressional Quarterly Weekly Reports*, 10 June 1989, 1414).

Bush's reaction to the Tiananmen Square massacre, and to Congress' attempts to influence that response, are as we would expect from a hierarchical president. His moral condemnation of the violence was restrained. He argued that the United States should not lose sight of its long-term interests in maintaining ties to China, and he claimed that as both policy expert and president he was positioned to understand those interests and had the authority to determine the country's foreign policy. He expected Congress to defer to his expertise and the executive's prerogatives, and he indicated his intention to compel that deference if it was not forthcoming.

"We Should Stand For Something"

Many congressional critics considered Bush's response to be too mild. Clearly, his criticisms lacked the punch we might have expected from his predecessor. "The U.S. cannot condone," he intoned in his first news conference after the massacre, "the violent attacks and cannot ignore the consequences for our relationship with China. . . . We deplore the decision to use force. . . . I condemn [the attack]" (*Congressional Quarterly Weekly Reports*, 10 June 1989, 1425, 1427). At a press conference three days later, Bush continued to mute the moral dimension of the issue: "We have to speak out in favor of human rights. And we aren't going to remake the world, but we should stand for something" (p. 1428).

Bush was also careful not to blame the entire Chinese government for the violence. He twice reminded listeners of the political persecution Deng Xiaoping suffered during the Cultural Revolution, and he noted that the Deng-led government "did move dramatically faster on economic reforms than I think any of us in this room would have thought possible" (p. 1430).

"Let's not," Bush cautioned, "jump to conclusions as to how individual leaders in China feel when we aren't sure of that." He highlighted Deng's reputation as a "forward-looking" leader and praised him for moving China "towards openness, towards democracy, towards reform" (pp. 1426, 1428).

At a news conference, Bush, while observing that "elements of the

Chinese Army" suppressed the protestors, cited reports that other parts of the military were "sympathetic . . . to the demonstrators" (pp. 1425, 1427). Calling the troops the "People's Liberation Army of China," Bush argued that they should not all be judged by "that terrible incident" (*Congressional Quarterly Weekly Reports*, 6 June 1989, 1428). He encouraged those sympathetic troops: "Continue to show the restraint that many of you have shown" (p. 1425).

When a reporter stated that China waited "a long time" before cracking down, Bush interrupted the questioner, saying, "Yes, they did. . . . The Army did show restraint" (p. 1426).

At times, Bush seemed to treat the actions of the demonstrators and government troops as moral equivalents. Consider especially his remarkable account of what many thought to be the single most stirring episode of the whole Tiananmen affair. Referring to the young man who kept jumping in front of a column of tanks to prevent them from repositioning themselves, Bush said: "The forces of democracy are so powerful, and when you see them as recently as this morning—a single student standing in front of a tank—and then, I might add, seeing the tank driver exercise restraint" (p. 1425).

"I've Told You What I'm Going To Do"

Bush's strategy was to dampen the public's revulsion, which he feared would lead Congress to adopt punitive actions against China. He thought such steps would jeopardize U.S.-Chinese relations, which he considered "vital to the U.S." (*Congressional Quarterly Weekly Reports*, 10 June 1989, 1427).

"This is not the time for an emotional response," he said, "but for a reasoned, careful action that takes into account both our long-term interests and recognition of a complex internal situation in China" (p. 1425). Instead of aiming at "the short-range problem in China," he was looking "down the road" and "beyond the moment" to the "enduring aspects of this vital relationship" (pp. 1426, 1427). The president was absolutely clear about the objective that guided his policy response to the Chinese government's crackdown: "There's a relationship over there that is fundamentally important to the U.S. that I want to see preserved" (p. 1430).

Bush was confident that as both policy expert and president he had the authority to identify and serve the country's national interest. He served as a U.S. representative to the United Nations in the early 1970s, and headed the U.S. Liaison Office in Beijing in 1974–75. He considers himself well-versed in Chinese politics, and he constantly referred to his expertise in the days following the massacre. "I remember being in China"; "I am one who lived in China"; "My recommendations are based on my knowledge of Chinese history" (pp. 1427, 1428, 1429). In defending his claim that harsher sanctions would be unproductive, Bush told his audience, "I would remind you of the history. . . . You just have to look back to the Middle Kingdom syndrome. . . . I've recognized the history of China moving into its own Middle Kingdom syndrome" (pp. 1426, 1427).

In addition to invoking his policy expertise, Bush also based his actions on the executive's power to direct foreign affairs. When asked whether he could accommodate congressional calls for tougher sanctions, he curtly replied: "I've told you what I'm going to do. I'm the president. I set the foreign policy objectives and actions taken by the Executive Branch" (p. 1427). He characterized congressional proposals as "flamboyant," as "180 degrees wrong," as ones that "don't make much sense" (pp. 1426, 1427, 1429). He announced that he was "not listening" to such suggestions, indicating that they would undermine China's move toward commercial prosperity, human rights, and democracy (p. 1430). He also expected Congress to abide by his decision.

I think they know—most of them in Congress—that I have . . . a keen personal interest in China. . . . I will just reiterate to the leaders [of Congress] this afternoon my conviction that this is not a time for anything other than a prudent, reasoned response. (p. 1427)

Conflict With Congress

On 29 June, the House overwhelmingly passed a foreign aid authorization bill that included a number of sanctions against China, most of which had already been put into effect by executive order. The additional sanctions called for were minor. The bill made it easy for the president to lift them by declaring that it was "in the national interest" to do so (*Congressional Quarterly Weekly Reports*, 1 July 1989, 1641, 1643).

Nevertheless, the administration staunchly opposed the bill on constitutional grounds, arguing that it constrained the president's flexibility to conduct foreign affairs. "We really and firmly believe," said Secretary of State Baker, "that the leadership on this issue must come from the Executive Branch and it should come from the president as Commander-in-Chief, and as one who is thoroughly and completely versed in the affairs of China" (p. 1642).

Student Visas

This interbranch dispute quickly centered on the question of the resident status of Chinese students living in the United States. Two hundred and fifty-nine co-sponsors supported HR 2712, which called for waiving the "J" status visa requirement for all Chinese nationals. Those holding "J" visas are required to return to their homelands for at least two years when their visas expire before applying for permanent resident status in the United States. The purpose of the "J" status is to protect countries who send students to American schools from suffering "brain drain." In effect, the "J" status guarantees countries that they will derive some benefit from the American education they provide their citizens (*Congressional Quarterly Weekly Reports*, 5 August 1989, 2049).

The Senate substituted its own language in place of the House version. The major difference in the Senate's measure was a section widely understood to express anti-abortion sentiments. Although the House initially refused to accept the Senate bill, the desire to respond more forcefully to the crackdown could not be contained, and on 19 November, the House passed the conference committee report by a vote of 403–0. The next day, it passed the Senate by voice vote and was sent to the president. Seventy-four senators, including 26 Republicans, wrote Bush, urging him not to veto the bill. On 30 November, the president vetoed HR 2712 (*Congressional Quarterly Weekly Reports*, 4 November 1989, 2960; 18 November 1989, 3163; 25 November 1989, 3245; 2 December 1989, 3316).

The veto touched off a furor on Capitol Hill. Members accused the president of "kowtowing to Beijing" and "bowing to the cruel Chinese regime." They vowed to override the veto when Congress reconvened the next year. Bush, however, aggressively defended his veto on policy and constitutional grounds, and he promised to veto the measure again if it reached his desk. His policy-based defense involved the claim that maintaining the student exchange program leads to continuing economic liberalization in China, and so undermines tyranny there. Moreover, the president issued an administrative order waiving the visa requirement and so claimed to protect Chinese nationals by executive action (*Congressional Quarterly Weekly Reports*, 2 December 1989, 3316; 16 December 1989, 3435). The president also insisted that the bill infringed on the executive's foreign affairs powers. "I want to keep control of managing the foreign policy of this country as much as I can," he declared in defense of his veto (p. 3435).

Congressional critics raised a constitutional objection of their own. Members claimed that the president had no authority to issue general residency waivers and that Bush's action was a usurpation of Congress' authority over immigration policy. Neither the White House nor the Justice Department was able to explain the legal basis for the action, and no previous president appears to have granted a blanket waiver to a whole group of nationals. "The administration can't go rewriting the immigration statutes any time it wants to," argued Representative Bruce Morrison (D-Conn.) (*Congressional Quarterly Weekly Reports*, 2 December 1989, 3316).

The override forces were buoyed by the revelation on 9 December, that Bush sent Brent Scowcroft to meet with Chinese government officials in Beijing. Pictures of Scowcroft toasting those responsible for the crackdown were widely publicized, and at this time word leaked of another secret delegation he had led to China only a month after the Tiananmen massacre (*Congressional Quarterly Almanac*, 1989, 525, 282). Congressional critics condemned Bush's business-as-usual approach toward the Chinese government (Stanfield, 1990). Bush, however, dismissed these critics: "They simply do not know what they are talking about." In mid-December, he even began to ease some of the economic sanctions he had imposed (*Congressional Quar-*

terly Weekly Reports, 16 December 1989, 3435; *Congressional Quarterly Almanac*, 1989, 525–26).

On 24 January 1990, the House overrode his veto of the residency-waiver law by a 390–25 majority. The administration aggressively lobbied the Senate, reminding members that the executive order protected the students, and that as president, Bush should be free to determine the country's policy toward China. With a 62–37 vote in favor of override, the effort to nullify Bush's veto fell four votes short (*Congressional Quarterly Almanac*, 1989, 282).

China and a Line-Item Veto?

Congressional opponents won a victory of sorts on 16 February, when Bush signed HR 3972 into law. Parts of the bill denounced human rights abuses in harsher terms than the administration had ever used, and Congress wrote into law many of the sanctions Bush himself had already imposed. The bill, however, permitted the president to lift any of the sanctions simply by citing "national security" considerations. Only eight days after signing the measure, Bush waived three of its provisions (Stanfield, 1990, 445).

More importantly, at the signing ceremony, Bush identified nine provisions as unconstitutional limitations on the president's power to conduct foreign policy, and he explicitly reserved the right to interpret those provisions (*Congressional Quarterly Almanac*, 1989, 526). Bush seemed to be announcing his intention to exercise a line-item veto over the legislation, a prerogative that some in his administration consider inherent in the constitutional powers of the office of the presidency (*Congressional Quarterly Weekly Reports*, 3 February 1990, 295).

MFN Status

In 1990 the main controversy centered on the scheduled expiration of China's "most favored nation" (MFN) status on 3 June. Under the 1974 Trade Act, MFN status can be extended to non-market economy countries only when they guarantee their citizens free emigration. The president has the power to waive that requirement annually, provided the White House reports improvements in the country's emigration practices. China had been granted MFN status under this annual waiver since 1980, and in late May Bush announced his decision to renew it again.

Over administration objections, legislation linking the extension of MFN status to Chinese improvements in human rights conditions was immediately introduced. The bill drawing the most attention was HR 4939, sponsored by Rep. Donald Pease (D-Ohio). The Pease bill was an attempt to find a middle ground in this dispute. It proposed to extend China's MFN status in 1990 without conditions, just as Bush desired. But before that status could be renewed in 1991, the president would have to report to Congress that China had made "significant progress" toward achieving human rights, and that China had taken the following steps: (1) ended martial law in China and Tibet; (2) released those imprisoned in the aftermath of Tiananmen Square; (3) eased press restrictions; (4) stopped harassing Chinese nationals in the United States; and (5) eliminated fees imposed on Chinese citizens seeking to travel abroad. The bill proposed that these conditions remain in effect for only one year, and after 1991, MFN status could again be extended by presidential waiver alone.

The Pease bill did not please many of the critics in Congress. They contended that it failed to express the depths of the country's anger at the "butchers of Beijing." The bill's proponents defeated several attempts to toughen its conditions and to restrict further the president's powers, including an amendment that would have completely terminated MFN for China. The Pease bill passed the House by a 384–30 vote. Representative Steven Solarz (D-N.Y.) expressed the opinion of many when he warned the president that if he failed to support this moderate approach he would "run the risk of immediate termination" of MFN (*Congressional Quarterly Almanac*, 1990, 765, 768).

Unswayed, Bush vowed to veto it as an illegitimate restriction of the president's ability to establish trade relations with foreign countries. As he did on the visa override vote, Bush lobbied the Senate not to tie the executive's hands with unconstitutional legislation, and he again prevailed in that body. The Senate never took up HR 4939 (pp. 764–68).

In early 1991, Bush notified Congress of his intention to grant normal trade relations to China once again. He asked Congress not to try to block his waiver. His critics were once again outraged at what they considered to be the timidity of the administration's position, and they began to question whether Bush had the vision to fashion a foreign policy program to meet the challenges of a transformed international order. "The president is drawing on his own experience," observed Representative John Porter (R-Ill.), "but unfortunately that experience is from a long time ago" (*Congressional Quarterly Weekly Reports*, 8 June 1991, 1514; 1 June 1991, 1433). Legislation modelled on the Pease bill was introduced into both chambers. Also introduced were measures calling for the complete revocation of MFN status.

In November 1991, as both the House and Senate were considering a conference committee report calling for conditions to be attached to MFN renewal, Baker led a high-profile delegation to Beijing. In part, the purpose of this trip was to show Congress that the administration's policy toward China was working. As these meetings began, reports appeared accusing China of continuing to export prison-made products and of mistreating political prisoners. Chinese sales of nuclear-related technology to Iran, South Africa, and other countries were publicized, as was China's efforts to assist Algeria in its building of a nuclear weapons and research and production facility.

While the Baker meetings were underway, China's foreign minister criticized efforts to pressure North Korea to halt its nuclear weapons production.

As the talks headed into their final sessions, the Chinese government had not made one concession on any of the issues raised by the U.S. delegation, leading a disappointed American official to warn, "We cannot want an improved U.S.–China relationship more than the Chinese" (*New York Times*, 17 November, 1991, 1). The House on 26 November approved the conference committee report by a vote of 409–21. The Senate had not yet taken action on the report when Congress adjourned in December.

Panama

Panama presented the Bush administration with its first foreign policy crisis. The crisis revolved around four key events: the Panamanian elections of 7 May 1989; the failed coup attempt against General Manuel Noriega on 3 October 1989; the U.S. invasion of Panama on 20 December 1989; and Noriega's decision to turn himself over to American authorities on 3 January 1990. At each stage of this crisis, Bush behaved as we would expect a hierarchal president to act.

Congressional critics complained that the administration failed to articulate a comprehensive set of goals and principles to guide U.S. foreign policy toward Panama, and as a consequence, the country was reacting to events as they unfolded instead of shaping events according to some grand design. The president's cautious, reactive approach, they claimed, left the United States unprepared to respond to the obvious fraud that marred the 7 May elections. It led the coup leaders into believing U.S. troops would come to their aid, and it prevented the administration from acting decisively to assist them. Finally, it created such an unstable condition that the invasion, with its attendant destruction and loss of life, became an unfortunate necessity (*Congressional Quarterly Weekly Reports*, 29 April 1989, 983; 13 May 1989, 1130; 14 October 1989, 2723–24; 1 January 1990, 51).

The president, for his part, responded to each of these events by asserting and exercising broad executive powers. This statement, made ten days after the failed coup, captures the spirit that characterized Bush's reaction to the entire Panamanian episode:

I want as broad a power as possible and I think under the constitution a president has it. . . . The [president] has broad powers, broader than some in the Senate or the House might think. I may have a difference with some on interpreting what the powers of the president might be. (*Congressional Quarterly Weekly Reports*, 14 October 1989, 2741)

Some of the powers he interpreted broadly were military ones. In response to the disturbances following the fraudulent elections, Bush unilaterally deployed 1,881 combat and support troops to Panama. These were in addition to the 1,300 military police officers and other security personnel he had sent there in April. Considering that some 10,000 military personnel were regularly stationed in Panama, Bush in a two-month period increased U.S. armed forces by more than 33 percent (*Congressional Quarterly Weekly Reports*, 13 May 1989, 1129, 1131).

Bush defended his deployment by citing the president's power to protect U.S. citizens and to enforce U.S. treaty rights (pp. 1150, 1151). In his 20 December broadcast to the American people discussing his decision to launch Operation Just Cause, Bush referred to a president's duty to defend the lives of citizens at least seven times (*Congressional Quarterly Weekly Reports*, 23 December 1989, 3534). And his invocation of the president's power to protect treaty rights was intended to head off congressional efforts to reassess the Panama Canal treaty, as much as it was meant to express his intention to keep the canal open (*Congressional Quarterly Weekly Reports*, 13 May 1989, 1130).

Defending his deployment decision, Bush referred to his constitutional powers:

I might add on the troops. I have a profound obligation and that is—as Commander-in-Chief of the armed forces and as president—to protect American life, and I'm going to do what is prudent and necessary to do this. And so we have a different obligation. And we also have certain treaty rights . . . and I am prepared to see [them] exercised. (*Congressional Quarterly Weekly Reports*, 13 May 1989, 1151)

Bush also indicated that he interpreted the commander-in-chief clause to permit the president to commence armed conflict without prior congressional authorization. Amid the outcry over the rigged elections in May, the administration announced that a "military option" was a possible course of action (p. 1130). Appearing before a Senate panel to respond to accusations that the administration failed to act decisively to support the October coup attempt, Baker insisted that the executive branch reserved the right to use military force to oust Noriega under circumstances of its own choosing (*Congressional Quarterly Weekly Reports*, 14 October 1989, 2660). Bush expanded on this point in a revealing exchange with a reporter about a week later, hinting that had the coup forces been American-led, he would have pursued the general with combat troops (p. 2742).

Bush also used the crisis in Panama as an opportunity to expand the president's power over covert operations. Administration officials claimed that intelligence officers were hampered from cooperating too closely with the coup leaders because of ambiguities in a U.S. policy banning assassination. While the policy explicitly prohibits U.S. agents from killing foreign leaders, they argued that it is not clear if it further prevents them from lending any assistance to activities that might result in the death of a political figure, or if it requires them to warn someone that they might be killed in a coup.

Congressional leaders denied that the assassination ban had any impact on the coup affair, saying that even "the most extreme" interpretation of it would not have applied to the Panamanian-led efforts to remove Noriega. Yet by pressing Congress to clarify its understanding of the ban, the administration successfully persuaded the legislature to commit itself to an interpretation that gave the executive branch "more flexibility" in applying the policy in the future (*Congressional Quarterly Weekly Reports*, 14 October 1989, 2726; 21 October 1989, 2812; 28 October 1989, 2884–86).

Bush also used this crisis to expand the executive's fiscal control of foreign policy. Since the mid-1970s, Congress has increased its capacity to shape foreign affairs by prescribing in detail how foreign aid assistance is to be spent. The Bush administration considers many of these spending limits an infringement on the executive's constitutional power. In order to resist these intrusions, Bush has exercised his deferral powers—the power not to spend money appropriated by Congress. By law, the executive is prohibited from using the deferral power simply to pursue policy goals that it has been unable to persuade the Congress to accept, and the legislative branch complained that Bush was exercising it in this illegal manner. A General Accounting Office investigation ruled in the spring of 1990 that all but two of the administration's nineteen deferrals proposed earlier in the year were not legitimate for this reason (*Congressional Quarterly Weekly Reports*, 24 February 1990, 605–6; 10 March 1990, 760; 17 March 1990, 845).

The Panamanian crisis was drawn into this larger interbranch rivalry when the United States decided to provide financial assistance to Panama after the fall of Noriega. Congress sought to set both overall spending limits and to attach specific conditions on how the money was to be spent (*Congressional Quarterly Weekly Reports*, 6 January 1990, 43–44; 13 January 1990, 112–14; 27 January 1990, 253). Bush resisted these directives and insisted that the money be appropriated without them. Conditions in Panama worsened, as both sides refused to budge, and Panamanian President Guillermo Endara went on a 13-day hunger strike to protest the delay. Incensed at congressional intransigence, Bush threatened to release the funds unilaterally if Congress continued to resist his desires (*Congressional Quarterly Weekly Reports*, 17 March 1990, 844; 24 March 1990, 928). He demanded that Congress limit its power over foreign aid assistance to approving overall spending amounts, leaving the executive with total discretion to spend money on specific programs in individual countries (*Congressional Quarterly Weekly Reports*, 31 March 1990, 1008). This fiscal dispute contributed to the administration's decision to introduce the International Cooperation Act of 1991, which sought, in Bush's words, "[t]he restitution of presidential authorities" in foreign aid programs.

CONCLUSION

Analyzing Bush's presidency through the conceptual lens afforded by cultural theory allows us to explain what might otherwise seem like incongruous behavior. Instead of claiming that there are "two" presidents, we have argued that Bush, by affirming and acting on hierarchical propensities, has, in both domestic and foreign affairs, approached interbranch relations in predictable way.

Our discussion has shown that Bush's rhetoric reveals his adherence to hierarchical values. We have also provided evidence to indicate how his affinity for hierarchy has carried over into his dealings with the legislative branch. In particular, Bush believes that each branch of government performs specific functions, with each one deferring to the legitimate powers of the others. According, as much of our foregoing discussion suggests, Bush has resisted what he construes as an attempt to obscure the distinction between the constitutional functions of the two branches, and he has acted to restore and even enhance what he understands to be the formal powers of his office. This has been true in domestic affairs as well as foreign affairs, though he is naturally more attracted to foreign affairs than domestic ones because that is where he is most likely to succeed in buttressing executive prerogatives.

We have also noted that Bush has been confronted with a Congress that, given its prevailing cultural composition, is not amenable to the exercise of authority and presidential leadership. This has forced the president to rely on the veto to shape legislation. We have suggested that his record of success in using the veto has created a perception of strength. This strategy is not without dangers, however, and it may be difficult to maintain indefinitely. Since it is contingent on the president's ability to build support required to sustain his veto, Bush has the challenge of maintaining coalitions of the competing cultures of hierarchy and individualism that make up his own party. To be effective in realizing his own agenda, he must appeal to or effectively neutralize a predominantly egalitarian majority party.

One fundamental dilemma facing Bush, then, is whether he can bridge the cultural chasms that distinguish Congress. Can he hold together his own party, which is composed of hierarchical and individualist elements, and still appeal to enough egalitarians to put together a legislative majority to pass initiatives? The budget agreement of 1990 suggests not. Indeed, individualists within the party—members of the so-called "ideas wing"—have grown more strident in their criticism of the president since he consented to raise taxes as part of the budgetary accord. They have recently called for an ideological show-down in the Republican Party, hoping to purge it of its more conciliatory elements (Madison, 1991). House Minority Whip Newt Gingrich (R-Ga.) often speaks for this group, and he believes that a purified Republican Party that refuses to accommodate the egalitarian policies of the Democratic Party will restore the Republicans to majority status in the Congress.

A second problem that Bush has to confront is a perception that he is preoccupied with international relations and foreign crises. As we have indicated, Bush has used foreign affairs to advance his hierarchical convictions.

He has directed two military engagements that were ostensibly successful. Neither Operations Just Cause nor Desert Storm lasted long, and U.S. casualties were relatively light. This strategy, however, is problematic. Bush cannot expect such military opportunities to continue to appear, and even those two conflicts have not proven to be unqualified successes. The Panamanian economy suffers, Noriega has yet to be convicted, and Saddam Hussein still rules in Iraq. Moreover, the public support generated by foreign affairs is short-lived, and international matters are generally less salient to many citizens. Indeed, Bush's emphasis on foreign affairs may be one of the reasons his standing in the polls has plummeted recently.

A final obstacle that Bush will eventually have to surmount is the anti-hierarchical ethos that pervades the milieu in which he operates. His determination to expand executive prerogatives notwithstanding, members of Congress are not likely to yield their powers. Neither, for that matter, are they likely to defer to the wishes of the president. As Ellis and Wildavsky (1989, 216) note, one of the difficulties that hierarchical leaders face is the fact that they must carry on in a regime in which "power does not inhere in position." Accordingly, future congressional-presidential relations can be expected to grow more acrimonious in the years ahead. If Bush wins a second term, the cultural tensions dividing his administration and the Congress outlined in this chapter are likely to increase rather than recede, while at the same time the strategies Bush has employed to overcome them may lose their effectiveness.

ACKNOWLEDGMENT

We would like to thank Patrick Burke for his assistance with this chapter.

NOTES

1. For further elaboration of this theory, see Douglas (1970: 1982), Thompson, Ellis and Wildavsky (1990), Ellis and Wildavsky (1989), and Wildavsky (1989).

2. *Congressional Quarterly*'s yearly analyses of presidential success (*Congressional Quarterly Almanac*, 30 December 1989, 3540–45; 22 December 1990, 4183–87; 28 December 1991, 3751–54) underscore his difficulties with Congress. Bush's success rates on roll call votes on which he took an unequivocal position were the lowest *Congressional Quarterly* found for the first three years of a first-term president.

3. The parallels between the military incursions into Panama and Kuwait are especially striking. Without going into detail here, in both instances: (1) Congress passed resolutions giving Bush the authority to use military force before hostilities began; (2) Congress passed these proposals, in part, because the administration had been attempting to resolve the crises with international diplomacy and because economic sanctions were perceived to be unsuccessful; and (3) Bush indicated that as president he did not require such congressional authorization in order to commit the U.S. armed forces to action.

REFERENCES

Bond, Jon R., and Richard Fleisher. 1990. *The President in the Legislative Arena.* Chicago: University of Chicago Press.

Cohen, Richard E. 1989. "Congress: Lonely Runner." *National Journal* 29 April: 1048–54.

Cohen, Richard. 1989. "Bush and Congress: The Honeymoon is Over." *National Journal* 14 October: 2508–12.

Cohen, Richard E. and William Schneider. 1991. "Partisan Patterns." *National Journal* 19 January: 134–61.

———. 1990. "Congress: The More Things Change." *National Journal* 27 January: 195–221.

Congressional Quarterly Almanac. 1990. Washington, D.C.: Congressional Quarterly Press.

———. 1989. Washington, D.C.: Congressional Quarterly Press.

Congressional Quarterly Weekly Reports. 1991. Washington, D.C.: Congressional Quarterly Press.

———. 1990. Washington, D.C.: Congressional Quarterly Press.

———. 1989. Washington, D.C.: Congressional Quarterly Press.

Dionne, E. J. 1991. *Why Americans Hate Politics.* New York: Simon and Schuster.

Douglas, Mary. 1982. "Cultural Bias." In *The Active Voice.* Edited by James Moffett. London: Routledge and Kegan Paul, pp. 183–254.

———. 1970. *Natural Symbols: Explorations in Cosmology.* New York: Pantheon Books.

Edwards, George. 1989. *At The Margins: Presidential Leadership of Congress.* New Haven, Conn.: Yale University Press, 1989.

Ellis, Richard, and Aaron Wildavsky. 1989. *Dilemmas of Presidential Leadership: From Washington Through Lincoln.* New Brunswick, N.J.: Transaction Press.

Fiorina, Morris P. 1990. "The Presidency and Congress: An Electoral Connection?" In *The Presidency and the Political System.* Edited by Michael Nelson. Washington, D.C.: Congressional Quarterly Press, pp. 443–69.

Friedman, Thomas L. 1991. "Baker Fails to Win any Commitments In Talks in Beijing." *New York Times,* 17 November, A13.

Ginsberg, Benjamin, and Martin Shefter. 1990. *Politics by Other Means: The Declining Importance of Elections in America.* New York: Basic Books.

Jones, Charles O. 1991a. "Meeting Low Expectations: Strategy and Prospects of the Bush Presidency." In *The Bush Presidency: First Appraisals.* Edited by Colin Campbell, S.J., and Bert Rockman. Chatham, N.J.: Chatham House Press, pp. 37–67.

———. 1991b. "Presidents and Agendas: Who Defines What for Whom?" In *The Managerial Presidency.* Edited by James P. Pfiffner. Pacific Grove, Calif.: Brooks/Cole, pp. 197–213.

———. 1990. "The Separated Presidency—Making it Work in Contemporary Politics." In *The New American Political System,* 2nd edn. Edited by Anthony King. Washington, D.C.: American Enterprise Institute, pp. 1–28.

Kinsley, Michael. 1991. "Heroes and Wimps." *New Republic* 16 and 23 September: 4.

Kristof, Nicholas D. 1991. "Rights Complaints Plaguing Beijing." *New York Times* 15 November: A7.

Madison, Christopher. 1991. "Pint-Sized Elephant." *National Journal* 1 January: 130–33.

McGregor, James. 1991. "Baker's Visit to China Produces Signs of Progress on Arms, Trade." *Wall Street Journal* 18 November: A13.

Mullins, Kerry, and Aaron Wildavsky. 1991. "The Procedural Presidency of George Bush." *Society* 28: 49–59.

New York Times. 1991. "Baker Fails to Win Any Commitments in Talks with Beijing." 17 November: 1.

———. 1988. "Transcript of Vice-President Bush's Speech Accepting Republican Nomination for President." 19 August: A14.

Oldfield, Duane M., and Aaron Wildavsky. 1991. "Reconsidering the Two Presidencies." In *The Two Presidencies: A Quarter Century Assessment.* Edited by Steven A. Shull. Chicago: Nelson Hall, pp. 181–190.

Pfiffner, James P. 1988. "The President's Legislative Agenda." *Annals* 499: 22–46.

Rauch, Jonathan. 1989. "Economy: Bush's Economic Headaches." *National Journal* 21 January: 116–20.

Rose, Richard. 1991. *The Postmodern President: George Bush Meets the World.* Chatham, N.J.: Chatham House Press.

Sciolina, Elaine, with Eric Schmitt. 1991. "Algerian Reactor: A Chinese Export." *New York Times* 15 November: 1.

Sinclair, Barbara. 1991. "Governing Unheroically (and Sometimes Unappetizingly): Bush and the 101st Congress." In *The Bush Presidency: First Appraisals.* Edited by Colin Campbell, S.J., and Bert Rockman. Chatham, N.J.: Chatham House Press, pp. 155–84.

Solomon, Burt. 1990. "Vulnerable to Events." *National Journal* 6 January: 6–10.

———. 1988. "The First 100 Days: Low Expectations." *National Journal* 12 November: 2838–41.

Stanfield, Rochelle L. 1990. "It's Beijing's Move." *National Journal* 24 February: 445–49.

———. 1989. "Muted Outrage." *National Journal* 1 July: 1719.

Stokes, Bruce. 1991. "Debating China Trade Policies." *National Journal* 18 May: 1177–78.

Sundquist, James L. 1988. "Needed: A Political Theory for the New Era of Coalition Government in the United States." *Political Science Quarterly* 103: 613–35.

Thompson, Michael, Richard Ellis, and Aaron Wildavsky. 1990. *Cultural Theory.* Boulder, Colo.: Westview Press.

Time. 1991. "A Tale of Two Bushes." 17 January: 18–20.

"Transcript of Bush Speech Accepting Presidential Nomination." 1988. *New York Times* 19 August: A14.

Weko, Thomas, and John H. Aldrich. 1990. "The Presidency and the Election Campaign: Framing the Choice." In *The Presidency and the Political System.* Edited by Michael Nelson. Washington, D.C.: Congressional Quarterly Press, pp. 263–86.

Wildavsky, Aaron. 1989. "A Cultural Theory of Leadership." In *Leadership and Politics: New Perspectives in Political Science.* Edited by Bryan D. Jones. Lawrence, Kan.: University of Kansas Press, pp. 87–113.

———. 1987. "Choosing Preferences by Constructing Institutions: A Cultural Theory of Preference Formation. *American Political Science Review* 81 (March): 3–21.

Will, George. 1989. "Playing With Guns." *Newsweek* 27 March: 78.

Wilson, James Q. 1986. "Political Parties and the Separation of Powers." In *Separation of Powers—Does it Still Work?*. Edited by Robert A. Goldwin and Art Kaufman. Washington, D.C.: American Enterprise Institute, pp. 18–37.

Wilson, Woodrow. 1956. *Congressional Government: A Study in American Politics*. New York: Meridian Books.

Chapter 5

George Bush and Inertial Federalism

John W. Winkle III

It may seem somewhat extravagant to devote an entire chapter to contemporary presidential leadership and federalism. Despite its prominence throughout American political history, the relationship between the national and subnational governments is today a neglected item in an already obscure domestic agenda. Executive initiatives on intergovernmental matters over the past three years have been rare, disjointed, and largely non-directional. Like any new Oval Office-holder, George Bush enjoyed in 1989 an opportunity to continue or refine the inherited policies of his predecessor or, alternatively, to chart his own course. Despite its appealing rhetoric and even a modest pragmatic impact, the decentralized "New Federalism" of Ronald Reagan by and large failed to achieve its promised restoration of balance to the federal system (Caraley, 1986; Zimmerman, 1991). The opportunity, if not the need, to act therefore appeared both natural and consequential for his successor, the former vice president. The salient absence of any identifiable, much less coherent, policy of federalism since his inauguration, however, raises serious questions about the programmatic leadership of George Bush.

We have come to expect presidential guidance across the spectrum of domestic and foreign matters. The primary constitutional responsibility of the chief executive is the enforcement of laws; yet that duty alone no longer adequately describes the nature and scope of the presidential role in national policy making. Modern presidents may and in fact do develop intergovernmental legislative agendas. Over time, presidents have conceptualized and articulated new directions in the maintenance of the federal system. Those policy efforts have differed in motivation and consequence, at times representing no more than expedient political gambits, while sometimes reflecting genuine and systematic concern for more effective governance. While we may sometimes confuse rhetoric with resolution and promise with policy, presidential involvement has been crucial on occasion in reordering federal, state, and local relationships. The actions of two recent presidents, Richard Nixon and Ronald Reagan, illustrate that influence particularly well. Using the same metaphor of "New Federalism" (although "newer" or "new and improved" might have been more appropriate), each advanced similar, but not identical, philosophies of decentralization.

Understanding the context of contemporary American federalism is essential before proceeding to an examination of presidential leadership in that domain. Whether one prefers the descriptor "federalism" or "intergovernmental relations" (a distinction important to scholars in the field; see Wright, 1988), the historical framework is especially instructive. Political and economic relationships between and among governmental units have markedly fluctuated over time. The nineteenth century, for example, witnessed a conflict model of federalism with rather constant constitutional tensions between states and nation. The expressive notions of "nation-centered," "state-centered," and "dual" federalism portrayed well the two levels of government as equal and combative sovereigns (Leach, 1970). In contrast, the midtwentieth century reflected a spirit of cooperation and partnership, in which officials more or less worked together toward common purposes (Elazar, 1984).

During the past thirty years, as governments on all levels have struggled to meet public needs and claim scarce resources, the competition model has resurfaced (Wright, 1988). David Walker (1991) goes beyond that analysis to suggest that modern intergovernmental developments mirror the early nineteenth-century theory of nation-centered federalism, with its emphasis on the acquisition and preservation of national authority. Michael Reagan and John Sanzone (1981) describe the phenomenon as "permissive" federalism, suggesting that the balance of systemwide power is mythical and in fact dictated by a federal willingness to permit the subnational units to participate nominally in the governing process. John Kincaid (1990) is less euphemistic, preferring instead the term "coercive" to capture current intergovernmental patterns.

THE PRELUDE: "NEW" FEDERALISM UNDER REAGAN

The decade of the 1980s represented a "contractive" phase of intergovernmental relations, a time of centripetalism (Wright, 1988). Twin forces, and arguably, conflicting ones, demarcated the boundaries of federalism. First, the devolution of federal programmatic and financial responsibilities to the states reflected not only sensitivity to the enhanced role of subnational governments but to the escalating national budget deficit as well. Second, the simultaneous increase in federal mandates suggested an unwillingness by Washington to let go completely. Characterized by contention, preemption, and litigious behavior, the decade produced a telescopic federalism replete with shrinking federal aid, erosive local autonomy, and judicial compression of the federal system (see Carroll, 1982).

It may be useful to examine in some depth the motives, designs, and impact of this "new federalism" of the 1980s. After all, because the Bush administration has offered no systematic alternative, the Reagan legacy remains for better or worse virtually intact. Conlan (1988) identifies three paramount objectives underlying the reform proposal first announced in the 1981 State of the Union message. On a more philosophical level, Reagan sought to clarify, if not reorder, federal relations. The "new federalism" in theory promised a return to subnational governance, an orchestrated promotion of state and local autonomy. More balance and less congestion for federal America appeared as primary foci (Walker, 1991). Aside from this holistic goal, the remaining two motivations appeared both pragmatic and progammatic. Simply put, Reagan attempted to reverse both the welfare state mentality and concomitant federal spending (Cole and Taebel, 1986). No doubt, the burgeoning federal budget crisis played an instrumental role (Zimmerman, 1991), and one observer has called deficit-driven federalism the "most enduring legacy" of the Reagan years (Walker, 1991). The plan seemed laudable and seductive: Shift federal aid closer to the people and provide more spending flexibility for states.

Looking back, it is evident that the new federalism, with its emphasis on "turnbacks," never reached its ambitious philosophical and practical goals. Some suggest that inaccurate assumptions signaled its demise from the outset. According to Caraley (1986), the Reagan policy suffered on two counts: first, by wrongly assessing the capacity of state and local resources to meet the increased public services and benefits, and second, by misgauging the level of state discontent with federal intervention. Other critics are less sanguine. Zimmerman (1991), for one, calls the new federalism "Janus-faced," a creature that showed two fronts, one "public" and the other "silent." It juxtaposed the visible rhetoric of devolution with the less visible reality of regulation. A new generation of sanctions and mandates requiring state compliance further centralized federal power. In the face of dwindling federal assistance, it became even more burdensome for states to generate resources to meet these unfunded or underfunded mandates. To compound the problem, states found themselves proscribed from regulating certain industries, like transportation, telecommunications, and banking. On balance, despite receiving some discretionary authority over the use of federal grants, the subnational governments never truly enjoyed enhanced prestige and power within the federal system. Even the more practical objectives of the Reagan plan fell short. The administration, some critics charge, never reduced the welfare state and may in fact have strengthened it through increased per capita expenditures for Social Security, Medicaid, and Medicare, among others (Conlan, 1988; Feinstein, 1989).

To several observers, however, the record is not wholly disappointing. New Federalism did significantly reduce both national fiscal commitment and actual expenditures (Walker, 1991). It expanded state discretion in limited areas (Zimmerman, 1991) and stimulated creative planning by forcing innovation to offset federal losses (Feinstein, 1989). Whether it prompted a state renaissance is debatable, but it may have indirectly fostered a favorable environment for political growth and independence (Reeves, 1990).

THE CONCERT: INERTIAL FEDERALISM UNDER GEORGE BUSH

The law of physics, specifically, the principle of inertia, holds that matter will remain at rest or in uniform motion until an external force intervenes. To some extent, the first element in that theorem aptly applies to domestic policy in general and intergovernmentalism in particular under George Bush. Paul Quirk (1991) contends that Bush has produced the "least domestic policy achievements . . . of any president since the 1920s" (p. 69). Pagano, Bowman, and Kincaid (1991), among others, confirm that observation for intergovernmental relations. They note the absence of any "explicit, coherent federalism policy," despite an apparent White House receptivity to state and local governments. With some degree of confidence—and nothing in the record truly stands to dispute it—we may conclude that matters of federalism remained virtually untouched, if not unnoticed, during the first two years of the Bush administration. To be sure, certain legislative proposals contained unmistakable implications for intergovernmental relations, but none emanated from a clearly enunciated and systematic scheme. The question that remains now is whether that legacy of disregard continues.

In his State of the Union Address in January 1991, George Bush, reflecting perhaps the spirit of Reagan "turnbacks," outlined an approximate $15 billion package of federal fiscal and programmatic "turnovers" to subnational governments. From an overall $22 billion menu of selected federal categorical grants, the president identified four primary targets: welfare administration expenses ($5.9 billion for Medicaid, Aid to Families with Dependent Children [AFDC], and food stamps); public and subsidized housing ($5.5 billion); the Community Development Block Grant (CDBG) program ($3.1 billion); and construction grants earmarked for environmental protection ($2.1 billion). This recommended policy change represented no consolidation of related programs. According to its terms, the federal government would convert the funding for these specific but unrelated aid programs into a single lump-sum grant. By design, this grand scheme would transfer greater fiscal discretion but still require states to cover attendant administrative costs for human services management. In a critical assessment of the plan, *New York Times* columnist Anthony Lewis (1991, A21) compared the Bush proposal to Reagan's new federalism by commenting, "It has been bricks without straws; burdens without funds."

Apart from the issue of the wisdom of this proposition for American federalism, an important threshold question arises for observers of presidential leadership. Did these turnovers reflect an incipient but purposeful intergovernmental strategy or, alternatively, simply the politics of cutback management? Immediately following the disclosure of the proposal, that question may have been unanswerable; months later, it is less so. The aftermath provides important clues.

While local officials objected to the inclusion of the CDBG, their state counterparts initially endorsed the sentiment of the Bush plan but showed concern for its configuration. Two state associations offered independent alternatives. The National Governor's Association (NGA) agreed on a turnover package that included fifty-three grant and loan programs estimated at $15.2 billion. The National Conference of State Legislatures (NCSL) countered with the consolidation of eighty-five separate programs, valued at $21.3 billion (Pagano, Bowman, and Kincaid, 1991). Importantly, both substitute proposals excluded the popular CDBG, the direct federal assistance program for housing and economic development in metropolitan areas. State officials by and large advanced these measures in order to further the intergovernmental dialogue. Regrettably, however, no discussion materialized at all. Neither a response from the Bush administration nor a follow-up from these public lobby groups has surfaced since the announcement of the NGA and NCSL alternatives. To some extent perhaps, localities and states may be reluctant to force the issue. Since the introduction of the counterproposals, for example, mayors fearing adverse consequences have not openly raised the CDBG turnover. Similarly, states concerned with the increased costs and expanded coverage of the Medicaid program have not pressed the substitute agendas. The real paradox, however, lies in the absence of a supplemental statement, or at least a constructive response from Washington.

Why this inaction and delay in the intergovernmental arena? Two possible explanations come to mind. First is the notion of displacement, suggesting that other more pressing matters, both anticipated and unforeseen, simply took precedence over the concerns of federalism. The claim is not without merit. No doubt certain volatile and urgent issues, foreign and domestic alike, could have superseded those less so on the presidential agenda. Two consequential global matters, the Iraqi invasion of Kuwait and the collapse of communism with its attendant Balkanization of the Soviet Union, required rather constant U.S. surveillance and response. On the home front, the rising budget deficit, the savings and loan scandal, and the controversial nominations of John Tower and Clarence Thomas arguably could have distracted George Bush from any systemic policy formulations or prescribed timetables.

An alternative explanation may lie in the construct of divided government and cooperative presidential leadership offered by Paul Quirk (1991). It is truistic in our constitutional system that presidents alone do not make public policy. No one denies the significant, and even paramount, influence of law-makers and judges. While the three branches of the national government may act in concert, they often do not. The tension that disagreement breeds is healthy for responsible democracy, but it may also thwart effective and timely policy making. According to Quirk, however, the now common oc-currence of differential partisan control of Congress and the White House may no longer pose the policy deadlocks of bygone eras. Premised on the idea that bipartisan cooperation routinely occurs anyway, this notion rein-forces Neustadt's (1960) emphasis on the presidential abilities of persuasion and negotiation. Quirk concludes that Bush, despite an initially favorable environment and the requisite interpersonal skills, faltered in his congres-sional strategy. The alleged failure stemmed from an unintended implication of expanded federal involvement and spending at a time of budget crisis. By extension, that setback may have sidetracked the entire domestic agenda of George Bush.

Neither of these rationales is wholly satisfying. While displacement politics offers a plausible explanation, standing alone it is insufficient. Similarly, the divided government notion overstates the case, for it suggests a stymied George Bush facing resistant and unsurmountable legislative obstacles. The most compelling inference, it seems, is that these circumstances did little to elevate the already obscure intergovernmental issues on the hierarchy of presidential values. Federalism began as a low priority item in the Bush strategy and has remained so. Domestic and foreign events, along with a Democratic Congress, merely provided the president with convenient tactical distractions.

THE POSTLUDE: LEADERSHIP AND INTERGOVERNMENTALISM

Woodrow Wilson once called the relationship between states and nation the "cardinal question" of our constitutional system. Intergovernmentalism is no less vital today. Including localities in the federal formula only inten-sifies its significance. Federalism involves more than formal structures and informal interactions; it is by design a means to the end of good government. Public demands for governments at all levels to address unmet needs will not diminish. Working for the common good in times of scarce resources necessitates careful coordination of policies and programs. And it requires creative and effective leadership from federal, state, and local officials as well.

While one should not overstate the role of the president in intergovernmental matters, it is important to recognize its expanding significance. In times of uncertainty and crisis, people expect their representatives, and especially their presidents, to restore their confidence. Sometimes inaction and drift are necessary and deliberate components of presidential leadership; after all, gradualism is the hallmark of U.S. pragmatism. However, the absence of action does not always indicate conscious policy choice; it may reflect ineffectual leadership. In the case of George Bush, it is difficult to determine which prevails. In either event, the opportunity for creative action persists, but it appears that the president will not likely disrupt the forces of inertia.

REFERENCES

Caraley, Demetrios. 1986. "Changing Conceptions of Federalism." *Political Science Quarterly* 101: 289–306.

Carroll, James D. 1982. "The New Juridical Federalism and the Alienation of Public Policy and Administration." *American Review of Public Administration* 16: 89–105.

Cole, Richard L., and Delbert A. Taebel. 1986. "The New Federalism: Promise, Progress, and Performance." *Publius: The Journal of Federalism* 16: 3–10.

Conlan, Timothy. 1988. "Federalism After Reagan." *The Brookings Review* 6: 23–30.

Elazar, Daniel J. 1984. *American Federalism: A View from the States*, 3rd edn. New York: Harper & Row.

Feinstein, Susan I. 1989. "The Ambivalent State: Economic Development in the United States Federal System under the Reagan Administration." *Urban Affairs Quarterly* 25: 41–62.

Kincaid, John. 1990. "From Cooperative to Coercive Federalism." *Annals of the American Academy of Political and Social Sciences* 509: 148–52.

Leach, Richard H. 1970. *American Federalism*. New York: W. W. Norton.

Lewis, Anthony. 1991. "Nixon and Bush." *New York Times*. June 3: A21.

Neustadt, Richard. 1960. *Presidential Power*. New York: John Wiley and Sons.

Pagano, Michael A., Ann O'M. Bowman, and John Kincaid. 1991. "The State of American Federalism—1990–1991." *Publius: The Journal of Federalism* 21: 1–26.

Quirk, Paul J. 1991. "Domestic Policy: Divided Government and Cooperative Presidential Leadership." In *The Bush Presidency: First Appraisals*. Edited by Colin Campbell, S.J., and Bert A. Rockman. Chatham, N.J.: Chatham House Publishers.

Reagan, Michael D., and John G. Sanzone. 1981. *The New Federalism*. New York: Oxford University Press.

Reeves, Mavis Mann. 1990. "The States as Polities: Reformed, Reinvigorated, Resourceful." *Annals of the American Academy of Political and Social Sciences* 509: 83–93.

Stewart, William H. 1982. "Metaphors, Models, and the Development of Federal Theory." *Publius: The Journal of Federalism* 12: 5–24.

Walker, David B. 1991. "American Federalism from Johnson to Bush." *Publius: The Journal of Federalism* 21: 105–19.

Wright, Deil S. 1988. *Understanding Intergovernmental Relations*, 3rd edn. Pacific Grove, Calif.: Brooks/Cole Publishing.

Zimmerman, Joseph F. 1991. "Federal Preemption Under Reagan's New Federalism." *Publius: The Journal of Federalism* 21: 7–28.

PART 3

THE BUSH PRESIDENCY IN AMERICAN POLITICS

Chapter 6

A Man for All Seasons?
The Guardian President and
His Public

Henry C. Kenski

> Managers aren't fired because they're incompetent. They're fired because leadership
> situations change. . . . Now it's recognized that there are very few managers for
> all seasons. You need to have the manager for where your team is now.
>
> Frank Cashen,
> general manager of New York Mets
> (cited in Boswell, 1989, 338)

The necessity of citizen support in modern governance is an undeniable reality, particularly for the president of the United States. Rose notes that for other political executives, like European prime ministers, popularity is not sought at the price of political relevance. "A Prime Minister's aim is to enjoy 100 percent of the authority with 51 percent of the popular vote" (Rose, 1991, 267). American presidents, by contrast, are continually forced to cultivate popularity in an attempt to influence other power-holders. Moreover, they must cultivate popularity to preempt or forestall attacks on their persona and policies. Neustadt suggests that "popularity may not produce a Washington response. But public disapproval heartens Washington resistance. Leeway guarantees one thing: avoidance of the trouble that can follow from its absence" (1990, 76–77).

This chapter examines this very complex but timely and important topic by focusing on presidential popularity during the first three years of President

George Bush's term. It will do so by assessing the importance of public approval, Bush's strategy to cultivate public support, and the nature of presidential popularity in the modern era. Bush's ratings will be analyzed from a comparative perspective.

The chapter then looks at the demographic bases of Bush's presidential approval, the significance of events and the president's response, and the importance of media interpretation in assessing the president. Finally, the chapter ends with a commentary on the paradox that confronts presidential popularity.

THE IMPORTANCE OF PUBLIC APPROVAL

Public approval is important for a variety of reasons. First, public assessments of the president are important as surrogates for broader opinions on politics and policy (Edwards, 1989). Second, they are viewed as important by virtually all of our postwar presidents, particularly in dealing with Congress and building grass-roots support (Edwards, 1989).

Third, they are important as a source of political cues for our political leaders, both presidential and congressional. They provide information for a president pushing an activist agenda on Congress or for presidents discouraging attacks on both their persona and agenda (Neustadt, 1990). Brody contends that presidential poll ratings are important

because political leaders look for indications of when it is safe or dangerous to oppose their policy interests or career ambitions to those of the president and because indications of political support—which in other political contexts might be preferred— are too limited in scope to be relied upon in this context. (1991, 22)

The important point, he contends, is that while "a president's rate of success in Congress may be indistinguishable when his public support is high or low, . . . [it is a] fact that a greater number of the elements of his program are passed when a large share of the public responds with approval to his overall policy performance" (Brody, 1991, 22).

Finally, public approval ratings are important for presidential reelection survival. Sigelman (1979) and Brody and Sigelman (1983) have demonstrated a strong association between an incumbent's level of approval on the last pre-election poll, often six months or more before the election, and the president's share of the popular vote in the general election. In short, public approval is important as a surrogate for broader opinions on politics and policy, because presidents view approval polls as important, as a source of political cues for political leaders, and as a guidepost to presidential reelection.

BUSH'S PUBLIC SUPPORT STRATEGY

Analysis of Bush's strategy to attract and maintain public support necessarily begins by identifying the political constraints that limit this endeavor. The president has been forced to operate in what Charles O. Jones (1990) calls a separated president environment with an electorate that prefers divided government, in this case it is a Republican president and a Democratic Congress.

Although scholars maintain that the president determines the governmental agenda, it is quite difficult to do so when the president serves with a Congress in which his party is the minority in both chambers. This constraint is reflected in the early assessments of his presidency. Jones notes that "the postelection judgments were that he lacked a mandate despite having won forty states. Yet the hundred-day review of his presidency criticizes him for failing to provide an agenda. Presidents are supposed to drive the system, even when electoral analysis questions their right to do so" (1990, 19). In the 102nd Congress (1991–92), the Democrats had a 267 to 167 advantage in the House (with one third-party member) and a commanding 56 to 44 edge in the Senate. In the 101st Congress (1989–90), Democrats controlled the House 260 to 175 and the Senate 55 to 45 (Stanley and Niemi, 1991). Such partisan disadvantages make it difficult to persuade the public about one's policy effectiveness.

A second factor, however, is the president's policy orientation and view of the presidency. Edwards observes that Bush is "devoted to consolidating the gains of the Reagan administration and dealing with the problems it left behind, rather than mobilizing a coalition behind bold new enterprises" (1991, 149). Richard Rose has aptly described the Bush philosophy as guardianship and says that a "guardian wants to limit the scope of presidential intervention favoring less, rather than more, government" (1991, 307). While favoring a limited domestic agenda, a guardian president will be active internationally, desiring to be more influential abroad than at home. A guardian prefers a middle-of-the-road label of moderate in contrast to the more committed views of liberals or conservatives, and sees much societal change emanating outside the arena of government. Most importantly, a guardian president rejects the idea that leadership must be expansive and modeled after Franklin Roosevelt.

Still another factor supplementing a president's philosophy is style. Edwards has described the style of the first half of Bush's presidency as one "characterized to a large degree by a spirit of moderation, openness, and bipartisanship" (1991, 149). Cook stresses conflict avoidance with both the public and Congress and notes that Bush in his first year "has not risked his popularity to mount either a direct assault on Congress or aerial warfare" (1989, 307–8). In contrast to Reagan, Bush uses more symbolic gestures to reach out, exemplified by more frequent informal meetings with the media and with black leaders (Rose, 1991). An important component of the Bush style is an aversion to the idea of long-term strategic planning and what he refers to as "the vision thing," believing that if you do the day-to-day things, the long run will take care of itself (Rose, 1991). Bush's proactive personal behavior does not carry over to proactive policy pursuits. It is more of a "watch and wait" style that Jones labels an *"actively reactive strategy*, as well illustrated by the Iraqi invasion and his subsequent efforts to mobilize a worldwide response" [emphasis added] (1991, 62).

Although gregarious and talkative, the president's communication skills are hampered by a language style that sometimes includes fractured half-sentences and opaque metaphors that leave his views unclear. For example, he once described the budget deficit as being "like walking the dog" (Rose, 1991). Bush, in short, is no primetime president like Ronald Reagan (Denton, 1988).

Finally, all of the preceding observations are consonant with Bush's strategy to attract and maintain public support, namely, lowering public expectations. Jones notes that

by the end of its first year, the lowered expectations of the administration had the approval of a near-record number of Americans. George Bush's popular approval far exceeded that of Ronald Reagan at the end of his historic first year in office. (1991, 37–38)

Edwards contends that low expectations were encouraged by the modest policy agenda that may have been a boon to Bush: "Since he began with such low expectations, it was more difficult to disappoint the public" (Edwards, 1991, 145). Thus, a February 1990 ABC News/*Washington Post* poll found that 67 percent felt that George Bush was "turning out to be a stronger President than I expected," and a July 1990 Gallup poll discovered that 50 percent agreed that Bush "is doing a better job as President than I expected" (Edwards, 1991, 145). Low expectations clearly played a role in the high levels accorded Bush, particularly during the first eighteen months.

Although initially helpful politically, it is unlikely that such a strategy will prove effective over the long-distance run of a four-year term. Changing economic and societal conditions, international policy failures, media priming of what is important and what the public could or should expect, and the emergence of strong political opposition in Congress and/or on the presidential reelection campaign trail are all factors that make it difficult to keep a political lid on the public's expectations.

NATURE OF PRESIDENTIAL POPULARITY IN MODERN ERA

Before examining the presidential approval data for the first three years of George Bush, this analysis begins with some observations about the nature of presidential popularity in the modern era. They include the volatility of presidential popularity ratings, the emergence of an increasingly critical public, and the importance of partisan support and independent approval as the key to political survival.

First, presidential approval ratings are volatile. Key events, both national and domestic, as well as a growing perception of failure to make progress on salient problems, can substantially increase or decrease a president's popularity over a short span of time. In his classic work, Mueller (1973) referred to surges of support as "rally events," which he defined as ones that relate to international relations; direct involvement by the United States and particularly the president; and are specific, dramatic, and sharply focused. Subsequent research by Ostrom and Simon (1985) discovered that an international crisis can lead to a rise of five points on average in a president's popularity. Specific events, of course, could be characterized by even larger increases. The rally events, however, are short-lived, largely because the new support typically comes from those who have previously opposed the president, and such people tend to be the first to revert to disapproval when the rally subsides (Hugick and Gallup, 1991; Edwards with Gallup, 1990; Sigelman and Conover, 1981).

Key events need not be confined to those of an international nature, and the percentage change need not be positive. Urban riots during Johnson's tenure, for example, lowered his popularity by 6.6 percent, while Nixon's return to bombing Hanoi was accompanied by a drop of 10.4 percent. Nixon's inability to address the Watergate problem, on the other hand, resulted in an erosion of 24.5 percent over a period of 17 months (MacKuen, 1983; Rose, 1991).

Volatile movements appear in the approval ratings of all presidents, but the most dramatic shifts have occurred since the midpoint of Lyndon Johnson's presidency. After one year in office, Johnson's approval rating stood at 62 percent positive, his lowest rating that year. By November 1966, when Democratic representatives and senators sought re-election, he dropped to 48 percent. Key events caused further slippage, and "he received the lowest Gallup job rating of his entire presidency immediately after the Detroit riots (39% approved and 47% disapproved), and it was virtually identical in the poll just after the Pentagon march (38%–50%)" (Barone, 1990, 426). Dramatic slippage within a year is illustrated in the Nixon presidency as

Nixon's job approval rating plummeted, from 68% in the Gallup poll just after the peace agreement with North Vietnam in January 1973 to 48% in April, 44% in May and June, 39% in July, 36% in August, 33% in September, and 27% in October; never again in his presidency did he rise to the 30% level (Barone, 1990, 516–17).

Nixon's successor, Gerald Ford, "experienced tremendous volatility in his first two months in office. Within a few months, his support fell 29 points, mostly in response to his pardon of his predecessor" (Edwards with Gallup, 1990, 171).

Jimmy Carter proved to be one of our least popular presidents, but even his ratings underscore the potential for positive surges stimulated by key events. After the greatest achievement of his presidency, the Camp David agreement between Egypt and Israel, his job rating "jumped from 39%–44% negative in late July 1978 to 56%–30% positive in September" (Barone, 1990, 574). After experiencing a major decline in popularity through much of 1979, the seizure of the U.S. Embassy in Iran and his response to it resulted in a big jump in Carter's popularity, although it would not prove to be a permanent one. In the fall of 1979, however, "Carter's job rating rose to 38%–49% negative within two weeks, to 51%–37% positive in less than a month, and to 61%–30% in early December" (Barone, 1990, 588).

Neither was Ronald Reagan immune to erosion in public support due to a poor economy. When a recession began in midsummer of 1981, Reagan's approval stood at 60 percent but dropped to 49 percent by the end of the year. Reagan's biographer, Lou Cannon, notes that

by the end of 1982, only 41 percent of Americans said they approved of Reagan's governance, a substantially lower rating than his four elected predecessors had received after two years in the White House. When the economy went to hell in a handbasket, 'Teflon' did not apply. (Cannon, 1991, 233)

Economic recovery was paralleled by Reagan's popularity recovery and successful re-election. His highest popularity ratings occurred in 1985 and 1986 and stood at 63 percent approval even in October 1986. Edwards with Gallup observe that "then the Iran-Contra affair broke, and he hovered around the 50 percent level (which is where he began) for most of the next two years. At the very end of his term, however, Reagan's approval level increased and once again exceeded 60 percent" (1990, 128). These preceding examples from Bush's predecessor underscore the basic volatility in presidential approval rating.

In addition to public approval volatility, modern presidents must contend with an increasingly critical public. In a recent book, Martin Wattenberg (1991) builds on previous research (Miller, Wattenberg, and Malanchuk, 1986) and presents a persuasive argument that the increasingly critical nature of the public is best demonstrated by going beyond the traditional monthly job evaluations. This is accomplished by employing "open-ended data from the 1952–1988 National Election Studies (NES) to place the popularity of presidential candidates in historical perspective" (Wattenberg, 1991, 67). By doing so, he pinpoints the factors behind people's evaluation. In examining the basic likes and dislikes about candidates, Wattenberg finds a more generous public in earlier elections, one more inclined to say something positive than negative about both candidates, and where even opponents recorded favorable comments about the eventual presidential winner.

Contrary to conventional wisdom, "neither Reagan nor Bush was as popular overall as their recent predecessors. Averaging the three elections of the 1980s, one finds that only 50.2 percent of voters' comments about Reagan and Bush were positive" (Wattenberg, 1991, 72). Wattenberg adds: "In contrast, from 1952 to 1964, responses concerning the most popular candidate were regularly about 70 percent positive. This was true not only for war-hero Eisenhower, but for Johnson as well, and strangely enough, for Nixon in 1960" (1991, 72–73). In 1980, for example, Reagan set an all-time high for the percentage of supporters with some stated reservation about their choice (53 percent), a pattern repeated in the 1984 sample, where Reagan commanded a high 63 percent approval rating, but the open-ended data revealed "that nearly half (45 percent) of those who approved of his handling of the presidency had some reason why they might be inclined to vote against him" (1991, 71).

Bush came to office in 1988 with the highest percentage of voters recording two negative comments as well as the lowest percentage of opponents making a positive comment about him. Wattenberg emphasizes that "compared to Reagan in 1980, though, Bush did better among his own voters. But as with Carter and Reagan before him, among Bush's supporters more had something negative to say about him than expressed strong positive support" (1991, 79). He further suggests that there is reason to expect that a major component of the decline in candidate popularity is tied to the focus on personal attributes. He divides these attributes into five general categories: integrity, reliability, competence, charisma, and the candidate's demographic characteristics.

In a later chapter, Wattenberg argues for recoding the data for reanalysis in order to identify a presidential performance variable. Here he underscores the salience of this variable for Reagan's success, as many voters who differed with Reagan on policy preferences selected him over Mondale based on perceptions of past or future performance. Thus, the Democratic advantage on policy questions "was vastly overshadowed by positive assessments of Reagan's performance on the economy and foreign relations" (1991, 155). High general presidential approval ratings may prove to be a mile wide and only an inch deep, due to an increasingly critical public. Despite ambivalence or contradictory attitudes, candidate-based evaluations, particularly performance, are critical for a presidential candidate's success.

Finally, against this turbulent political backdrop, partisan support and Independent backing hold the key to political survival. Edwards with Gallup find that

presidents typically receive high support from their fellow partisans, and this support is usually stable over time. Republican presidents do especially well, averaging 81 percent approval from fellow Republicans. Eisenhower never fell below a yearly average of 82 percent approval from Republicans, while Reagan's lowest yearly average was 77 percent. (1990, 120)

Partisanship is less potent but still the strongest base for presidential approval in a worst-case scenario. Nixon, at his lowest point in the Watergate crisis, had an overall popularity rating of 24 percent, but he received 50 percent approval from Republicans, 13 percent from Democrats, and 22 percent from Independents (Edwards with Gallup, 1990, 121). Democratic presidents face a more challenging task in

obtaining approval from those who identify with their party; they average 67 percent approval from Democrats. The base of the Democratic party has traditionally been larger and more diverse than that of the Republican party, including most liberals and many moderates and conservatives. (Edwards with Gallup, 1990, 120)

Independent support is especially important for a Republican candidate, as the Republicans have captured a majority of the Independent vote in presidential elections in every election since 1952, with the sole exception of Johnson's 1964 landslide victory (American Enterprise Public Opinion Report, 1990b).

High presidential approval ratings mean that an incumbent has far exceeded his partisan and coalitional base to attract out-party support. Overall, in 22 of 36 years of approval ratings from 1953 to 1988, identifiers with the out-party were more likely to disapprove than to approve of the president's handling of his job (Edwards with Gallup, 1990). Party affiliation also does much to explain popularity declines. Citizens outside the president's party have a greater tendency to become disillusioned than do in-party identifiers. In-party identifiers tend to be more loyal to their president, while out-party identifiers are quicker to register disapproval (Presser and Converse, 1976– 77; Tatalovich and Gitelson, 1990).

BUSH APPROVAL RATINGS IN COMPARATIVE PERSPECTIVE

Table 6.1 presents the average yearly Gallup approval ratings for presidents from Eisenhower through Bush, including the highest and lowest ratings recorded in each year. An inspection of the high and low rating differences underscores again that approval ratings are quite volatile. Eisenhower and Kennedy do exceedingly well, as does Johnson for his first two years. The time frame 1953 through 1965 is clearly the golden age of presidential support, as solid majority approval is recorded consistently. Even Eisenhower, in the difficult recession-ridden year of 1958, registered 55 percent approval, with his lowest rating being 48 percent. Johnson's last two years underscore

Table 6.1
Average Yearly Presidential Approval and the Highest and Lowest Ratings
(in percentages)

President	Year	Average Approval	High	Low
Eisenhower	1953	68	74	59
	1954	66	75	57
	1955	71	78	66
	1956	73	79	68
	1957	64	73	57
	1958	55	60	48
	1959	64	77	57
	1960	61	66	49
Kennedy	1961	76	79	72
	1962	72	79	61
	1963	65	74	56
Johnson	1964	74	79	69
	1965	66	71	62
	1966	51	61	44
	1967	44	51	38
	1968	42	50	35
Nixon	1969	61	67	56
	1970	57	64	51
	1971	50	56	48
	1972	56	62	49
	1973	42	67	27
	1974	26	28	24
Ford	1974	54	71	42
	1975	43	52	37
	1976	48	53	45
Carter	1977	62	75	51
	1978	46	55	39
	1979	37	54	28
	1980	41	58	31
Reagan	1981	58	68	49
	1982	44	49	41
	1983	44	54	35
	1984	55	62	52
	1985	60	65	52
	1986	61	68	47
	1987	48	53	43
	1988	52	63	48
Bush	1989	64	71	51
	1990	66	80	53
	1991	72	89	50

Sources: Edwards with Gallup, 1990, for Eisenhower through Reagan. Bush averages and identification of high/low ratings were computed from data published in Hugick and Gallup,
1991, and the American Enterprise Public Opinion and Demographic Report, 1992.

his popularity decline due to public perceptions about the lack of progress on Vietnam, the president's handling of urban riots, and the decline in support for his Great Society agenda.

Nixon's first-term ratings are solid but unspectacular when compared with Eisenhower and Kennedy, while his second-term percentages underscore the toll of Watergate on his presidency. His successor, Gerald Ford, was stung by the Nixon pardon and finished his abbreviated term of office with less than majority yearly presidential approval scores (43 percent and 48 percent). Carter had one good year, his first, and then registered mediocre ratings for the remainder of his term.

Reagan's first term started off with a 58 percent approval in 1981, but then slumped to 44 percent in both 1982 and 1983 due to the recession. He bounced back to register a 55 percent rating in his 1984 re-election year, and then accelerated to 60 percent and 61 percent, respectively, in 1985 and 1986. Irangate took its toll, as his approval ratings for 1987 and 1988 indicate (48 percent and 52 percent).

By comparison, Bush's yearly ratings (even in 1991) are impressive. Based on his first three years, his popularity is surpassed only by Kennedy's, and his ratings are on a par with those of Eisenhower. Although not noted for exceptional scores on candidate attributes (Wattenberg, 1991), Bush's overall popularity surpasses his fellow Republicans, Reagan and Nixon. Recall, of course, the conflict-avoidance/low expectation strategy that proved successful initially. Bush's guardian philosophy resulted in few domestic proposals. It prompted Robert M. Teeter, the president's pollster, to remark that the president "doesn't have anyone, no specific group, mad at him right now" (Devroy and Morin, 1989). With the exception of the John Tower confirmation fight for Secretary of Defense, there was very little public controversy. Dan Balz of the *Washington Post* commented that the paradox of the Bush presidency is that "he has made a favorable impression on the American public—and virtually no impression at all" (1989, A1). GOP strategist John Sears concurred, saying, "You can look at his polls, and they're as high as they are because people can't think of anything wrong that he's done. They can't think of anything he's done" (Perry, 1989, A24).

It is a well-known axiom in data analysis that aggregates reveal, but also conceal. These impressive aggregate average yearly ratings conceal Bush's weaknesses, as additional data in Table 6.2 suggest. These data focus on the approval rating at a particular point in time. After twelve months in office, Bush's rating was 80 percent, topping all presidents going back to Truman. After twenty-four months, he again ranked first for the seven presidents for whom there is a comparable situation, with a robust 83 percent approval rating. In the thirty-fifth month, the Persian Gulf war effect had dissipated, and economic and health insurance issues ranked more prominently. Here Bush recorded a mediocre 50 percent, topping only the unpopular presidents, Truman and Johnson. The table also contains data of

Table 6.2
Bush and His Predecessors: A Presidential Approval Profile (in percentages)

President	Inaugural Date	After 12th Month	After 24th Month	After 35th Month
Truman	4/45	50	--	36
Eisenhower	1/53	68	69	75
Kennedy	1/61	77	76	--
Johnson	11/63	69	64	44
Nixon	1/69	61	56	50
Ford	8/74	46	--	--
Carter	1/77	52	43	54
Reagan	1/81	47	35	54
Bush	1/89	80	83	50

January Re-election Year Approval Ratings

President	Date	Rating
Eisenhower	1/56	76
Johnson	1/68	48
Nixon	1/72	49
Ford	1/76	46
Carter	1/80	56
Reagan	1/84	52
Bush	1/92	46

Sources: The American Enterprise Public Opinion and Demographic Report, 1992; Edwards with Gallup, 1990.

each president's standing after the first poll in their schedule reelection year. Of seven presidents, Bush's rating ties for the worst with Gerald Ford, with a very weak 46 percent, a sign of potential incumbent vulnerability.

As this chapter is being written, other polls in December 1991 and January 1992 were even more discouraging for Bush. The December *Washington Post/ ABC News* poll showed that "Bush's approval rating stood at 47 percent, the first time in his presidency that it had dropped below 50 percent in *Post/ ABC News* surveys" (Morin, 1992, 37). Moreover, these numbers also suggested that, absent an economic turnaround, this rating would go lower. "Just 17 percent of those interviewed in December said they strongly approved of Bush's performance, while 30 percent said they only somewhat approved" (Morin, 1992, 37).

Similarly, a November 18–22, 1991, *New York Times*/CBS News poll found Bush's approval rating to be 51 percent, "a drop of 16 percentage points since mid-October. The decline seemed to reflect a month of bad economic news and turmoil in the White House" (Toner, 1991a). Moreover, his handling of the economy was given 25 percent approval, the lowest since Jimmy Carter's rating in the era of stagflation (Toner, 1991b). A January 6–8, 1992, poll recorded more bad news for the president as the *New York Times*/CBS News poll pegged his popularity at 48 percent (Toner, 1992a), and their January 22–25 pre-State of the Union poll turned up even lower numbers and claimed that "support for Mr. Bush continues to erode, with just 43 percent saying they approve of his performance as President, an astonishing drop of 45 points since his popularity rating reached 88 percent, a historic peak, after the Persian Gulf War" (Toner, 1992b).

Regardless of what poll one examines, Bush's stratospheric presidential approval scores had declined to an all-time low by January 1992, endangering his prospects for re-election. To have a better understanding of how this decline came about, a brief examination of the demographic bases of Bush's approval is in order.

DEMOGRAPHIC BASES OF BUSH'S PRESIDENTIAL APPROVAL RATINGS

Drawing on available data, it is clear that Bush's approval ratings before his free fall in the last three months of 1991 was based on his ability to expand substantially beyond his 1988 demographic electoral base. Gallup data for the first 14 months show that Bush's Democratic support the first month was only 38 percent, but mushroomed to 68 percent by the twelfth month, declining slightly to 64 percent and 61 percent, respectively, in the thirteenth and fourteenth months (American Enterprise Public Opinion Report, 1990a).

Gallup data on differences between white and non-white approval indicate that one of the special features of the Bush presidency was how little it polarized groups in the electorate, particularly when contrasted with Reagan. A 32-month analysis of Bush's ratings begins with a non-white/black approval score of 51 percent the first month. It then varies a bit, with a high of 77 percent in March 1991 and a successful outcome in the Persian Gulf, to a low of 25 percent in November 1990. In July 1991, Bush's non-white/black approval rating was 49 percent, and in August 1991, it stood at 46 percent. "The average approval difference between non-white and white approval of Reagan in his first 32 months in office was 37 percentage points; for Bush it is half that" (American Enterprise Public Opinion and Demographic Report, 1991a, 86–87).

Gallup data on the first thirty-four months of their respective presidencies ending in October 1991 underscore that

Ronald Reagan and George Bush were more popular among men than women. The gender gap for President Reagan in this period was 9 percentage points, for Bush, 6. Bush, however, has much higher ratings among both groups than Reagan and Carter, who did not have a gender gap. (American Enterprise Public Opinion and Demographic Report, 1991b, 94)

Bush's Gallup approval rating in October 1991 was 65 percent for men and 64 percent for women. Data on the congressional vote intention of women, however, show consistent Democratic leanings (1991b, 95).

Table 6.3 contains *New York Times*/CBS News poll data for two cross-sectional surveys conducted in October and November 1991, the latter dramatizing the beginning of a substantial erosion in Bush's popular support. His decline was a steep double-digit figure for virtually all demographic categories except blacks. Of particular interest is his base of partisan support. In November, Republicans accorded him his highest level of approval at 75 percent, down from 88 percent in October and below the 81 percent approval Republican baseline established in pre-Bush presidencies. Moreover, his approval among the very important Independent identifiers dropped from 66 percent to 49 percent. That the various approval declines were associated with economic perception is revealed in respondent perceptions of whether the economy was getting better, worse, or staying about the same. Those who said it was better declined from a high of 87 percent to a still very high 77 percent. Respondents who felt the economy was staying about the same registered 70 percent approval in October and 61 percent in November, a decline but still a majority. The most dramatic change occurred among those who said the economy was getting worse. Their 57 percent October approval fell by 22 percent to only 35 percent in October. A key factor in Bush's future popularity and 1992 election prospects will be the proportion of voters who still feel the economy is getting worse when they enter the voting booth in November.

SIGNIFICANCE OF EVENTS AND PRESIDENTIAL RESPONSE

Bush began his term with a mediocre 51 percent approval rating, due largely to the 43 percent of respondents who refrained from evaluating him (Edwards with Gallup, 1990). His popularity improved throughout the year, and he ended with a very high 71 percent approval score by December. The early January 1990 poll shows a jump in popularity to 80 percent, mainly due to the December invasion of Panama. The effect of this rally point was short-lived, and his approval dropped to 73 percent by February.

Table 6.3
The Demographic Bases of Bush's Popularity (in percentages)

| Demographic Categories | Approve | | Percentage Shift |
	Oct. 15-18	Nov. 18-22	In Approval
TOTAL	67	51	-16
Republican	88	75	-13
Democrat	49	34	-15
Independent	66	49	-17
Liberal	59	40	-19
Moderate	64	51	-13
Conservative	78	60	-18
18-29 yrs. old	75	63	-12
30-44 yrs. old	73	55	-18
45-64 yrs. old	60	43	-17
65 yrs. or older	51	37	-14
Northeast	63	42	-21
Midwest	66	51	-15
South	70	58	-12
West	67	50	-17
Income under $15,000	59	34	-25
$15,000-$30,000	61	53	- 8
$30,000-$50,000	71	51	-20
Over $50,000	75	59	-16
Male	70	53	-17
Female	64	49	-15
White	70	52	-18
Black	45	45	0
Those who said economy is:			
Getting better	87	77	-10
Getting worse	57	35	-22
Staying about the same	70	61	- 9

Source: *The New York Times* CBS News Poll in Toner, 1991a. Telephone survey of 1,106 adults, of whom 840 were registered voters.

Bush's approval ratings gradually declined to 60 percent by late July. Once again, an international crisis boosted his popularity, as Iraq invaded Kuwait, and Bush's approval jumped to 74 percent. The crisis wore on, and Bush's approval dipped again. Increasing unemployment and a budget crisis also contributed to increased public disillusionment. The president flip-flopped on his "no new taxes" pledge, and his ratings dropped into the 50 percent range in October and November. By a healthy majority (60 percent to 40 percent), the public felt that Bush was wrong to abandon his "no new taxes" pledge (Barrett, 1990).

The president benefited from yet a third major rally event that began in January 1991, the Persian Gulf war. A successful outcome boosted his approval to an almost unbelievable level. The March issue of the *Gallup Poll Monthly* proclaimed: "Bush approval at 89 percent, highest in polling history" (1991, 2). The effects of this rally event were more enduring, and Bush's approval gradually declined but was still an impressive 70 percent in September.

The economy continued to decline, and the public's evaluation of Bush in this area was less than enthusiastic. Table 6.4 contains data on how the public has evaluated Bush on his handling of the economy, as compared with his handling of foreign affairs. The difference between the two ratings is computed to underscore a foreign affairs approval advantage by subtracting his economic handling score from his foreign affairs rating. A gap is evident throughout. In 1989, he received healthy percentages on his handling of both in the 60 percent-plus range, with only a single-digit gap. In 1990, the gap increases, presumably because the higher foreign affairs percentages were influenced by his handling of the Panamanian invasion and the Iraqi invasion of Kuwait. The gap is largely double digit, and by the end of the year, his economic scores dip to a low of 36 percent in November. These data also suggest a masking effect of the public's evaluation of foreign affairs that overshadows their economic evaluations, particularly in 1991. The gap in Bush's ratings is large throughout (+ 36 in March, for example), and his economic management rating never attained majority approval.

What happened in the last three months of 1991 and early January 1992 was a continual economic decline, the emergence of the economy as the most salient political issue, and a diminished role for foreign affairs (Morin and Balz, 1991; Toner, 1992b). An October *Wall Street Journal*/NBC News poll still pegged Bush's overall approval at 63 percent, but it also detected substantial voter discontent with Bush and Congress: "The pollsters identify two major potential vulnerabilities for Mr. Bush: the public perceptions that he has no domestic agenda and that his economic policies favor the wealthy" (Jaroslovsky, 1991a, A1). The poll was one of the first to uncover the perception of a middle-class squeeze that may hold the key to the 1992 presidential election (Jaroslovsky, 1991b). A special U.S. Senate election in Pennsylvania won by a Democrat resulted in a widespread interpretation of

Table 6.4

The Two Presidencies: A Comparison of Bush's Ratings on His Handling
of the Economy with His Ratings on Foreign Policy (in percentages)

Date	Nation's Economy	Foreign Affairs	Difference
1989			
April	61	67	+ 6
May	61	65	+ 4
June	61	69	+ 8
August	63	63	0
October	64	72	+ 8
1990			
January	61	75	+14
February	58	75	+17
March	65	70	+ 5
May	52	68	+16
July	46	70	+24
August	55	N/A	N/A
September	53	74	+21
October	38	N/A	N/A
November	36	N/A	N/A
1991			
January	45	76	+31
March	49	85	+36
June	46	70	+24
July	36	66	+30
September	42	73	+31

N/A = Not Applicable

Source: Surveys by ABC News/*Washington Post* as reported in The American Enterprise Public
Opinion and Demographic Report, 1992. The difference is computed as the percentage
Foreign Affairs approval advantage, when handling the nation's economy is subtracted
from handling foreign affairs (March, for example). His economic management rating never
attained majority approval.

voter discontent on the need to fix the economy, high taxes, and inadequate
health care. It was referred to as a wake-up call for Republicans, particularly
Bush (Shribman and McQueen, 1991).

The president was reluctant to act and initially sided with some of his
advisers, who viewed the situation as a public relations problem (Murray
and Harwood, 1991). He appeared quite indecisive, and his domestic policy

was in disarray. His positions on the economy, his re-election bid, and affirmative action were plagued by flip-flops (Devroy, 1991; Harwood and Wessel, 1991; McQueen, 1991a). In early December, his controversial chief of staff was forced to resign (Rosenthal, 1991). A December 1991 *Wall Street Journal*/NBC poll found high percentages of voters demanding that political leaders do something, almost anything, to promote economic recovery (McQueen, 1991b).

The unraveling political situation attracted considerable political opposition to Bush's re-election. At the time of writing, he is being attacked strongly by five Democrats, particularly on economy and health policy, and is being challenged on the right in his own party by conservatives Pat Buchanan and David Duke (Harwood, 1992; Rosenthal, 1992a). The president finally accepted some blame for the weak economy and promised to do better (Perry, 1992). His advisers were still divided internally about the appropriate political strategy to deal with the economy (Rosenthal, 1992b).

After considerable caution and occasional waffling, the president finally responded to the economic malaise in his State of the Union speech on January 28, 1992. He put forth a plan to end the recession that included cuts in payroll withholding taxes, a new IRA, and so on. Whether this plan will work economically and stem the erosion in Bush's popularity will be the big question in 1992. Instead of simply consolidating Reagan's domestic agenda, this guardian president is now cast in a new role as an agent of economic change. Wessel and McQueen note:

For the first time in a decade, the president's State of the Union address has focused on fiscal stimulus rather than spending restraint. Politically, that may prove astute. But economically, it poses an array of risks, notably increasing the federal deficit to a projected $399 billion in the current fiscal year (Wessel and McQueen, 1992).

Paralleling the emergence of the economy as the dominant issue is the decline in the importance of foreign affairs. An October *Washington Post*/ABC News poll found that 69 percent approved the job Bush is doing on international relations. But at the same time, 70 percent said he spends too much time on foreign problems and not enough on problems in this country (Morin and Broder, 1991). The December *Washington Post*/ABC News poll recorded an increase, as 75 percent said Bush spent too much time on foreign problems (Morin, 1992). Although still proud of our Persian Gulf involvement, some Americans nevertheless are having second thoughts. An *Americans Talk Issues* survey in late November by Fred Steeper and Stanley Greenberg

found that eight out of ten Americans believe the United States and its allies should have continued fighting until Iraqi President Saddam Hussein was out of power. And 65 percent of those interviewed said the Gulf War was a "great victory" for the United States—down from 85 percent in March. (Morin, 1992)

Finally, a *New York Times*/CBS poll in January 1992, shortly before the president's State of the Union address, painted a picture of national gloom. While this poll underscored that the economy was the driving issue, it also discovered that Bush's overall approval had dropped to 43 percent, an astonishing decline of 45 percent from their March poll, when Bush's rating was 88 percent, a historic peak, after the Persian Gulf war. This pre-State of the Union poll also found that the public was losing confidence in Bush's handling of foreign policy, his strong suit during his first three years in office. Although it could eventually prove to be an aberration and not very significant, this poll showed that only 46 percent approved of the president's conduct of foreign policy, while 46 percent disapproved (Toner, 1992b). It may well be that what the public focuses on in foreign policy is changing. Instead of the traditional thrust of defense spending and national security, Bush's Democratic opponents have attempted to blur the meaning of foreign policy by introducing a strong economic component involving the trade issue (Seib, 1992). The president's attempt to preempt this Democratic assault by a trip to Japan to persuade the Japanese to be more cooperative by reducing trade barriers and buying more U.S. products was not well received by the public. The previously mentioned pre-State of the Union poll suggests that "Mr. Bush's effort to cast his Japanese trip as a mission for jobs clearly backfired. Sixty-three percent said the trip was a failure, while 19 percent judged it a success" (Toner, 1992b, A10). To the extent that trade becomes an increasing part of the foreign policy agenda, the president will continue to have a more difficult time registering foreign affairs ratings that even remotely approximate what he garnered in his first three years. Having analyzed the president's responses to events, the next topic concerns the all-important role of the media.

MEDIA INTERPRETATION OF THE PRESIDENT

The power of media to influence public opinion is undeniable. A recent but powerful theory about the nature of this influence is the priming theory, which posits that the more attention media pay to an issue, the more the public is primed to focus on it, and more citizens will incorporate the issue into their overall judgment of the president. As Krosnick and Kinder put it, "When asked to evaluate a president's performance, U.S. citizens generally focus only on the aspects of their knowledge that happen to be most accessible at the time of judgment" (1990, 499). Thus, the media influence the standards used to evaluate the president by the stories the media choose to cover. Repeated exposure to a problem, like economic malaise, enhances the importance that people attach to the problem.

Iyengar and Kinder (1987) have marshaled considerable direct, experimental evidence to support this claim, and to the corollary proposition that as a result, people accord more weight to that problem in presidential evaluations. When primed about the economy, people evaluate the president by their perceptions of how well he managed the economy.

Brody (1991) notes that along with media coverage, citizens are also affected by real world conditions that may or may not be reflected accurately in the media. It is also possible to have strong congruence between media coverage and real world conditions, a lethal combination that constitutes the greatest threat to a president's popularity. In fact, four combinations are possible: (1) stable economy/positive media; (2) stable economy/negative media; (3) weak economy/positive media; and (4) weak economy/negative media. Conditions (1), (2), and (4) have all occurred during Bush's tenure.

During Bush's first 100 days, the research of Robert Lichter and his associates found that positive portrayals of Bush were about 61 percent. The economy was stable. From August 1 through December 16, 1989, the level of positive coverage decreased to 39 percent, and overall, "his administration had more negative than positive coverage" (cited in Devroy, 1989, A2). Bush's popularity ratings did not decline, however, because the real world conditions of a stable economy proved more potent than the negative media.

Beginning in late September and early October 1991, however, economic conditions declined, with increased unemployment and layoffs in large corporations like General Motors and IBM. It is reasonable to assume that the media coverage was also highly negative. Even a cursory analysis of print and electronic media for this time frame (October 1990 to January 1991) supports this claim. Next to a story about the president's return from his trip abroad hailing gains in an agreement with Japan, the headline of the lead story in the upper right corner of the prestigious *New York Times* on January 11, 1992, proclaimed: "U.S. unemployment increases to 7.1%, worst in 5½ years; economy still stagnant" (Hershey, 1992). A front-page headline in the more conservative *Wall Street Journal* on November 22, 1991, declared: "Bush's domestic policy is in growing disarray, plagued by flip-flops" (Harwood and Wessel, 1991). Similarly, the more mass circulation-oriented *USA Today* featured a bold front-page headline on January 20, 1992, "Joblessness struck 1 in 5 workers in '91" (Belton, 1992). Finally, the tabloid *New York Post* headline in January 1992 blared, "Economy is in 'Free Fall,' " but followed this with a larger-type punch line: "No Kidding, George!" (Kennedy, 1992).

THE PARADOXES OF BUSH'S POPULARITY

This chapter concludes by identifying six paradoxes of Bush's popularity. First, Bush compiled some rather impressive approval ratings for the first thirty-three months of his term, although his guardian view of the office constrained him from even attempting to exploit this political resource. Instead, he was content to let these high ratings, particularly for the first eight months of 1991, serve as a shield to discourage proactive domestic agendas from a Democratic Congress.

Second, Bush must stem the decline in his popularity that prevailed at the time of his fourth State of the Union address in order to survive and be re-elected. Even if he does so, however, he is unlikely to have his domestic programs accepted intact by a Democratic-dominated Congress. Faced with this major political constraint, his strongest weapon is the veto, which he exercised twenty-four times during his first thirty-six months in office.

Third, the most important task for Bush's political survival is to be sure that his Republican base is solidified. To reinforce his partisans, however, he must address contradictory expectations. Republican partisans are not nearly as homogeneous as some scholars would have us believe. There are *enterprisers*, fiscal conservatives who hold pro-business attitudes and are anti-welfarist. They are usually affluent, well educated, and well informed. There are also *moralists*, or populist Republicans, who are socially conservative, highly religious, and are not as concerned about personal freedom. They tend to be less affluent, older, and may live in the South. The November 1991 *Times Mirror Survey* discovered contradictory expectations for these two Republican groups. It noted that the moralists

show the most discontent with the country's course, the most desire for government action, and some second thoughts about George Bush. In contrast, pro-business, fiscally conservative, Enterprise-Republicans show more loyalty to the President, more contentment with the status quo, and less enthusiasm for many of the programs and policies favored by their less affluent GOP brethren. (*Times Mirror Survey*, 1991, 2–3)

Fourth, President Bush must appear decisive and act as if he can control his re-election. However, the outcome is to a great extent beyond his control. Wattenberg's party-disunity hypothesis in presidential election outcomes is relevant here (1991). The hypothesis stipulates that the party ticket experiencing the least divisive nomination fight has been the general election winner since 1964. The nomination contest consists of four phases: early primary contests, late primary contests, and convention battle, and the vice presidential selection. Strong division in all four phases, as in Goldwater's Republican nomination in 1964 and Humphrey's Democratic nomination in 1968, are prime examples of what both party tickets want to avoid. In 1992, both parties have potential for divisiveness, in all four phases, and the party that minimizes disunity has the best prospect of winning in the fall.

Who emerges as the Democratic winner could well be more important in Bush's political fate than what he does for himself. As Brody points out, "An incumbent whose job performance was responded to negatively by a large number of voters could still be more appealing than the opposition candidate to enough voters to win reelection" (1991, 16).

Fifth, the president needs to address the structural problems of the country's economy, but there is tension between the long-range economic interests of the country and the short-term policy action needed for re-election. Economists see a long-run need to raise taxes (Greenhouse, 1992), while the Congressional Budget Office foresees recovery in the middle of the year and advises restraint and no radical policy change (Pear, 1992). Still other economists on nightly news broadcasts call for substantial infrastructure investment or a long-range tax-cut investment strategy that would not necessarily jump-start the economy. For the president and other elected officials, however, such programs do not match their political needs to respond to an angry electorate demanding immediate economic relief.

What happened in American politics between March 1991 and January 1992 involved a major shift in the policy agenda. The name of the game was the economy and not foreign affairs. At the beginning of this chapter, Frank Cashen, general manager of the New York Mets, was quoted as saying that managers are not fired because of incompetence but because leadership situations change. A similar question faces George Bush, a president who does not favor an expansive domestic agenda, who has a guardian view of the office, demonstrates capable managerial skills in foreign policy, and possesses a style that prefers an actively reactive strategy. The paradox is that to succeed, he must become something that he is not. The country's leadership needs have changed, and he now must be an agent of change rather than consolidation. His rhetoric and performance in 1992 will be assessed by the American people, who will decide if he should be fired or whether he has been sufficiently persuasive as to convince them that indeed he is a president for all leadership situations and all seasons.

REFERENCES

American Enterprise Public Opinion Report. 1990a (March/April). "The Out Party Rates the Ins." *The American Enterprise* 1:98–99.
———. 1990b (Nov./Dec.). "Declarations of Independents." *The American Enterprise* 1:93.
American Enterprise Public Opinion and Demographic Report. 1992 (Jan./Feb.). "The Bush Barometer." *The American Enterprise* 3:90–91.
———. 1991a (Sept./Oct.). "Racial Polarization and the Presidents." *The American Enterprise* 2:86–87.
———. 1991b (Nov./Dec.). "The Presidents and the Gender Gap over Time." *The American Enterprise* 2:94–95.
Balz, D. 1989 (May 29). "The President's Paradox." *Washington Post*: A14.
Barone, M. 1990. *Our Country: The Shaping of America from Roosevelt to Reagan*. New York: Free Press.
Barrett, L. I. 1990 (Aug. 6). "On the Way Down?" *Time*: 23.
Belton, B. 1992 (Jan. 20). "Joblessness Struck 1 in 5 Workers in '91." *USA Today*: 1A.
Benedetto, R. 1992 (Jan. 13). "Bush Support Slips to 46%." *USA Today*: A1, A6.
Boswell, T. 1989. *The Heart of the Order*. New York: Penguin.

Brody, R. A. 1991. *Assessing the President: The Media, Elite Opinion, and Public Support.* Stanford, Calif.: Stanford University Press.

Brody, R. A., and L. Sigelman. 1983. "Presidential Popularity and Presidential Elections: An Update and Extension." *Public Opinion* 47:325–28.

Cannon, L. 1991. *President Reagan: The Role of a Lifetime.* New York: Simon and Schuster.

Cook, R. 1989 (Nov. 11). "Approval of Bush is High but Ratings are Slipping." *Congressional Quarterly Weekly Report* 47:3097–98.

Denton, R. E., Jr. 1988. *The Primtime Presidency of Ronald Reagan.* New York: Praeger.

Devroy, A. 1991 (Nov. 25–Dec. 1). "The White House in Disarray." *Washington Post National Weekly Edition* 9:6–7.

———. 1989 (Dec. 16). "Sparser, Tougher TV Coverage Seems Not to Hurt Bush Ratings." *Washington Post*: A2.

Devroy, A., and R. Morin. 1989 (April 5). "New President Getting High Marks from Public." *Washington Post*: A6.

Edwards, G. C., III. 1991. "George Bush and the Public Presidency: The Politics of Inclusion." In *The Bush Presidency: First Appraisals.* Edited by C. Campbell, S.J., and B. A. Rockman. Chatham, N.J.: Chatham House.

———. 1989. *At the Margins: Presidential Leadership of Congress.* New Haven, Conn.: Yale University Press.

Edwards, G. C., III, with A. M. Gallup. 1990. *Presidential Approval: A Sourcebook.* Baltimore: Johns Hopkins University Press.

Gallup Poll Monthly. 1991. "Bush Approved at 89 Percent, Highest in Polling History." 306:2–4.

Greenhouse, S. 1992 (Jan. 27). "Economists See Long-Run Need to Raise Taxes." *New York Times*: A1 and C5.

Harwood, J. 1992 (Jan. 14). "Bush Returning to New Hampshire, Could Get a Flinty Reception from Granite State's Voters." *Wall Street Journal*: A16.

Harwood, J., and D. Wessel. 1991 (Nov. 22). "Bush's Domestic Policy Is in Growing Disarray, Plagued by Flip-Flops." *Wall Street Journal*: A1 and A4.

Hershey, R. D., Jr. 1992 (Jan. 11). "U.S. Unemployment Increases to 7.1%; Worst in 5 1/2 Years." *New York Times*: 1 and 16.

Hugick, L. and A. M. Gallup. 1991. " 'Rally Events' and Presidential Approval." *Gallup Poll Monthly* 309:15–31.

Iyengar, S. I., and D. R. Kinder. 1987. *News that Matters: Television and American Opinion.* Chicago: University of Chicago Press.

Jaroslovsky, R. 1991a (Nov. 1). "Voters Voice Dismay about Nation's Course a Year before Election." *Wall Street Journal*: A1 and A16.

———. 1991b (Nov. 5). "Voters Caught up in the 'Middle Class Squeeze' May Hold the Key to the White House Next Year." *Wall Street Journal*: A16.

Jones, C. O., 1991. "Meeting Low Expectations: Strategy and Prospects of the Bush Presidency." In *The Bush Presidency: First Appraisals.* Edited by C. Campbell, S.J., Chatham, N.J.: Chatham House.

———. 1990. "The Separated Presidency: Making It Work in Contemporary Politics." In *The New American System.* Edited by A. King. Lanham, Md.: University Press.

Kennedy, J. M. 1992 (Jan. 19). " 'Prez' Off to Poor Start in Economy-Based Campaign." *Arizona Daily Star*: G2.

Krosnick, J. A., and D. R. Kinder. 1990. "Altering the Foundations of Support for the President through Priming." *American Political Science Review* 84:497–512.

MacKuen, M. P. 1983. "Political Drama, Economic Conditions, and the Dynamics of Presidential Popularity." *American Journal of Political Science* 27:165–92.

McQueen, M. 1991a (Nov. 27). "Bush's Greatest Strength, the Personal Touch, Becomes his Biggest Weakness on Volatile Issues." *Wall Street Journal*: A12.

———. 1991b (Dec. 13). "Voters Demand Political Leaders Do Something, Almost Anything, To Spur Economic Recovery." *Wall Street Journal*: A16.

Miller, A. H., M. P. Wattenberg, and O. Malanchuk. 1986. "Schematic Assessments of Presidential Candidates." *American Political Science Review* 80:521–40.

Miller, M. D., and M. Burgoon. 1979. "The Relationship between Violations of Expectations and the Induction of Resistance to Persuasion." *Human Communication Research* 5:301–13.

Morin, R. 1992 (Jan. 20–26). "How Quickly They Regret." *Washington Post National Weekly Edition* 9:37.

Morin, R., and D. Balz. 1991 (Dec. 23–29). "Bush's Rating Skids with the Economy." *Washington Post National Weekly Edition* 9:37.

Morin, R. M., and D. S. Broder. 1991 (Oct. 28–Nov. 3). "Candidate Bush's Achilles' Heel." *Washington Post National Weekly Edition* 8:39.

Mueller, J. 1973. *War, Presidents, and Public Opinion*. New York: John Wiley and Sons.

Murray, A., and J. Harwood. 1991 (Nov. 19). "Bush Sensing Only a Public Relations Problem, Will Delay Any New Economic Plans Until 1992." *Wall Street Journal*: A16.

Neustadt, R. E. 1990. *Presidential Power and the Modern Presidents*. New York: Free Press.

Ostrom, C. W., Jr., and D. M. Simon. 1985. "Promise and Performance: A Dynamic Model of Presidential Popularity." *American Political Science Review* 79:334–58.

Pear, R. 1992 (Jan. 22). "Study in Congress Foresees Recovery in Middle of Year." *New York Times*: A1, A11.

Perry, J. M. 1992 (Jan. 16). "Bush Accepts Some Blame for the Economy." *Wall Street Journal*: A12.

———. 1989. (July 18). "Bush Wins Points for Efforts on Environment and Foreign Affairs." *Wall Street Journal*: A24.

Presser, S., and J. M. Converse. 1976–77. "On Stimon's Interpretation of Declines in Presidential Popularity." *Public Opinion Quarterly* 40:538–41.

Rose, R. 1991. *The Postmodern President*. Chatham, N.J.: Chatham House.

Rosenbaum, D. E. 1992 (Jan. 18). "Democrats Vying in '92 Race Offer Painless Recovery." *New York Times*: 1, 7.

Rosenthal, A. 1992a (Jan. 21). "Bush Aides Divided on How to Correct Slip in Popularity." *New York Times*: A1, A9.

———. 1992b (Jan. 25). "Bush Camp Renews Strategy Debate." *New York Times*: 1, 8.

———. 1991 (Dec. 4). "Sununu Resigns under Fire as Chief Aide to President; Cites Fear of Hurting Bush." *New York Times*: A1, A12.

Seib, G. 1992 (Jan. 7). "With Bush Strong on Global Issues, Democrats Seek to Blur Domestic and Foreign Distinctions." *Wall Street Journal*: A12.

Shribman, D., and M. McQueen. 1991 (Nov. 7). "Pennsylvania Election Sends Nation's Leaders an Ominous Message." *Wall Street Journal*: A1, A5.

Sigelman, L. 1979. "Presidential Popularity and Presidential Elections." *Public Opinion Quarterly* 43:532–34.

Sigelman, L., and P. J. Conover. 1981. "The Dynamics of Presidential Support during International Conflict Situations: The Iranian Hostage Crisis." *Political Behavior* 3:303–17.

Stanley, H. W., and R. G. Niemi (eds.). 1991. *Vital Statistics on American Politics*, 3rd edn. Washington, D.C.: CQ Press.

Tatalovich, R., and A. R. Gitelson. 1990. "Political Party Linkages to Presidential Popularity: Assessing 'Coalition of Minorities' Thesis." *Journal of Politics* 52:234–42.

Times Mirror Survey. 1991 (Dec. 13). "The People, the Press and Politics on the Eve of '92: Fault Lines in the Electorate." Washington, D.C.: Times Mirror Center for the People and the Press.

Toner, R. 1992a. (Jan. 10). "Poll Shows Price Bush Pays for Tough Economic Times." *New York Times*: A1, A10.

———. 1992b. (Jan. 28). "Bad News for Bush as Poll Shows National Gloom." *New York Times*: A1, A10.

———. 1991a. (Nov. 26). "Poll Finds Confidence in Bush in Decline over the Economy." *New York Times*: A1, A9.

———. 1991b (Dec. 1). "Bush Takes Hits from All Sides, Including His Side." *Wall Street Journal*: Sect. 4, 1.

Wattenberg, M. P. 1991. *The Rise of Candidate-Centered Politics*. Cambridge, Mass.: Harvard University Press.

Wessel, D., and M. McQueen. 1992 (Jan. 29). "Bush Offers a Plan to End the Recession in this Election Year." *Wall Street Journal*: A1, A16.

Wines, M. 1992 (Jan. 11). "Bush Returns, Hailing Gains in Japan Agreement." *New York Times*: 1, 7.

Chapter 7

The National Chairman Becomes President: George Bush as Party Leader

HAROLD F. BASS, JR.

Presidential party leadership is a paradoxical concept and phenomenon (Odegard, 1956; Seligman, 1978; Cronin, 1980; Brown and Welborn, 1982; Ranney, 1983; Harmel, 1984; Brown, 1985; Milkis, 1988). It is peripheral yet central, divisive yet integrative. It lacks a constitutional foundation, emerging in the wake of the 1787 Constitution with the subsequent appearance of political parties on the national scene in the 1790s. The position of the presidential nominee at the head of the party ticket thereby enabled the individual occupying that titular position, and subsequently elective office, both to claim party leadership and to have that claim generally acknowledged. What remains uncertain is what presidential party leadership entails.

James MacGregor Burns (1974, 4, 308–43) had identified two general types of leadership: transactional and transforming. Transactional leadership features bargaining and negotiation in exchange contexts. Transforming leadership, more complex and potent, has an elevating, even moralistic, quality. Burns considers party leadership transactional, although it can embody transformations as well.

Clearly, party leadership involves diverse arenas of exchange: organizational, governmental, and electoral. In relations with both party organization and party-in-government, the separation of powers and federal structure of the U.S. political system complicate interactions.

Further, president-party relations are dynamic; they change over time with regard to shifting power balances between the two institutions and personal considerations. At minimum, aspirants to the presidency require party nomination to legitimate their candidacies. The party additionally can be expected to provide its nominees with electoral assistance and subsequent support in achieving political objectives. In turn, the party seeks assistance in party building, an enterprise with electoral, organizational, and policy components. The inclinations and capabilities of president and party to satisfy these needs and expectations vary over time.

In attempting to characterize presidents as party leaders, at least three general variables appear significant (cf. Brown and Welborn, 1982, 304–5). The first is the attitude of the incumbent toward partisanship in general and the party in particular. A continuum can be established ranging from positive to negative. The second is the tone of president-party relations, here ranging from congenial to hostile. The third is the environment in which presidential party leadership takes place, the political circumstances surrounding its exercise. The environmental considerations include the current distribution of partisanship in the electorate, the issue of an electoral mandate, party control of Congress, and the current vitality of the party organization. This continuum ranges from favorable to unfavorable along each dimension.

Beyond these variables, there can be an ideological dimension to party leadership, which involves visions and agendas. What are the perceived goals and objectives of party leadership, the ends to which it is directed? In this ideological dimension, Burns' transforming leadership can be manifested.

Clearly, this classification scheme oversimplifies complex realities. Note that the variables are not presented as dichotomous. An element of imprecision is inevitable. Rather than encountering "either/or" situations, we find ourselves addressing their "more/less" counterparts. Thus, our classifications invoke inexact evaluations. This situation is as true of George Bush in the White House as it is of any other president.

THE CASE OF GEORGE BUSH

George Bush's background and experiences inclined him favorably toward partisanship and the Republican Party, as well as providing unprecedented preparation for presidential party leadership. First, he entered political life fortified with a long-standing familial heritage of Republican Party identification and service. Chairmanship of a county committee (1963) inaugurated his own extensive leadership role in the party organization. He went on to be a delegate to the 1964 and 1968 Republican National Conventions, and was President Nixon's choice to chair the national party committee (1972).

Bush's party-in-government background is even more extensive, spanning the legislative and executive branches. Twice nominated for the U.S. Senate (1964 and 1970), he lost both general elections. In between, however, he won two terms in the House of Representatives (1966 and 1968), holding a seat on the prestigious Ways and Means Committee. On the executive side, he received political appointments from Presidents Nixon and Ford to executive branch positions as United Nations ambassador (1971), head of the U.S. Liaison Office in China (1974), and director of the Central Intelligence Agency (1976).

In 1980, after strongly contesting Ronald Reagan for the Republican presidential nomination, he became Reagan's choice and the convention's nominee for vice president. Victory that November launched two terms, replete with traditional deputy party leadership assignments. This paved the way for his capture of the 1988 presidential nomination and the ensuing election.

No previous president has come to office with anywhere near this expansive record of party service and leadership. His strong positive orientations toward both partisanship and the Republican Party, his organizational direction, and his broad-based governmental experiences have combined to make him especially attentive to and prepared for the obligations and opportunities of presidential party leadership.

PRESIDENT-PARTY RELATIONS IN THE BUSH YEARS

National Party Organization

We will now survey the general tone of president-party relations during the Bush administration to date, looking primarily at the presidential interactions with the national party organization (Bass, 1984). These interactions typically center on the roles assigned to the national party chairman in the campaign and subsequent presidential party management. These roles were once central; for over a half century, they have been in decline.

The presidential campaign constitutes the accession stage of party leadership (Bass, forthcoming). The two related aspects of the 1988 presidential campaign that require brief examination pertain to party organization involvement in the campaign and to staff changes at the party headquarters.

Traditionally, the national party organization directed the presidential campaign, and the national party granted to its presidential nominee the prerogative of naming the national party chairman. In addition, many presidential nominees have installed deputies in positions of responsibility at the national party headquarters. These staffing assignments customarily ensured the responsiveness of the national party organization to the new party leader for the ensuing campaign.

In recent years, however, the national organization's campaign role has diminished. Accordingly, modern presidential nominees are less attentive to and assertive over its staffing. The current tendency is for the nominee to retain the incumbent chairman, at least through the fall campaign. Not since 1964 has a Republican presidential nominee named a new party chairman in the immediate wake of the convention. More recently, in 1980, the

Republican National Convention established a rule setting the term of the chairman from the January following the presidential election to two years hence. As nominee, George Bush abided by this rule and retained the incumbent chairman, Frank Fahrenkopf, through the fall general election.

However, following his nomination, Bush designated a key campaign aide, Frederic Malek, as his high-level agent at the party headquarters. Months earlier, at the outset of the nomination contest, Bush had assigned Malek the task of planning and conducting convention operations. When it became clear that Bush would be the nominee and that the convention would not feature even symbolic contests, Malek moved smoothly into the party role of convention manager. He orchestrated the convention proceedings in a manner befitting the agent of an incumbent president, precisely choreographing the program to emphasize the themes established by the campaign leadership (Oreskes, 1988).

Following the convention, Bush positioned Malek as Fahrenkopf's deputy to represent the nominee's interests at the national committee. However, soon afterward, allegations of anti-Semitism while in the service of the Nixon administration embroiled Malek in a campaign scandal, and he quickly resigned (Dowd, 1988). He was not replaced with a similarly highly stationed agent from the Bush campaign.

Nevertheless, the president's campaign organization worked smoothly with the national party headquarters. No doubt, elements of Bush's background contributed to the tranquility: Recall that he had previously chaired the national committee in 1973–74. Further, throughout his vice presidency, he had performed the role of deputy party leader that has become customary for that incumbent. In doing so, he maintained his already strong ties with the national party headquarters and its constituents throughout the nation.

However, there was no doubt that the central direction of the campaign came from Bush's personal organization, with the national party chairman and machinery operating on the periphery. The major party contribution was in fund-raising. The Republican National Committee has earned a reputation for excellence in this realm, and it performed exceptionally well in the 1988 campaign. In addition, it developed and sponsored what Fahrenkopf described as generic advertising (Runkel, 1989, 151–52).

In the November 1988 ballot, Bush won a comfortable electoral victory. It was the first success by a non-incumbent nominee of the party holding the presidency since Herbert Hoover's, in succession of Calvin Coolidge, in 1928. It was the first by an incumbent vice president since Martin Van Buren followed Andrew Jackson in 1836.

After the election, with party chairman Fahrenkopf's term expiring in January, Bush asserted his presidential prerogative and designated his youthful campaign manager, Lee Atwater, as his choice for the post. Conforming to custom, the Republican National Committee ratified the president-elect's nomination and elected Atwater to a two-year term on January 18, 1989, two days before the presidential inauguration (Berke, 1989).

This staffing decision had both traditional and innovative features. In placing his campaign manager in the chairmanship, Bush reverted to a once-commonplace practice followed by William McKinley, Woodrow Wilson, and Franklin Roosevelt but largely abandoned in the past half-century. In turn, Atwater represented a new wave in American politics—the professional political consultants, who have supplanted the old-style party bosses in managing campaigns (Agranoff, 1976). In managing the victorious presidential campaign, Atwater had become a controversial figure, criticized for an inclination to engage in negative tactics. Nevertheless, the campaign outcome had confirmed his reputation as an astute and creative electoral strategist.

Atwater's selection to the party chairmanship thus promised to elevate the prestige of that office, perhaps even to restore the national party organization to its traditional roles as political arm of the administration and principal organizational vehicle for the re-election campaign, now typically the purview of a personal organization monitored by the White House staff. Where most recent party chairmen lacked status as presidential insiders, Atwater was a close confidant of the president.

In addition, Atwater's "new politics" orientation, along with his key role in building the South Carolina Republican Party, raised expectations for party development. It was hoped that under his leadership, the national party machinery would accelerate existing tendencies toward modernization and spearhead the transformation of the GOP into the majority party nationally. Meanwhile, as the only president to have served as party chairman, Bush would presumably be especially sensitive to the party's needs and interests.

Initially, optimism prevailed. Atwater had direct access to the president, reportedly talking with Bush three or four times a week, in addition to several conversations a day with White House Chief of Staff John Sununu, to coordinate operations and to mobilize the resources of the national party on behalf of the president's agenda (Lambro, 1989a; Alterman, 1989). Atwater energetically undertook efforts to attract minority voters to the Republican Party, in hopes of breaking a longstanding Democratic Party stranglehold (Atwater, 1989). In addition, by addressing the divisive abortion issue, he sought to extend the Republican Party's appeal to the pro-abortion constituency by asserting that the party, whose platform statement was unequivocally anti-abortion, was "a big enough tent" to accommodate differing views on that extremely controversial question (Toner, 1989a, 1989b, 1989c).

Further, the plaudits Bush received from party headquarters emphasized his unusual attentiveness to party concern (Lambro, 1989a; Benedetto, 1990). Of particular note was Bush's willingness to engage in party fundraising, gilding the lily in a garden in which the Republican Party had already established standards of excellence (Benedetto, 1990).

A year into the Bush presidency, the bright hopes centered on the party chairman had dimmed in the wake of several incidents that led Atwater to assume a much lower profile. Abiding concerns about his negative campaign style were reinforced by the release of a party headquarters' memo using sexually suggestive language to attack Thomas Foley, the new Democratic House Speaker, although Atwater insistently denied sponsorship. Student protests over his proposed election to the board of trustees of predominantly black Howard University prompted his withdrawal. Questions about his maturity and judgment arose when he appeared repeatedly on stage with rock and blues bands and posed for *Esquire* magazine in running shorts with sweatpants dropped around his ankles. Finally, Republican losses in scattered off-year elections undermined his reputation as strategist (Dowd, 1989; Oreskes, 1989; Daley, 1990).

In early March 1990, Atwater collapsed while delivering a speech. Physicians diagnosed a brain tumor as the cause, and Atwater, while continuing to occupy the party chair, turned from partisan struggles to a fight for his life.

With Atwater incapacitated, a sense of drift overtook the national party headquarters. Like nature, political power abhors a vacuum, and one significant consequence of the party headquarters' weakening handle on political operations was a corresponding empowerment in that arena of the White House, led by Chief of Staff John Sununu and the political affairs office he oversaw.

Party loyalists began to question both the partisan sensitivity and the political astuteness of the White House. In July, with the support of both Atwater and Bush, the Republican National Committee responded to its deteriorating position by naming Atwater associate Charles Black as its official spokesman (Toner, 1990a, 1990b). While performing competently, Black lacked the standing to fill the void left by Atwater and to emerge as the preeminent presidential agent in partisan matters.

Eighteen months into Bush's presidency, initial expectations and indications to the contrary, the national party organization was unable to reestablish itself as the institutional base for the conduct of presidential political operations and party management. Rather, in accordance with the modern pattern, the president was exercising presidential party leadership in organizational matters primarily through the White House staff.

As 1990 drew to a close, speculation abounded regarding the occupancy of the party chair. On November 10, the ailing Atwater announced his intention to seek election to a second two-year term. Meanwhile, informed sources suggested that Atwater would be elevated to a largely ceremonial position of general chairman, creating a vacancy in the chair that could be filled by an individual capable of assuming its daily responsibilities ("G.O.P. Chief," 1990).

The post of general chair had been established in 1983, when President Reagan indicated that U.S. Senator Paul Laxalt from Nevada was his choice to fill a vacancy in the party chairmanship. However, party rules required that the chairmanship be a full-time, salaried position, and Laxalt was understandably unwilling to resign his Senate seat. An acquiescent national committee named Laxalt general chairman and Laxalt associate Frank Fahrenkopf party chairman. Laxalt's incumbency proved to be largely ceremonial. When he retired from the Senate after the 1986 elections, he also took leave of his party assignment, and he was not replaced.

Within a week of the reported speculation, another press report (Berke, 1990a) noted that Bush had chosen William J. Bennett, departing federal drug-policy chief, to be the new party chairman. This account credited Sununu at the White House with engineering the choice and attributed it to ideological considerations. A strident conservative, Bennett would presumably placate the restive right-wing of the party.

The report took most observers by surprise. It generally succeeded in delighting party conservatives, many of whom had been critical of Bush for a perceived lack of ideological commitment. However, it was thoroughly unconventional. Bennett had only recently converted to the party and lacked any campaign experience. Moreover, his combative reputation and his presumed political ambitions led critics to question his capacity to conciliate party factions supporting rival issue positions and candidacies. One informed commentator (Broder, 1990) described it as a gamble.

Nevertheless, it indicated Bush's continuing willingness to put the party's reins in the hands of a strong and controversial personality. Indeed, Bush was guaranteeing that the party chairmanship would remain the high-visibility position it had again become under Atwater. However, Bush was also signaling his altered perception that the position of chairman now called less for the talents of an electoral strategist than those of an ideological spokesman. Bennett reportedly agreed to take the job after Sununu assured him that he would have both access to the president and a major agenda-setting role (Berke, 1990a, 1990b).

However, less than three weeks later, Bennett unexpectedly reversed his decision to accept the nomination. Although many reports attributed it to brewing conflict with Sununu, both he and the White House provided convincing alternative explanations tied to financial considerations (Dowd, 1990).

With the deadline for the election of new chairman rapidly approaching, the president cast about for a prospect, reportedly receiving several rejections. Eventually, he opted for another surprise candidate, Agriculture Secretary Clayton Yeutter. Where Atwater had fit neatly into the electoral strategist mold, and Bennett that of a new conception of the chairman as party ideologue, Yeutter could claim neither banner. Like Bennett, he did appear destined to assume the primary role of party spokesman, but without so clear an ideological frame of reference. Lacking Atwater's close personal relationship with the president, Bennett's ideological constituency, and the forceful presence of either, he did not appear inclined to challenge the preeminence of the White House staff in the conduct of partisan political operations.

The national committee dutifully elected Yeutter and, as expected, elevated Atwater to general chairman (Toner, 1991b). Atwater died two months later, and that position remains vacant. During his brief tenure, Yeutter operated in a low-key fashion.

By the onset of the 1992 campaign, however, the president's political future seemed to be in doubt. In a surprise move in early February, Bush moved Yeutter to the White House and replaced him with Richard Bond. Bond promised to be a chairman in the Atwater mold, and his selection suggested that Bush wanted the national committee to play a more aggressive and more important role in his re-election campaign than observers had thought up to that time. Leaders of the president's personal campaign organization included three former Republican National Committee (RNC) staff, presumably with abiding links to party headquarters: Frederic Malek, campaign manager; Charles Black, senior adviser; and Mary Matalin, the departing RNC chief of staff who was named campaign political director.

The challenge to Bush's renomination mounted by Patrick Buchanan not only attested to the growing disenchantment of Republican conservatives with his party leadership, it also raised questions regarding the relationship between the president and the national party organization. When an incumbent seeks renomination, the normal expectation that the national party headquarters will be neutral toward competing candidacies does not apply. However, Bush can count on his loyalists at the party headquarters to advance his candidacy against an intra-party rival.

Presidential leadership over the national party organization has been a central feature in the long record of successes for presidents seeking renomination. Not since Chester A. Arthur in 1884 has an incumbent president who sought that party nomination been denied it. However, the serious challenges faced by several modern incumbents suggest that reforms in convention delegate selection may have diminished the traditional advantages accorded the incumbent through control of the party machinery.

Looking back over the first three years of the Bush presidency, the presidential designations of Atwater and Bennett for the national party chairman promised to usher in a new era in White House-national party organization relationships, restoring the stature of the party in presidential politics. However, these promises have not been realized. Structurally, the relationship has developed in a fashion similar to other modern presidencies, featuring White House domination of political operations and party management. The controversial departure in December 1991 of Sununu from the White House and his replacement as chief of staff by the less ideological and flamboyant Samuel Skinner did not alter this structure (Rosenthal, 1991).

In tone, the relationship has been very amicable. There have been no indications of the pervasive tensions and even hostilities experienced during the Nixon years, when Bush himself served as national chairman, and their clear parallels during the Johnson and Carter presidencies. Indeed, in the appearance of mutual appreciation, this president-national party organization relationship arguably sets the pace for modern presidencies.

Party in Government

Turning to the tone of presidential relationships with the party in government, as noted, the White House staff, led first by Sununu and then by Skinner, has characteristically emerged as the central institution for presidential party management, leaving a negligible role for the national party organization that once prevailed. Within the government, the party organization's traditional jurisdiction over presidential appointments ended during the New Deal. Inside the White House, a personnel office established under President Truman has assumed managerial responsibility. In claiming and distributing government patronage, the party organization's own needs and interests were paramount. The White House personnel office is less attentive to purely partisan concerns.

Presidential appointments continue to offer opportunities for party-building, through rewarding party loyalists and reaching out to potential party constituencies. In staffing his administration, Bush has not ignored these opportunities. Not only have faithful retainers figured prominently, but so also have symbolically significant women, blacks, and Hispanics. Nevertheless, party-building does not appear to have been the driving force behind his appointments.

At the outset of his administration, conservatives pressured Bush to perpetuate the Reagan administration's practice of subjecting potential appointees to ideological litmus tests to ensure policy responsiveness. However, Bush has been less willing to be blatantly ideological in making appointments. Indeed, the moderate reputations of some key early appointees, most notably Richard Darman, director of the Office of Management and Budget, generated sustained criticism from the party's right wing. The subsequent Skinner move to the White House did the same. Moreover, Bush's perceived lack of a domestic policy agenda has distressed conservatives and liberals alike. His pragmatic bent notwithstanding, Bush's appointees have generally been ideologically conservative.

In his relations with the Republican Party in Congress, Bush has benefited from his previous membership in those ranks. While his aforementioned pragmatism has hurt him with right-wing party ideologues, some of whom are members of Congress, on balance it probably has helped him in his dealings with the congressional party. He understands, appreciates, and embraces the congressional norms of compromise and accommodation. He has appeared very comfortable working with his old congressional colleagues,

Table 7.1
The President's Party Support in Congress

	House	Senate
Eisenhower, 1953-60 (R)	65%	69%
Kennedy, 1961-63 (D)	73	67
Johnson, 1964-1968 (D)	77	59
Nixon, 1969-1974 (R)	63	63
Ford, 1974-1976 (R)	63	66
Carter, 1977-1980 (D)	63	67
Reagan, 1981-1988 (R)	64	73
Bush, 1989-1990 (R)	68	78

Source: *Congressional Quarterly Almanac* (Washington: Congressional Quarterly, various issues); *Congressional Quarterly Weekly Report*, 28 December 1991, p. 3784.

making regular visits to Capital Hill for both business and pleasure. The congressional relations staff he assembled at the White House has operated competently in a low-key fashion.

As will be addressed in more detail subsequently, the minority status of the Republican Party in both houses of Congress creates tensions for the party leadership of the president. The criticisms Bush has received tend to come from the right wing of the congressional party, bemoaning his apparent lack of ideological vision and commitment (Lambro, 1989b).

From an aggregate data perspective, Bush's three-year record of party support in Congress looks impressive in comparison with that of other recent presidents (see Table 7.1). In the House, his 68% party support average is higher than that of any of his modern Republican predecessors and has been exceeded only by Kennedy and Johnson. In the Senate, his 78% party support average ranks higher than that of any other recent president. This relatively impressive party support is especially noteworthy since, in dealing with Congress as a whole, Bush has the worst three-year record in the thirty-eight year history of the *Congressional Quarterly* presidential support vote study (*Congressional Quarterly Almanac*, 1990, 22; *Congressional Quarterly Weekly Report*, 1991, 3874).

The favorable aggregate record has masked intermittent and highly publicized conflict between Bush and prominent congressional Republicans. The most noteworthy intra-party dispute occurred in October 1990, over budget legislation. It pitted the president against the House Republican Whip, Newt Gingrich of Georgia. Gingrich refused to support a controversial compromise budget agreement developed after lengthy negotiation between the administration and the congressional leaders of both parties because the agreement called for new taxes, negating a key Bush campaign pledge.

Despite a feverish presidential lobbying effort, a majority of House Republicans followed Gingrich in opposing the compromise budget resolution, dooming it to defeat. The subsequent budget agreement that passed both the House and Senate did so with the support of Democratic majorities and in the face of opposition by Republican majorities (Sinclair, 1991, 174–83).

This debacle occurred in the midst of the mid-term election campaign. While Bush campaigned extensively and enthusiastically for his fellow partisans, some recoiled from his embrace (Devroy, 1991). In late October, Bush became embroiled in an unseemly feud with the co-chairman of the Republican Congressional Campaign Committees, Ed Rollins, who had circulated a memo urging House Republican candidates not to hesitate to distance their campaigns from the president. Under White House attack, Rollins resigned in early 1991 ("The Rollins Remedy," 1990; Balz, 1990; Toner, 1991a).

Midterm losses in congressional seats for the president's party are a virtual given in U.S. politics. In losing only eight House seats and one Senate seat, the Republicans fared comparatively well under Bush's leadership (see Table 7.2).

Thus, the relationship between Bush and the Republicans in Congress has been mixed. Conflict has been much more apparent here than with the national party organization. Still, it has not reached the heights of antagonism evidenced in some previous administrations, and Bush retains a substantial reservoir of personal good-will.

Party in the Electorate

Moreover, for most of his presidency to date, Bush's support from the party in Congress has been enhanced by his sustained high popularity among the party in the electorate. An awareness of Bush's background and experiences should have informed speculation that the tone of his presidential relations with the national party organization and the party in the government would be generally harmonious. Little in that background provided a basis for predicting such relations with the party in the electorate. One of the major surprises of the first three years of the Bush presidency was his extraordinarily high public opinion approval ratings (Edwards, 1991, 129).

Republican partisans spearheaded that record public support (see Table 7.3). Indeed, not only has Bush's peak support from fellow partisans been higher than that of any of his recent predecessors, his lowest level of partisan support has also exceeded theirs. Certainly, Bush's high public and partisan

Table 7.2
Midterm Election Outcomes in House and Senate, 1946–90

Year	President	Party	House	(Majority)	Senate	(Majority)
1946	Truman	Democratic	-54	No	-11	No
1950	Truman	Democratic	-20	Yes	- 5	Yes
1954	Eisenhower	Republican	-18	No	- 1	No
1958	Eisenhower	Republican	-47	No	-13	No
1962	Kennedy	Democrat	- 5	Yes	+3	Yes
1966	Johnson	Democrat	-48	Yes	- 4	Yes
1970	Nixon	Republican	-12	No	+1	No
1974	Ford	Republican	-48	No	- 5	No
1978	Carter	Democrat	-16	Yes	- 3	Yes
1982	Reagan	Republican	-26	No	0	Yes
1986	Reagan	Republican	- 5	No	- 8	No
1990	Bush	Republican	- 8	No	- 1	No

Source: Congressional Quarterly, *Guide to Congress*, 3rd edn. (Washington: Congressional Quarterly, 1982), p. 896; *Congressional Quarterly Almanac*, various issues.

support in large measure can be attributed to the "rally round the flag" factor associated with foreign policy crises, particularly the Persian Gulf war. Moreover, as previous analyses of presidential support would predict, it began falling in the fall of 1991 (Mueller, 1970, 20–22; *Gallup Poll Monthly*, 1989–91, various issues). Nevertheless, until the aforementioned decline, Bush's remarkably high level of support from the party in the electorate made his relations with this component of the party extremely felicitous.

Moreover, Republican Party affiliation increased significantly in the decade of the 1980s. The longstanding gap between Republicans and Democrats has almost disappeared. One-third of the electorate now consider themselves Republicans, 10 percent more than did when Bush chaired the national party during the second term of the Nixon presidency (Gallup and Newport, 1990, 36; Clymer, 1991). While Bush is surely more the beneficiary than the catalyst for this shift, it nevertheless enhances the significance of his support from

Table 7.3
Presidents' Public Approval Ratings from Partisans

	High	Low
Johnson, 1963-69 (D)	87	48
Nixon, 1969-73 (R)	91	48
Ford, 1973-77 (R)	77	57
Carter, 1977-81 (D)	84	34
Reagan, 1981-89 (R)	94	67
Bush, 1989-91 (R)	95	69

Source: George C. Edwards III and Alec M. Gallup, "Twenty-Five Years of Measuring Presidential Approval," *Gallup Poll Monthly* (September 1990): 14–15; *Gallup Poll Monthly*, 1989–91, various issues.

the party in the electorate, thus affecting positively an evaluation of his presidential party leadership.

THE POLITICAL ENVIRONMENT

The political environment obviously affects the exercise of presidential party leadership, providing opportunities and/or impediments. With regard to the distribution of partisanship in the electorate, as noted, the fortunes of Bush's Republican Party generally appear to be advancing, while those of the opposition Democrats are waning. Still, a wholesale partisan realignment, long awaited by the minority Republicans, has yet to occur. Instead, signals of declining partisanship in the electorate abound. Weakening party ties lead voters to make their decisions more on the basis of short-term candidate and issue factors than on long-term party identification. This de-alignment phenomenon would appear to hinder the prospects for presidential party leadership by diminishing the attraction of partisan appeals.

Presidents who win comfortable electoral victories are presumably in a stronger position to assert party leadership than those winning by narrow margins. Bush decisively defeated his Democratic opponent, winning forty states with 426 electoral votes and a 53 percent popular-vote majority. While he fell well short of record totals, his victory was clear (*Congressional Quarterly Almanac*, 1988, 4A, 7A).

Despite his success, Bush lacked presidential coattails. In the concurrent gubernatorial elections, the Republicans lost one statehouse; they suffered substantial setbacks in state legislative contests; and in the congressional

Table 7.4
Gains and Losses in the House and Senate in Presidential Election Years, 1944–88

Year	President	Party	House	(Majority)	Senate	(Majority)
1944	Roosevelt	Democratic	+24	Yes	- 2	Yes
1948	Truman	Democratic	+75	Yes	+ 9	Yes
1952	Eisenhower	Republican	+22	Yes	+ 1	Yes
1956	Eisenhower	Republican	- 3	No	0	No
1960	Kennedy	Democrat	-20	Yes	+ 1	Yes
1964	Johnson	Democrat	+37	Yes	0	Yes
1968	Nixon	Republican	+ 5	No	+ 7	No
1972	Nixon	Republican	+12	No	- 2	No
1976	Carter	Democrat	+ 1	Yes	+ 1	Yes
1980	Reagan	Republican	+32	No	+12	Yes
1984	Reagan	Republican	+14	No	- 2	Yes
1988	Bush	Republican	- 3	No	- 1	No

Source: Congressional Quarterly, *Guide to Congress*, 3rd edn. (Washington: Congressional Quarterly, 1982), p. 896; *Congressional Quarterly Almanac*, various issues.

elections, they lost three House seats and one Senate seat (*Congressional Quarterly Almanac 1988*, 4A, 7A, 8A, 14A, 21A, 24A). While the congressional losses were slight, this was the first time since 1916 that the party of the presidential victor lost seats in both the House and Senate (see Table 7.4). The outcome left the president facing a Congress with both Houses comfortably controlled by the opposition Democrats.

In a hostile partisan environment on Capitol Hill, presidential party leadership must be muted in the exercise of legislative leadership. In developing, submitting, and lobbying on behalf of legislative proposals, the president must take into account the perspectives of Democratic legislators whose support is essential for their enactment. As was seen in the 1990 budget debacle, accommodating opposition perspectives can alienate partisan supporters. Thus, Bush has found himself whipsawed.

Party organizations in the United States have been resurgent in recent years. The Republican National Committee has spearheaded this invigoration. As such, Bush's political environment has been enhanced. However, the significance of this development should not be overestimated. Party organization remains relatively weak (Beck and Sorauf, 1992, 89–94, 109–14).

In assessing the political environment for Bush's party leadership, he has benefited from rising Republican support in the electorate, his surprisingly high level of popular support, and a revitalized party organization. However, generally weakening party ties and the enduring presence of opposition majorities in Congress have constrained his exercise of party leadership. On balance, his environmental liabilities outweigh the assets.

PROJECTING A VISION

During the presidential campaign, Bush openly acknowledged his limitations regarding "the vision thing." His message for voters was that he combined the greatest experience in public life (wags called him "the resume candidate") with a commitment to continue the policy direction charted by Ronald Reagan. He was not a candidate driven by ideology or wedded to an encompassing vision of national destiny. Criticism of his lack of direction has continued to plague his presidency, particularly in the realm of domestic policy. As party leader, he has yet to invoke a transforming agenda and present it in a partisan frame of reference.

GEORGE BUSH IN COMPARATIVE PERSPECTIVE

Recall that in characterizing presidents as party leaders according to the framework proposed, complex realities are inevitably simplified. With this caveat, Franklin Roosevelt would appear to set the standard for success in presidential party leadership. He most clearly combined a personal partisan commitment, positive intra-party relations, and favorable circumstances for the exercise of party leadership. Moreover, his New Deal best approximates the transformational potential for party leadership in U.S. politics.

At the other extreme, Lyndon Johnson, Richard Nixon, and Jimmy Carter all appeared personally much less comfortable with their exercises of presidential party leadership. All experienced and contributed to rather antagonistic intra-party relations. They did so amid differing circumstances, with Nixon's the least favorable and Johnson's the most. They rank as failures, although Johnson merits recognition for articulating a transforming agenda, the Great Society, in partisan terms.

Evaluations of the other presidents are less clear-cut. Dwight Eisenhower lacked a strong partisan orientation and commitment. While he enjoyed relatively congenial intra-party relations, his environment was somewhat unfavorable. Further, he was unable to express effectively his definition of or commitment to what he called "Modern Republicanism."

Harry Truman, John Kennedy, Gerald Ford, and Ronald Reagan generally shared positive partisan orientations and congenial intra-party relations amid somewhat unfavorable circumstances. Reagan ranks highest among them in projecting a vision.

To date, George Bush fits best in this latter group. While he falls short of the Roosevelt standard, he belongs in the second tier. As he embarks on his 1992 quest for renomination and re-election effort, Bush and his presidency are under severe assault. He confronts an economy lingering in recession, a strident intra-party challenge from the ideological right, and an invigorated opposition party increasingly optimistic about its presidential prospects. Nevertheless, Bush deserves generally high marks in the realm of party leadership. To retain his standing, Bush must surmount the immediate tests of renomination and re-election. To improve it, he must transcend party leadership's transactional context and address its transforming potential.

REFERENCES

Agranoff, R. 1976. "The New Style of Campaigning: The Decline of Party and the Rise of Candidate-Centered Technology." In *The New Style of Election Campaigns*, 2nd ed. Edited by R. Agranoff. Boston: Holbrook, pp. 3–47.

Alterman, E. 1989. "G.O.P. Chairman Lee Atwater: Playing Hardball." *New York Times Magazine*, 30 April: 30–31, 66–70, 73.

Apple, R. 1991. "Reading Bush's Lineup." *New York Times*, 6 December: A1, A26.

Atwater, L. 1989. "Toward a G.O.P. Rainbow." *New York Times*, 26 February: E23.

Balz, D. 1990. "Bush Seeks Firing of Party Official." *Washington Post*, 26 October: A1, A23.

Bass, H. F. 1984. "The President and the National Party Organization." In *Presidents and Their Parties*. Edited by R. Harmel. New York: Praeger, pp. 59–89.

———. Forthcoming. "Comparing Presidential Party Leadership Transfers: Two Cases." *Presidential Studies Quarterly*.

Beck, P. A., and F. J. Sorauf. 1992. *Party Policies in America*, 7th edn. New York: Harper Collins.

Benedetto, R. 1990. "Already Busy Bush Stays Even Busier Helping Party." *Arkansas Gazette*, 8 April: 6C.

Berke, R. L. 1990a. "Outspoken Ex-Drug Chief Selected to Head the G.O.P." *New York Times*, 18 November: A26.

———. 1990b. "Behind the Bennett Selection: Bush Wants a Battler." *New York Times*, 19 November: A16.

———. 1989. "Atwater Elected Chairman of G.O.P." *New York Times*, 19 January: A20.

Broder, D. S. 1990. "And Now, Chairman Bill." *Washington Post National Weekly Edition*, 4 December: 10–16.

Brown, R. G. 1985. "The Presidency and the Political Parties." In *The Presidency and the Political System*. Edited by M. Nelson. Washington: CQ Press, pp. 313–14.

Brown, R. G. and D. M. Welborn. 1982. "Presidents and Their Parties: Performance and Prospects." *Presidential Studies Quarterly* 12: 302–16.

Burns, J. M. 1978. *Leadership*. New York: Harper and Row.

Clymer, A. 1991. "Poll Finds G.O.P. Growth Erodes Dominant Role of the Democrats: Republicans Gain Support Among White Voters." *New York Times*, 14 July: 1, 16.

Congressional Quarterly Almanac, 1990. 1991. Washington: Congressional Quarterly.

Congressional Quarterly Almanac, 1988. 1989. Washington: Congressional Quarterly.

Congressional Quarterly Weekly Report. 1991. 28 December, pp. 3751–58.

Cronin, T. E. 1980. "The Presidency and the Parties." In *Party Renewal in America*. Edited by G. M. Pomper. New York: Praeger, pp. 176–93.

Daley, S. 1990. "Atwater Redefining Role of GOP Party Chairman." *Arkansas Gazette*, 23 January: p. 7B.

Devroy, A. 1991. "Candidates Spurn Bush's Embrace." *Washington Post*, 24 October: A1, A4.

Dowd, M. 1990. "Bennett Rejects Top G.O.P. Post, Adding to Republicans' Disarray." *New York Times*, 14 December: A1.

———. 1989. "Politics: Are Lee Atwater's Antics Making Him an Enemy in the White House He Cannot Afford?" *New York Times*, 19 June: B8.

———. 1988. "Adviser to Bush Quits G.O.P. Post amid Anti-Semitism Allegations." *New York Times*, 12 September: A1, A16.

Edwards, G. C., III. 1991. "George Bush and the Public Presidency: The Politics of Inclusion." In *The Bush Presidency*. Edited by C. Campbell and B. A. Rockman. Chatham, N.J.: Chatham House, pp. 129–54.

Edwards, G. C., III, and A. M. Gallup. 1990. "Twenty-Five Years of Measuring Presidential Approval." *Gallup Poll Monthly*, September: pp. 7–15.

Gallup, G., Jr., and F. Newport. 1990. "No Clear Leader Yet for Democratic Nomination in 1992." *The Gallup Poll Monthly*, May: 32–36.

"G.O.P. Chief Will Run Again Despite an Inoperable Tumor." 1990. *New York Times*, 12 November: A20.

Harmel, R. 1984. *Presidents and Their Parties: Leadership or Neglect?*: New York: Praeger.

Lambro, D. 1989a. "Atwater Says Bush a Real Partisan." *Arkansas Democrat*, 25 May: 6B.

———. 1989b. "Where Is Bush Taking Republicans?" *Arkansas Democrat*, 12 December: 10B.

Milkis, S. M. 1988. "The Presidency and Political Parties." In *The Presidency and the Political System*, 2nd edn. Edited by M. Nelson. Washington: CQ Press, pp. 331–49.

Mueller, J. E. 1970. "Presidential Popularity from Truman to Johnson." *American Political Science Review* 64:18–34.

Odegard, P. H. 1956. "Presidential Leadership and Party Responsibility." *Annals of the American Academy of Political and Social Sciences* 307: 66–81.

Oreskes, M. 1989. "Man as Symbol: Atwater's First Year as the Republican National Chairman." *New York Times*, 29 December: A6.

———. 1988. "A Convention Made for TV, Precisely." *New York Times*, 15 August: B6.

Ranney, A. 1983. "The President and His Party." In *Both Ends of the Avenue: The Presidency, the Executive Branch, and Congress in the 1980s*. Edited by A. King. Washington,: AEI, pp. 131–53.

"The Rollins Remedy." 1990. *Washington Post*, 25 October: A21.

Rosenthal, A. 1991. "Bush Names New Staff Chief and Campaign Team." *New York Times*, 6 December: A1, A26.

Runkel, D., ed. 1989. *Campaign for President: The Managers Look at '88*. Dover, Mass.: Auburn House.

Seligman, L. G. 1978. "The Presidential Office and the President as Party Leader, with a Postscript on the Kennedy-Nixon Era." In *Parties and Elections in an Anti-Party Age*. Edited by J. Fishel. Bloomington, Ind.: Indiana University Press, pp. 295–302.

Sinclair, B. 1991. "Governing Unheroically (and Sometimes Unappetizingly): Bush and the 101st Congress." In *The Bush Presidency: First Appraisals*. Edited by C. Campbell and B. A. Rockman. Chatham, N.J.: Chatham House, pp. 155–84.

Toner, R. 1991a. "Gathering Opens with G.O.P. in Flux." *New York Times*, 25 January: A14.

———. 1991b. "Yeutter Steps In and Atwater Gets a New Post." *New York Times*, 26 January: A11.

———. 1990a. "On the Defensive, Republicans Name a Spokesman." *New York Times*, 21 July: A6.

———. 1990b. "The New Spokesman for the Republicans: a Tough Player in a Rough Arena." *New York Times*, 31 July: A10.

———. 1989a. "G.O.P. Blurs Focus on Abortion, To Dismay of Some Party Faithful." *New York Times*, 18 January: A1, B6.

———. 1989b. "G.O.P. Chiefs Meet to Plan a Strategy on Abortion." *New York Times*, 19 January: B9.

———. 1989c. "Atwater Urges Softer Abortion Line." *New York Times*, 20 January: 10.

Chapter 8

"Poppy" and His Conservative Passengers

MATTHEW C. MOEN AND
KENNETH T. PALMER

The nickname "Poppy" was tagged on George Bush early in life, much to his father's chagrin (Bush, 1987). The nickname belies his role as a Navy combat pilot in World War II, a fact noted here because an aeronautical simile best summarizes Bush's relationship with the conservative faction of the Republican Party. He treats conservatives as commercial airlines treat their passengers at hub airports: Try to make them feel individually important, but also recognize that many are clamoring to get aboard and there is no other airline to choose. Such treatment, especially evident since summer 1990, has irked conservatives. They enjoyed first-class status during the Reagan years and resent the demotion to coach.

It was unclear during the 1988 presidential campaign season whether "Poppy" and his conservative passengers would experience a turbulent ride together. Conservatives were suspicious of Bush on several counts: his moderate, "silk-stocking" background; his switch to the anti-abortion side on the abortion issue; his attacks on rival candidate Ronald Reagan during the 1980 primaries. However, he proved a loyal vice president and gave signals during the 1988 campaign that the relationship might be smooth. Candidate George Bush inherited Reagan's legacy and positioned himself as his disciple in order to benefit from the relative prosperity and peace that reigned. In his acceptance speech at the 1988 Republican National Convention, Bush acknowledged his debt to his mentor ("Bush Takes the Lead and Defines His Mission," 1989). Then too, he used several visceral issues against Democratic opponent Michael Dukakis, such as trumpeting the case of furloughed convict Willie Horton and arguing the need for a constitutional amendment outlawing the wanton destruction of the U.S. flag. Those themes and tactics won approbation from conservatives, who appreciated Bush's cognizance of Reagan's role and lauded campaign tactics that drew sharp thematic differences between Republicans and Democrats. Even the so-called "movement conservatives"—those who operated in conservative circles long before Reagan became president and conservatism became a popular cause—willingly gave Bush some leeway. They blithely overlooked the rhetoric about a "kinder, gentler nation" in his 1988 acceptance speech, with its implicit indictment of the harshness of the Reagan years.

More than anything, though, Bush's unanticipated selection of Senator Dan Quayle (R-Ind.) as his vice-presidential running mate signaled the possibility of a smooth ride with his conservative passengers. Quayle had established solid credentials with conservatives during his years in Congress. His rating by the liberal interest group, Americans for Democratic Action, averaged only twelve on a scale of one to 100, where the higher figure connoted liberalness. In two separate years, he scored zero on the ADA scale (Sharp, 1989). Quayle was also cozy with conservatives because he unseated incumbent Birch Bayh (D-Ind.) during the Reagan landslide of 1980, when liberal Senate Democrats were turned out in droves. How better to ingratiate oneself with conservatives than to rid the Senate of one of its outspoken liberals, and a 1976 Democratic presidential contender? Quayle never became part of the "New-Right" Republican clique swept into office with Reagan in 1980 that included Jeremiah Denton (Ala.), Don Nickles (Okla.), and John East (N.C.), plus such sitting members as Roger Jepsen (Iowa), Jesse Helms (N.C.), and Gordon Humphrey (N.H.). However, an aide from a conservative senators' office remarked that Qualye was "standing nearby" that clique and "looking their direction" (confidential interview, 1984). The youthful senator's conservative credentials were cemented when he led the 1986 fight over Senate confirmation of Daniel Manion to a federal appeals court. Manion was a marginally qualified judge whose family was closely linked to the John Birch Society; his confirmation was a litmus test for conservative groups, which sought to whisk him through all Senate checkpoints despite Manion's ideological baggage (Shenon, 1986).

The selection of Quayle meant a great deal to conservatives. It was an overt act of appeasement, which flattered them. It guaranteed access to the White House, as occurred in "revolving door" fashion during the Reagan years (Moen, 1989, 51), even if it meant access at one notch below the presidential level. It signaled a willingness on the part of the perpetually cautious Bush to take a chance, by running with a young senator with a modest record of congressional service who hailed from the habitually Republican state of Indiana (Fenno, 1989). Not surprisingly, conservatives hailed the nomination and wrote articles and editorials defending Quayle's record.

The purpose of this chapter is to chronicle and analyze the relationship of the Bush White House and the conservative community from the earliest days of the administration to the present, with an eye toward a second term. The narrative shows that Bush wisely navigated his way early on, building political capital that sustained him through more turbulent times with conservatives, and leaving them—to mix a metaphor—mostly ruminating about abandoning the ship of state.

WHO'S RIGHT?

The conservative wing of the Republican Party consists of three principal elements. These categories are not mutually exclusive or exhaustive, but they are often employed by scholars and journalists to describe the machinations of the conservative community (Himmelstein, 1990, 63–128). One wing of the Republican right, which traces its lineage primarily to the 1964 presidential candidacy of Barry Goldwater, is today frequently called the "Old Right." Its principal spokesman is the sultan of syntax, William F. Buckley, whose guiding hand established the periodical *National Review*, the Young Americans for Freedom organization, and the "Draft Goldwater" movement in the summer of 1963 (Himmelstein, 1990, 67–69). The Old Right's agenda is centered historically in opposition to communism and the New Deal, as well as concern over "law and order" issues. Its supporters are often upper-middle-class people dissatisfied with major U.S. institutions (Himmelstein, 1990, 75).

The second wing, which arose in the early to mid–1970s, is customarily called the "New Right." There is a vast scholarly literature on the rise of the New Right; the term itself was popularized by a conservative journalist (Crawford, 1980). Almost all observers of the New Right agree on these points: (1) its early ringleaders were Paul Weyrich, Howard Phillips, Richard Viguerie, and Terry Dolan; (2) its institutional base consisted of closely linked organizations, such as Weyrich's Committee for the Survival of a Free Congress, Phillip's Conservative Caucus, and Dolan's National Conservative Political Action Committee; and (3) its financial base consisted of donors who responded to direct-mail solicitations, usually by Viguerie. Observers distinguish the New Right from the Old Right partly by its fanaticism, its inventive use of tactics and technologies, and/or its political agenda, which includes strong support for supply-side economics and traditional morality (McIntyre, 1979; Crawford, 1980; Phillips, 1982; Himmelstein, 1983).

The third wing arose in the late 1970s, under the tutelage of the New Right leaders. It is commonly called the "Christian Right" or the "Religious Right," and its principal spokesmen in the 1980s included the Rev. Jerry

Falwell and the Rev. M. G. "Pat" Robertson. Early observers failed to differentiate between the New Right and the Christian Right, but subsequent scholarship rectified that error by pointing out past and ongoing fissures between the two groups, including the Christian Right's greater support for the Reagan administration and for the overt injection of religious rhetoric into the public domain (Moen, 1989). A congressional aide summed up the difference: "Terry Dolan's goals are not Falwell's goals [for America]" (confidential interview, 1984). The Christian Right in the 1980s was embodied by such organizations as Moral Majority and Christian Voice. Today, it is institutionalized in such groups as Concerned Women for America, Christian Coalition, Family Research Council, and the American Freedom Coalition (Moen, 1992).

Again, these wings of the Republican Party are not the only elements of the conservative wing; neither are they always easily distinguished on matters of policy. Yet they do represent somewhat different philosophic traditions and trace their origins to different time periods. Since parsimony is desired in explanation in the social sciences, the subsequent analysis is restricted to these three wings. The rest of the chapter focuses on Bush's relationship with them.

APPEASEMENT THROUGH APPOINTMENT

Bush entered the Oval Office with a large coterie of friends, associates, colleagues, and acquaintances who were qualified for key governmental positions. His network had been built during years of service in the House of Representatives and in such posts as chairman of the Republican National Committee, director of the Central Intelligence Agency, and vice president of the United States. Indeed, Bush probably knew more people in the federal government than any incoming president since Lyndon Johnson, prompting the *National Journal* to describe his executive branch appointments as a "gathering of friends" ("The Decision Makers," 1989, 1042). Accordingly, thirteen of sixteen Cabinet and top White House staff selections already resided in Washington, D.C. ("The Decision Makers," 1989, 1402).

Bush sought to woo and placate Republican conservatives by choosing several of their contingent for highly visible positions, a strategy that gained him broad support in conservative circles during the first year of his presidency. His selection of Quayle topped the appointments list, but his choice of New Hamshire Governor John Sununu for White House chief of staff was a close second. The governor hailed from a bedrock Republican state, with a richly deserved reputation for low taxes, minimal state regulation, and economic success. More importantly, Sununu had close ties to all factions of the conservative community and demonstrated a willingness to attack ideological moderates and environmentalism when those opportunities surfaced early on (Goodgame, 1990, 25). Within months after taking his position, he was touted as the conservatives' liaison to the president (Fly, 1989). The glee with which conservatives viewed Sununu's appointment was evident in a November 1989 Heritage Foundation sampling of elite opinion. Asked to grade John Sununu's performance, such prominent conservatives as Paul Weyrich and Pat Robertson gave him an "A." When asked to expand on that ranking, Weyrich said that "Sununu has been the best chief of staff I have seen."

Robertson opined that "one of President Bush's best decisions was his selection of Sununu as his chief of staff" ("Bush and His Cabinet," 1990, 32). That level of satisfaction among New Right and Christian Right leaders echoed evaluations of representatives from the Old Right ("Bush and His Cabinet," 1990, 32). Virtually all conservatives agreed that Poppy had selected someone capable of navigating him through difficult situations.

That degree of unanimity dissipated with the nomination of former Senator John Tower (R-Texas) to be Secretary of Defense. He was an early and important player in Old Right circles, known chiefly on Capitol Hill for his mastery of defense issues and subsequently for the Tower Commission Report investigating the Iran-Contra affair. The New Right and Christian Right were skeptical of his nomination as defense secretary, however, because of alleged moral failings that might be described as a yen for cocktails and stewardesses. In fact, the most damaging testimony to the nomination came from Paul Weyrich, who questioned the "moral character" of the nominee on grounds of "lack of sobriety" and companionship with "women to whom he was not married" ("Tower Nomination Spurned by Senate," 1990, 404). The dissent of a prominent conservative helped Tower's opponents defeat him in the Senate by a 53–47 vote. Tower was bumped from a seat he thought was reserved.

Bush's replacement for Tower was Dick Cheney (R-Wyo.), a highly regarded member of the House of Representatives with bedrock conservative credentials and a surprising reputation for conciliation and compromise (Ehrenhalt, 1987, 1676). During eight years in the House, Cheney compiled a 5 percent average approval rating by Americans for Democratic Action, receiving a zero rating more than once (Ehrenhalt, 1987, 1678). Those figures provide an inkling of his ties to the conservative wing of the Republican Party and belie his moderate reputation, which stemmed from service as President Ford's White House chief of staff. In the same *Policy Review* article in which Sununu was graded, Cheney received "A" marks from representatives of the New Right and Christian Right, except for Paul Weyrich, whose "B" rating reflected unhappiness with Cheney's deferential attitude toward moderates in the Cabinet, such as Secretary of State Jim Baker ("Bush and His Cabinet," 1990, 33).

Other highly visible appointments by Bush generated genuine enthusiasm and good-will among conservatives, including Dick Thornburgh as attorney general, Richard Darman as director of the Office of Management and

Budget, and William Bennett as director of a national anti-drug crusade ("Bush and His Cabinet," 1990, 34–39). The nomination of Jack Kemp for secretary of Housing and Urban Development was also welcomed, although not with the enthusiasm that conservatives once exhibited for Kemp, prior to his public rhetoric about the failure of conservatives to offer remedies for endemic urban problems (Shapiro, 1989; Hill, 1989). Unlike Reagan's predilection for appointing ideological warriors to some posts, such as Alexander Haig (State Department) or James Watt (Interior Department), Bush showed a willingness to appoint conservatives with long resumes and reputations for being "civil, cautious, and conciliatory" ("The Decision Makers," 1989, 1402).

Several Bush nominations, though, brought sharp rebukes from conservatives. A particular target was Health and Human Services Secretary Louis Sullivan, who was pressured to publicly recant his pro-abortion position as a basis for action before his nomination went forth (Morganthau, 1990). Some of Bush's ideologically moderate selections—including Secretary of State Baker, Secretary of Treasury Nicholas Brady, and Secretary of Commerce Robert Mosbacher—alienated but scarcely surprised conservatives because they were personal friends of the president. Each was given low to middling marks for his performance by conservative leaders ("Bush and His Cabinet," 1990, 32–34). Still other nominees, such as Bryce Harlow to the Treasury Department and Bruce Gleb to direct the United States Information Agency, were objectionable because they represented the liberal Republican tradition that controlled the party in the 1940s and 1950s (Rae, 1989).

What most angered conservatives, though, were not top-level appointments, of which they received their share (or more), but rather the outcome (and process) of lower-level appointments. The most stinging criticism came from Christian Right leaders, who rebuked the Bush administration on several counts. For one, they sharply criticized the nomination of Alfred Sikes to head the Federal Communications Commission (FCC) because he refused to take a public stand against television and radio "indecency." That position was symbolically important to the leaders of a movement dedicated to restoring traditional moral values and was the sine qua non of the Rev. Don Wildmon's American Family Association (Selcraig, 1990, 43). The nomination particularly offended Christian Right leaders because they had tangled previously with the FCC over the content of religious broadcasting; they were hurt by the lack of consultation in a substantive policy area that so greatly affected their operations (Moen, 1989, 23–26). The tension was compounded by the fact that Christian Right leaders had a candidate in mind for the job— Indianapolis attorney John Price, who spearheaded the 1986 congressional candidacy of fundamentalist minister Don Lynch (Witham, 1989).

A second point of criticism centered on the overall number of tangible appointments. Stated metaphorically, religious conservatives were like standby passengers patiently waiting in line to get aboard but never getting called. The almost total lack of appointments infuriated Pat Robertson, who threatened Bush's appointments coordinator Chase Untermeyer: "If you don't want us to be identified [in the appointments process], we won't be identified next election" (Lawton, 1990, 44). Similar sentiments were expressed by the Rev. Adrian Rogers, the former president of the Southern Baptist Convention, who said that only 1 percent of all executive branch appointments went to religious conservatives in 1989. He added that many in the Christian Right felt "used" by the administration, because there was no "understanding of who we are" (Lawton, 1990, 44).

A third criticism, shared widely by Christian Right, New Right, and Old Right conservatives, was that the pace of filling vacancies was unacceptably slow. They complained that the president was squandering precious time and political capital by taking so long to appoint people. Why the delay in taking off? Did it prove that the president lacked not only a time schedule, but also a flight plan? Did he have to take so long to fill every seat when prominent conservatives waited in the wings? Bush tried to turn aside the criticism, noting that it took a long time to clear people through the complicated ethics codes and the Senate's procedural obstacles (*Public Papers of the Presidents of the United States: George Bush, 1989*, 1990, 1100); moreover, those who clamored for prompt action did not have to live with the consequences of bad decisions. Even so, many conservatives complained that Bush frittered away his "honeymoon" period.

Conservatives' objections with the process and outcome of certain appointments, however, were partly offset by the fact that the Bush administration responded in some measure. Health and Human Services Secretary Sullivan, for instance, announced his intent to follow the administration's "pro-life" position even though it was the opposite of his own. He further redeemed himself in the eyes of conservatives by stifling a sex survey of teenagers that New Right and Christian Right leaders believed encouraged sexual experimentation and advocated licentiousness (Morganthau, 1990; Price, 1991). Similarly, once in office, FCC Chairman Alfred Sikes enforced existing "indecency" laws more stringently than did his predecessors. In an appearance before the annual meeting of the National Religious Broadcasters, he openly invited them to scrutinize existing FCC policies and practices (Witham, 1990, B5).

Discontent with the pace of appointments naturally dissipated as positions were filled, leaving the total number of appointees drawn from conservative ranks as the only major objection. Since that sentiment was restricted largely to Christian Right leaders, it was less worrisome.

At the end of the first year of his presidency (1989), Bush was relatively well positioned with conservatives. Their initial reservations were offset by the passage of time and/or remedial action by the president's subordinates, and in any case, were overshadowed by glee over such appointments as Quayle and Sununu. Their contentment was evident after a private meeting with Bush and Quayle in December 1989, at which time they stressed their favorable impressions and cordial relations (Murray, 1989). The following month, Bush received a warm reception from the National Religious Broadcasters, which was probably his "highwater mark" vis-à-vis the conservative community (Murray and Witham, 1990).

In retrospect, Bush performed masterfully during that first year with respect to appointments and conservatives. He won their affection by placing conservatives in key posts and allayed some of their fears by having distrusted nominees make overtures. Equally important, he fractured conservative opinion with some appointments, such as John Tower and Alfred Sikes, who were objectionable to some factions but not others. What better way to deflect a challenge from the party's conservative wing, as in Reagan's challenge to President Ford in 1976, than to drive wedges between its constituent elements? The political capital that Bush accumulated in 1989 paid benefits the next year, when his relationship with conservatives greatly soured.

NEED AND WEAD

The need for more revenue to alleviate budget deficits that pushed Bush to accept higher taxes and the firing of presidential aide Doug Wead seriously jeopardized relations with conservatives during 1990.

The story of tax increases is widely known and easily told. In his acceptance speech at the 1988 Republican convention, Bush went to great lengths to assert his opposition to tax increases:

And I'm the one who will not raise taxes. . . . My opponent won't rule out raising taxes. But I will. And the Congress will push me to raise taxes, and I'll say no, and they'll push, and I'll say no, and they'll push again. And I'll say to them: Read my lips. No new taxes. ("Bush Takes the Lead and Defines His Mission," 1989, 43-A)

The "read my lips, no new taxes" rhetoric soon became part of candidate Bush's "stump speech" and of the national dialogue. Not surprisingly, his subsequent capitulation on taxes infuriated conservatives. It was almost as if Poppy had lost his bearings and relied upon, as his air traffic controllers, House Speaker Tom Foley (D-Wash.) and Senate Majority Leader George Mitchell (D-Maine), who happily told him where to touch down.

The new position on taxes was announced on the morning of June 26, 1990. It came in the form of a three-sentence statement released to the press that acknowledged that "tax revenue increases" were needed in conjunction with spending cuts to bring down the budget deficit (Rosenthal, 1990). The language itself was designed to give Bush a modicum of "wiggle room." Presumably, "tax revenue increases" could be interpreted to mean inflationary expansion of the tax base, rather than higher tax rates or additional user fees.

The statement was released on a busy news day that included such events as Nelson Mandela's appearance before a joint session of Congress and the Interior Department's long-awaited announcement about offshore oil drilling restrictions (Rosenthal, 1990).

In spite of mildly ambiguous language and clever timing, the reaction to the announcement among conservative Republicans was swift and intense, especially in Congress, where they would be asked to vote on a tax package just weeks before the midterm elections. On the morning of the announcement, Representative Bob Walker (R-Pa.), a leading figure in the New Right-oriented Conservative Opportunity Society, stood in the well of the House to denounce Bush's new position (*Congressional Record*, 1990a). He also invited members to co-sign a brief and blunt letter that read: "We were stunned by your announcement that you would be willing to accept tax revenue increases as part of a budget summit package. A tax increase is unacceptable" (Berke, 1990a). By the next day, over ninety House members had signed. Across the Capitol, Senators Trent Lott (R-Miss.) and Mitch McConnell (R-Ken.) circulated their own letter professing astonishment at the policy shift (Berke, 1990b). The flurry of activity, according to one observer, presented "the most serious Republican congressional revolt of George Bush's presidency" (Berke, 1990b). For their part, Democrats gleefully mocked the abrupt position change; Representative Charles Schumer (D-N.Y.) even took a dictionary to the well of the House to emphasize that the words "tax revenue increases" translated literally into higher taxes (*Congressional Record*, 1990b, H4219).

The clamor on Capitol Hill initially drowned out the cries of protest and betrayal from conservative activists. Eventually, though, their voices were heard in opposition to the deal between Bush and congressional leaders that raised taxes $147 billion over five years ("Budget Adopted After Long Battle," 1991, 134). Yet their plea was ignored. It bred anger that was plainly evident in the December 1990 "midterm grades" they gave Bush. Every conservative leader meted out consistently low marks, mentioning the tax issue as the justification for the grade. Most of the leaders surveyed gave Bush a "D" or "F" for his handling of domestic policy; Burton Yale Pines, a senior vice president of the Heritage Foundation, used words like "dizzy" and "distracted" and "blinded" while giving Bush a "D" ("Sophomore Slump," 1991, 32–33). The anger among conservatives even spilled over into evaluations of other White House officials who previously received high marks. John Sununu and Richard Darman both received two "F" grades for their role in negotiating the tax package and pressuring Republicans on Capitol Hill to support it. One evaluator was so angry with Darmin that he refused to issue a grade, calling for the ouster of this "idiot savant of American politics" ("Sophomore Slump," 1991, 43). Only Quayle escaped the wrath of conservatives' assessments, retaining a solid "A" rating for his private counsel against tax increases.

The problems the White House faced with all elements of the conservative community during late June 1990 were exacerbated by the firing of Doug Wead in August. He was a special assistant to the president for public liaison, whose *raison d'être* was to serve as an intermediary to New Right and Christian Right groups. His dismissal enraged many leaders of those groups, both because it occurred and because of the reasons it occurred.

The sequence of events that caused Wead's departure began in April, when he publicly objected to the invitation of homosexual activists to the White House for the signing ceremony of the so-called "hate crimes" bill. The bill required the Attorney General to compile and publish statistics each year on violent crime aimed against persons on the basis of their race, religion, ethnicity, or sexual orientation. It was opposed by some conservative Republicans, such as Representative William Dannemeyer (R-Calif.), on the grounds that it lumped homosexuals in with other constitutionally protected groups. Bush's invitation to gay rights activists to attend the signing ceremony drew the ire of conservative activists; Wead condemned it in remarks to the *Baptist Press*, saying the decision to invite gay rights activists "very poorly served the president" (Murray and Archibald, 1990, 8). That comment paved the way for an early departure.

The episode causing Wead's quick exit was a July 26 bill-signing ceremony for the Americans With Disabilities Act. It prohibited discrimination in employment, public services, and public accommodations; moreover, it required that employers take steps to accommodate disabled workers. For the most part, debate in Congress focused on employers' compliance costs, but it also delved into the issue of whether AIDS patients could be transferred out of food-handling jobs ("Sweeping Law for Rights of Disabled," 1990, 460; Friedman, 1990). That issue brought gay activists into the debate and back to the White House. Wead responded to conservatives' complaints about a second visit by gay activists with a letter saying that Bush was being poorly served by his staff. This explicit criticism of the staff was an affront to Chief of Staff Sununu, who quickly dispatched aide Andrew Card to fire Wead (Murray and Archibald, 1990, 8).

That act inflamed Christian Right leaders, who said the wrong people had been fired. Gary Bauer, of the Family Research Council, said: "The world is upside down. If anybody should be leaving the White House staff, it should be the individuals who have embarrassed the president by inviting homosexual rights activists who have opposed Bush in 1988 and will oppose him again in 1992" (Murray and Archibald, 1990, 8). The Rev. Robert Grant, an early leader of the Christian Right, said it was "crazy" to alienate millions of "traditional" conservatives to win accolades from a small number of "homosexuals" (Murray and Archibald, 1990, 8). Wead's supporters drafted a "letter of outrage" to send to the White House (Elvin, 1990a).

As with other personnel issues, though, Wead's departure was only partly injurious to the White House. While Christian Right leaders stewed, New

Right activist Paul Weyrich seized the chance to install a former legislative director of Phyllis Schlafly's Eagle Forum, Lee Anne Metzger, in the job. He then praised the White House decision, calling her selection "excellent for the conservative community" (Elvin, 1990b). Much like the Tower appointment, Wead's dismissal fractured conservative Republicans.

Timing caused the Wead controversy to end quickly. He was fired the same day that Iraq invaded Kuwait, and the invasion occupied the White House and dominated the media well beyond the February 27, 1991, ceasefire. By then, the "need and Wead" issues that had brought Bush so much flak from conservatives during 1990 had lost some of their intensity.

POPPY'S PROSPECTS

President Bush's overtures to the conservative wing of the Republican Party in 1989, in combination with his high popular approval ratings, his early affirmation that Quayle would be kept on the ticket, and his incumbency status, preempted a challenge to his renomination until November 1991. At that time, conservative columnist Pat Buchanan announced his intention to seek the 1992 Republican presidential nomination, on a platform that put "America First" (Hallow, 1991a). Buchanan's announcement came amid a series of events that caused conservatives chagrin: the forced resignation of John Sununu, who was still seen as a friend despite his "sell-out" on the tax issue; the claim of Louisiana gubernatorial candidate and former Ku Klux Klansman David Duke to be a symbol and voice for the nation's conservatives and his entry into the presidential race; Bush's indecision on an economic recovery package that provided Democrats an opportunity to seize the initiative, as well as his decision to sign a civil rights bill virtually identical to the one that he had opposed previously on the grounds that it mandated quotas. Those public issues combined with Buchanan's own personal goals and ambitions to breed a challenge that one prominent conservative a year earlier had not thought possible: "I do think that conservatives are upset with George Bush, as they have every right to be, based on what he's done. But I don't see the main conservative movement . . . opposing an incumbent president" (Harvey, 1990).

Although the White House dismissed Buchanan's candidacy publicly, saying the nation was not clamoring for "another Buchanan" (in reference to the undistinguished fifteenth president of the same last name), it took the challenge very seriously. The White House dispatched Quayle to New Hampshire to repair relations with conservatives prior to its February 1992 primary. It also pressured state party organizations to keep Buchanan off the ballot, prompting him to threaten legal action in states with early primaries, such as South Dakota. Finally, the White House temporarily raised the visibility of conservative House and Urban Development Secretary Jack Kemp (Taylor, 1991).

Buchanan's earliest and most enthusiastic support came from New Right and Christian Right ranks. They were disturbed by the whole panoply of gay rights and civil rights issues that led to policy and personnel changes, matters that neither offended nor interested Old Right conservatives very much (Hallow, 1991b). In particular, Christian Right leaders backed Buchanan. As far back as 1986, they had pondered forming a third party composed of conservative Christians (Judis, 1989), but eventually settled on building grass-roots structures within the Republican Party that will be brought to bear when the Bush era ends (Moen, 1992). In the meantime, though, Buchanan's candidacy provided an outlet for their anger and a rallying point for their grass-roots work. One factor working in Bush's favor as he geared up for the campaign was that conservatives held low expectations for his presidency. Not expecting much, conservatives were never quite as disappointed with Bush as they were with Reagan when he failed to deliver. They viewed Reagan as an astronaut—a hero capable of a speedy and direct flight into uncharted areas in search of a conservative nirvana; they view Poppy as a commercial pilot operating a plane with limited hydraulics, slowly zigzagging his way through territory explored first by others. Ironically, Bush benefited from such perceptions, from the fact that conservatives grew accustomed to the idea of waiting out his presidency. It made them less enamored with Buchanan's quixotic quest.

The 1992 election will fracture the conservative community further, in all likelihood, since those who supported Bush and Buchanan will not soon forget their allegiances in the struggle between an incumbent president and a conservative darling. A second term for Bush is likely to bring sniping from conservatives, as they endeavor to move the administration and the Republican Party further to the right. The sniping will probably be ignored, which may serve to intensify it. However, conservatives realize that carping at Bush has its limits. They will never ride in first class in Air Force I; their best hope is to install a pilot someday whose internal compass keeps bearing right. Many of them believe that person now flies in Air Force II.

REFERENCES

Berke, Richard. 1990a. "Republicans Fear Kiss of Death as Bush Moves Lips on Texas." *New York Times*, June 27: 1.

———. 1990b. "GOP in Revolt on Taxes, Steps up Criticism of Bush." *New York Times*, June 28: 20.

"Budget Adopted After Long Battle." 1991. *Congressional Quarterly Almanac 1990*, vol. 46. Washington, D.C.: Congressional Quarterly, pp. 111–66.

Bush, George, with Victor Gold. 1987. *Looking Forward*. New York: Doubleday.

"Bush and His Cabinet." 1990. *Policy Review* (Winter): 30–39.

"Bush Takes the Lead and Defines His Mission." 1989. *Congressional Quarterly Almanac 1988*, vol. 44. Washington, D.C.: Congressional Quarterly, pp. 41A–45A.

Confidential interviews, 1984. Thirty-three personal interviews were conducted in Washington, D.C., in conjunction with a book on the influence of religious conservatives, two of which are cited anonymously in this chapter.

Congressional Record. 1990a. Vol. 136, no. 83 (June 9): H4319.

———. 1990b. Vol. 136, no. 84 (June 27): H4219.

Crawford, Alan. 1980. *Thunder on the Right*. New York: Pantheon Books.

"The Decision Makers: A Gathering of Friends." 1989. *National Journal*, June 10: 1402.

Ehrenhalt, Alan. 1987. *Politics in America: The 100th Congress*. Washington, D.C.: Congressional Quarterly.

Elvin, John. 1990a. "Kilberg Coup?" *Washington Times*, Aug. 6:6.

———. 1990b. "A Done Deal." *Washington Times*, Aug. 7:6.

Fenno, Richard F., Jr. 1989. *The Making of a Senator*. Washington, D.C.: Congressional Quarterly.

Fly, Richard. 1989. "How Bush Is Keeping the Radical Right Inside the Tent." *Business Week*, June 19:45.

Friedman, J. Roger. 1990. "Restaurants Shouldn't Suffer Because of AIDS Panic." *Nation's Restaurant News*, August 13:27.

Goodgame, Dan. 1990. "Big Bad John Sununu." *Time*, May 21: 21–25.

Hallow, Ralph. 1991a. "On the Right, a Challenge." *Washington Times*, Nov. 14:1.

———. 1991b. "Buchanan Readies One-Two for Bush: Taxes and Deficit." *Washington Times*, November 24:6.

Harvey, Chris. 1990. "GOP Right Is Angry—But Not Mutinous." *Washington Times*, July 30:3.

Hill, Gwen. 1989. "Kemp Pledges Campaign to Help Nation's Poor." *Washington Post*, January 28:4.

Himmelstein, Jerome L. 1990. *To the Right: The Transformation of American Conservatism*. Los Angeles: University of California Press.

———. 1983. "The New Right." In *The New Christian Right*. Edited by Robert C. Liebman and Robert Wuthnow. New York: Aldine, pp. 13–30.

Judis, John B. 1989. "Rev. Moon's Rising Political Influence." *U.S. News & World Report*, March 27:27.

Lawton, Kim. 1990. "Evangelicals Still Not Sure About Bush." *Christianity Today*, January 15:44–45.

McIntyre, Thomas. 1979. *The Fear Brokers*. Boston: Beacon Press.

Moen, Matthew C. 1992. "The Christian Right in the United States." In *The Religious Challenge to the State*. Edited by Matthew C. Moen and Lowell S. Gustafson. Philadelphia: Temple University Press, pp. 75–101.

———. 1989. *The Christian Right and Congress*. Tuscaloosa, Ala.: University of Alabama Press.

Morganthau, Tom. 1990. "Sullivan: Bush's Aide Makes Waves." *Newsweek*, March 5:19.

Murray, Frank J. 1989. "Bush Faces Tough Right, Wins Decision." *Washington Times*, December 15:4.

Murray, Frank J., and George Archibald. 1990. "Bush Link to Right Is Fired." *Washington Times*, August 2:1.

Murray, Frank J., and Larry Witham. 1990. "Bush Pledges to Fight for TV Preachers' Political Agenda." *Washington Times*, January 30:8.

Phillips, Kevin P. 1982. *Post-Conservative America*. New York: Random House.

Price, Joyce. 1991. "Surprised Sullivan Says Whoa to Teen Sex Survey." *Washington Times*, July 19:1.

Public Papers of the Presidents of the United States: George Bush, 1989. 1990. Washington, D.C.: Government Printing Office.

Rae, Nicole C. 1989. *The Decline and Fall of the Liberal Republicans From 1952 to the Present*. New York: Oxford University Press.

Rosenthal, Andrew. 1990. "Bush Now Concedes a Need for Tax Revenue Increases to Reduce Deficit in Budget." *New York Times*, June 27:1.

Selcraig, Bruce. 1990. "Reverend Wildmon's War on the Arts." *New York Times Magazine*, September 2:22.

Shapiro, Joseph. 1989. "A Conservative War on Poverty." *U.S. News & World Report*, February 27:20–23.

Sharp, J. Michael. 1989. *The Directory of Congressional Voting Sources and Interest Group Ratings*, vol. 2. New York: Facts On File.

Shenon, Philip. 1986. "Byrd Maneuvers Stalls Approval of a New Judge." *The New York Times*, June 27:1.

"Sophomore Slump." 1991. *Policy Review* (Winter): 32–34.

"Sweeping Law for Rights of Disabled." 1990. *Congressional Quarterly Almanac 1989*, vol. 46. Washington, D.C.: Congressional Quarterly, pp. 447–61.

Taylor, Ronald. 1991. "Kemp Tackles Domestic Ills, Not Presidential Bid." *Washington Times*, November 24:6.

"Tower Nomination Spurned by Senate." 1990. *Congressional Quarterly Almanac 1989*, vol. 45. Washington, D.C.: Congressional Quarterly, pp. 403–13.

Witham, Larry. 1990. "FCC Chief Welcomes Participation of Nation's Religious Broadcasters." *Washington Times*, February 2:B5.

———. 1989. "Nominees to FCC Irk Religious Conservatives." *Washington Times*, July 31:5.

PART 4

PRUDENCE AND/OR POLICY LEADERSHIP

Chapter 9

The Home Front: Domestic Policy in the Bush Years

ROBERT J. THOMPSON AND CARMINE SCAVO

"A new world order" is George Bush's theme, symbolizing the objective of his administration's various international policy initiatives. Is there a domestic equivalent? Is it "a kinder, gentler America?" "A thousand points of light?" Does he have a vision for the kind of America that he wishes to leave when he completes his presidency? Or only an internationally oriented one? As the 1992 presidential election draws close, these kinds of questions about George Bush's interest in domestic policy and his effectiveness as domestic political leader have not only become a matter of scholarly and editorial assessment; they threaten to become a key political issue in the election campaign. This chapter addresses questions about George Bush as a domestic political leader.

FACTORS IN THE EVALUATION OF BUSH'S LEADERSHIP

The evaluation of a leader's effectiveness involves consideration of several conditioning or contextual factors. It is, consequently, appropriate that we consider Bush's domestic political vision, his goals, and the contexts within which he has operated since January 1989. How does Bush perceive domestic politics? What does he perceive his role in domestic politics to be? What domestic goals has he set for his administration? And, how have various contextual factors affected his performance?

Bush's twenty years of national-level political experience, including eight years as vice president, have given him a solid basis for developing his own perceptions of the proper roles of a president. He sees the presidency as having clear leadership responsibilities for the country as a whole, but with considerably less clear distinctions of how far those responsibilities require a president to take national action (Bush, 1991). Foreign policy and national security affairs are the paramount tasks of a president and the national government in his eyes. Domestic matters, however, vary in terms of their significance as presidential issues. The state of the economy, education, drugs, crime, highways, the environment, and other domestic issues are important, but the president's role is much more restricted, as is that of the national government. Bush is a political conservative in this sense; in Richard Rose's terms, he sees his role as a guardian (Rose, 1991). In Rose's view, a president's role in these issues is primarily a symbolic one of educating the country about problems and urging others to deal with them. *Newsweek* summarized Bush as having "an almost 19th-century approach to social ills. The answer is not government, but the kindness of individuals" (McDaniel and Thomas, 1991, 20).

Which domestic issues has Bush singled out as being important and what has he proposed to do about them? If one merely lists the topics to which Bush gave attention during his campaign, in his inaugural address, in his budget speeches, and in his State of the Union addresses, his domestic agenda appears to be a rather lengthy one. It includes: child care, Head Start, parental leave, minimum wages, housing for the homeless, civil rights, health-care issues, drugs, education, the environment, crime, the savings and loan crisis, and economic growth. Indeed, Bush began his presidency with the themes of a "kinder, gentler nation" and "a thousand points of light," which seemed to indicate a major break from the relative neglect of domestic affairs that was perceived to have occurred during the second Reagan term. *Congressional Quarterly's, President Bush: The Challenge Ahead*, published early in Bush's first year, described the budget situation as a quandary that faced both Bush and the Democrats "because much of his social agenda conformed to the Democrats' agenda." It further observed that a number of his initial budget recommendations contradicted the trends of the Reagan domestic agenda. In his inaugural address, Bush also seemed to offer the Democrats an opportunity to work together (*Congressional Quarterly*, 1989, 109).

This approach has been more aggressive in symbolic terms than it has in practice, as is consistent with the president's views on his role. Aside from his education proposals, virtually every other domestic policy initiative has been moderate in nature and scope. They have built much more on the Reagan policy initiatives than they have differed from them. We would be willing to argue, in fact, that excluding Reagan, Bush has had the most limited domestic agenda of any president since Hoover. Moreover, relations with Congress have gotten progressively more intense. This can partly be attributed to the tight fiscal constraints facing the national government and the increasing tensions that come from the approaching presidential election, but they have been present virtually from the start of the administration. Fault can be found at both ends of Pennsylvania Avenue, but certainly Bush and his former chief of staff, John Sununu, must share in the responsibility for the deterioration of relations. If nothing else, the initial symbolic approach to domestic concerns signaled a shift that many Democrats and Republicans have not found to be followed through with substantive proposals. In an exaggerated way, bargaining by the administration has been replaced by harsh critical attacks and vetoes. In fairness to the administration, though, this tactic has not infrequently obtained for it legislation closer to what it initially preferred. Thus, the approach has become part of the administration's "bargaining" strategy.

This moves us closer to the contextual factors influencing Bush. One of the most important of these is the divided party control of the presidency and Congress. This topic has been discussed by a number of scholars in recent years and does not need much elaboration here (Thurber, 1991; Sundquist, 1988). Suffice it to say that the Democratic majority in Congress and the Republican control of the executive branch means that both must cooperate in order for the legislative proposals of either to be put into place. In some respects, a basic condition of stalemate exists, forcing both parties to engage in hard bargaining.

That bargaining, however, has been made even more complicated by various other factors, including the fragmented nature of Congress and the budget deficit. The fragmentation of authority in Congress complicates the bargaining process for Congressional leaders in both parties and for the president. The tight fiscal constraints confronting the federal government during the past decade have also made the bargaining process more complicated. This has particularly been the case since Congress and the Bush administration made the 1990 budget agreement limiting spending increases to cuts in existing programs or new taxes. And, given Bush's reluctance to raise new taxes, despite his "temporary lapse," major changes in domestic policies have not had much chance. As a result, domestic policy changes have been on hold in many respects.

Related to fiscal constraints is the overall legacy of the Reagan years. The limited domestic agenda of the Reagan administration contributes in several ways. In a sense, as Bush's own campaign indicated, some important domestic issues were not dealt with; thus, a kind of backlog of problems exists. However, the fiscal constraints that Bush inherited did not provide much opportunity for new programs. Moreover, because Bush ran for the nomination as the rightful heir to Reagan, the development of an aggressive set of domestic policies would be interpreted by many Republicans as a betrayal of that legacy. One may presume that this includes many Republicans working in important positions in the Bush administration.

The Reagan legacy also relates to another important aspect in Bush's leadership style, his partisanship, though it is less a contextual factor than the others. Bush began his term by extending an olive branch to congressional Democrats, as noted above. Yet his campaign for the presidency was a very partisan one, focusing not on key issues facing the country but more on negative images about his opponent. He has continued this bifurcated approach, employing aides like Lee Atwater, John Sununu, and William Bennett to make sharp attacks on the Democrats in Congress, while sounding like a peacemaker himself. At other times, his own approach has been very partisan, attacking the Democrats for neglecting the public interest for political advantage because they do not agree with him. He has also framed issues like drugs and education in terms that do not permit reasoned disagreement. The issues are seen as being so critical that almost a state-of-war mentality is needed to confront them; therefore, disagreements about methods and objectives should be put aside and the president's perspective should dominate (Mackey-Kallis, 1989). From one perspective, Bush thus uses the situation of divided government and his public position to great advantage, appearing to be above politics and partisanship almost simultaneously.

A final contextual factor that has influenced Bush's approach to the domestic policy agenda has been the press of major international events and problems. Bush argues that his attention to international affairs has had important implications for domestic affairs. One cannot disagree with that point entirely. The dramatic changes in Eastern Europe and the Soviet Union, the Persian Gulf war, the situation in Panama, the attempts to initiate negotiations in the Middle East, and a range of other international matters have required a great deal of presidential time and attention. They would have no matter who was president. The undetermined question, though, is whether another president would have made more time for some domestic issues. Since they have been time-consuming, they have contributed to the lurching image of the White House as it has dealt with domestic affairs. The result is that domestic issues appear to come second, to be less important, and to have less genuine presidential commitment even when they are the focus of attention.

When one considers these various factors and Bush's overall political orientation, one is left with a rather mixed bag of generalized goals, complicated institutional relationships, and severe political and fiscal constraints, but little concrete sense of how these factors have affected Bush's domestic policy leadership. For that, we turn to the case studies of drugs and education.

THE BUSH ADMINISTRATION AND DRUGS

The problem of drugs in American society is, in some ways, very different from the problems of education described below, yet in other ways, the problems are very similar. Both problems lead many Americans' lists of the most severe problems facing the United States. Both are domestic problems that several administrations have attempted to solve, and both have defied simple solutions. The two problems interact with each other: Drug use in public schools is often cited as a reason that education cannot take place. But the two problems also differ both in their nature and in the ways public policy has addressed them. While the severity of the American education problem has been increasing in recent years, the drug problem seems to be easing, most likely not as a result of public policy successes, but as demography and life styles change (*Time*, 1990; Moore, 1991).

A variety of methods have been advanced by policy analysts for controlling illegal drug use. Lieber (1986), for example, writes that cocaine, the most visible of the drugs federal policy seeks to control, can be made less available to Americans by: attempting to inhibit coca cultivation, interdiction at U.S. borders, strict enforcement of drug dealing and associated laws inside the United States, and punishment and education of those who use the drug. In these four ways, one can see the broad ideological debate over law enforcement issues that dates back to the early days of the Nixon administration (*The Economist*, 1988) in which liberals tended to focus on the causes and prevention of crime while conservatives tended to focus on its effects and deterrence. Thus, the four ways of reducing cocaine use—and by implication, other drug use—can be divided into supply-side policies, or strategies to make drugs less readily available to Americans, and demand-side policies, or strategies to reduce Americans' cravings for illegal drugs. Supply-side strategies in controlling drugs dominated the early days of the Reagan administration as a result of Reagan's declaration of a "war on drugs." It was not until first lady Nancy Reagan developed the "Just Say No" campaign that the demand side of drug control received attention, at least informally, from the White House (Guess and Farnham, 1989).

In his inaugural address, Bush promised to reinvigorate the war on drugs. He proclaimed illegal drug use a "national scourge." This approach initially represented a continuation of the war on drugs announced by Reagan in the early 1980s. The appointment of "drug czar" William Bennett, a former Reagan administration Secretary of Education, also signaled Bush's commitment to follow policies similar to his predecessor's. However, by the late summer of 1989, Bush began an effort to establish his administration's own distinct direction. On September 5, 1989, in a broadcast timed so that school-age children could hear the message, Bush addressed the public from the Oval Office. His speech revolved around two themes: intolerance for drug use, and the need for cooperation from all Americans to eliminate U.S. drug use. Brandishing a vial of crack cocaine that he said had been purchased in a park across Pennsylvania Avenue from the White House (reporters later found that this was not quite accurate), Bush announced that the federal government's previous efforts to address the drug problem had lacked a strategy and that his administration would provide the necessary guidance.

Bush's policies are largely of two types. First are those policies that seek to deter the use of drugs through the identification of drug users by workplace testing and the punishment of drug dealers with long prison sentences. Second are policies that emphasize reducing the supply of drugs in the United States. These policies put an emphasis on such strategies as interdiction (through use of the U.S. Customs Service, the Coast Guard and other military services, and border patrol agents), and source reduction (through use of foreign assistance and other international agreements aimed at changing the economies of the Latin American and Asian nations that are the source of many illegal drugs). The differences in the Bush policies announced in the September 1989 speech amounted not to wholly new directions, but rather to incremental changes in Reagan policies. The speech, and the later supporting document issued by Bennett's office, sought to increase the emphasis on control of domestic use of drugs more than Reagan had, and to decrease somewhat the emphasis on interdiction. In addition to announcing goals that addressed interdiction and other source-reduction strategies—a 10 percent reduction in illegal drugs entering the United States by 1991, a 50 percent reduction by 1999—Bush announced goals that addressed reduction in domestic use of illegal drugs. He sought a 10 percent reduction in the number of people reporting illegal drug use by 1991, with a long-term goal of a 50 percent reduction by 1999 (Biskupic, 1989).

To many observers and analysts, the Bush anti-drug policy initiative fell short not only in its effort to describe a bold new vision but also in the funds it budgeted for administration proposals. The major new program in Bush's speech was a proposal for $129 million for fiscal 1990–91 in military assistance to Latin American governments that asked the United States for help in addressing drug problems. These funds were over and above the $65 million that Bush had proposed as emergency assistance for Colombia (Felton, 1989). Funds to implement the remainder of the goals addressed in this program were more limited. In fiscal 1991–92, the administration called for some $7.9 billion to address drug problems, but this represented only $717 million in new spending; the remaining funds were to be shifted from other programs or would be funds already appropriated that would be repackaged as drug abuse funding. The Office of National Drug Control report accompanying Bush's speech reported that 73 percent of the total funding in the Bush administration plan was projected to be for supply reduction, with only 27 percent earmarked for demand reduction strategies (Biskupic, 1989).

Various events in the first two years of the Bush administration served to keep drugs on the national agenda. For example, the invasion of Panama in December 1989 was publicly justified in part by a desire to apprehend Manuel Noriega, who had often been accused by the Bush administration of involvement in the importation of illegal drugs into the United States. Noriega was captured by U.S. troops, removed to the United States, and held for trial on drug law violations. Drug czar William Bennett also served to keep drugs on the front burner. In speeches to predominantly conservative groups across the country, Bennett threatened to issue report cards that would grade state and local law enforcement efforts in meeting national anti-drug goals (Solomon, 1990). Industry groups signed on to help promote a drug-free society, and new advertising campaigns were developed to deter both children and adults from experimenting with illegal drugs. A major Amtrak passenger train derailment in Baltimore and a New York City subway accident were shown to be partially the result of illegal drug use by their respective operators. In early 1990, Bush asked heads of Latin American drug-producing countries to meet with him in Cartagena, Colombia, for a drug summit that would seek to develop strategies on reducing the supply and demand for drugs. Amid threats by Colombian drug traffickers to shoot down Air Force I, the drug summit took place in February 1990. Agreements were signed by the relevant national leaders to develop what Bush called an "anti-drug cartel" to combat the drug problem (Lauter and Long, 1990, A1).

At the same time, however, drug use was declining. By 1990, the National Institute on Drug Abuse (NIDA) was beginning to report data that drug use was declining among many sectors of the American public. Casual drug use, cocaine use on a monthly as well as a weekly basis, and drug-related emergency room visits all showed sharp drops from 1985 to 1990, prompting *The National Journal* to comment, "The drug crisis has ebbed if not ended among middle-class Americans of all ages" (Moore, 1991, 268). Both Bush and Bennett attributed the drop in drug usage to administration policies, with Bennett taking a much more optimistic stance than did Bush. In late 1990, contending that the war on drugs was a success and that it would be possible to accelerate to 1994 the accomplishment of Bush's goal of halving drug use, Bennett resigned as director of the Office of National Drug Control Policy. His successor, Bob Martinez, was nominated partly in recognition of his role as a tough law enforcement advocate in his term as Florida's governor.

In a speech in November 1990, Bush declared, "We're on the road to victory" (*Time*, 1990, 44) and later told reporters, "[O]ur hard work is paying off" (Moore, 1991, 267). In his 1991 State of the Union address, Bush took a more cautious tone, and while claiming progress in the war on drugs, stated, "[W]e will not rest until the day of the dealer is over, forever" (Moore, 1991, 267).

Experts in drug abuse generally have looked skeptically at the Bush administration's claims of success of federal efforts in dealing with drugs. To many experts, the dropping incidence of drug abuse has more to do with demographic and life-style changes in the American public than it does with public policy. It may be true that stiffer prison sentences for casual drug use and lower tolerance of drug use in the workplace may deter middle-class Americans from trying drugs. But analysts point to the downturn in drug use before the stiffer laws favored by the Bush administration were in place. Equally disturbing is the lack of decline in some indicators of drug use. While the NIDA reported monthly and weekly cocaine use dropping in early 1991, daily cocaine use actually increased, and the number of crack cocaine users remained constant (Moore, 1991). To careful analysts, this represents a redefinition of the drug abuse problem, from one of the casual user in the workplace to the habitual user who may commit violent crimes to support his or her habit. Peter Reuter, co-director of the RAND Corporation's policy research center, has remarked: "[A]n epidemic has run its course. It doesn't mean that the problem is over. What you do have to worry about is how you manage the problems of people who have become dependent on drugs" (Moore, 1991, 267).

In his administration's proposals on the control of illegal drugs, Bush appears not to see this side of the drug problem. His administration's policies, with their supply-side assumptions, at best may deter average Americans from becoming casual users, but even here there is little evidence that illegal drug consumption has dropped in response to public policy. Policy solutions to the problem of hard-core drug abuse are more complex than strategies addressing casual users. The development of such solutions remains a challenge for the Bush administration. The long-term problem is, of course, that Bush may prematurely announce victory in the drug war and walk away from the problem of hard-core drug abuse as Richard Nixon walked away from the problem of hard-core heroin use in the 1970s.

BUSH ADMINISTRATION
EDUCATION INITIATIVES

If George Bush had to single out one aspect of domestic policy to which his administration has given significant attention, it would be education. Here, Bush has enumerated a bold set of goals for reforming the nation's school system, accompanied by an ambitious time schedule of getting the job done by the year 2000. Like his approach to the U.S. drug problem, however, Bush's statement of broad goals and ambitious schedules has been accompanied by a lack of consistent follow-through both by himself and those in his administration charged with pursuing his policy goals. In education, Bush's problem has not been consistency of vision, but rather consistency of effort, as both other domestic concerns (the recession, the savings and loan bailout, and so on) and international events (the Persian Gulf war, Eastern Europe) have competed for places on the president's policy agenda.

In the 1988 presidential election, candidate Bush promised on more than one occasion to give education a top priority in his administration. By expressing his desire "to be the education president, . . . to make us number 1 in education all around the world," Bush created high expectations in the education community over what his administration would do to remedy these problems. Many, both in the education policy community and outside it, looked for wholly new federal initiatives on education in the first Bush administration. Such positive federal initiatives would represent a dramatic break from the initial policies of his predecessor, who came into office promising to abolish the Department of Education and blaming teachers for the problems of U.S schools. However, education policy was in the past tightly linked to federal spending on education. The Bush administration, like administrations of earlier presidents, faced a twofold problem with this. First, federal education spending represents only 6 percent of all spending on public education in the United States; the remaining 94 percent comes from the states and localities (*The Economist*, 1989a). Second, the size of the deficit puts severe limitations on any new direct federal spending on education. But many education policy analysts had, by 1989, begun to question whether any additional amount of money could cure U.S. school ills. Combined federal, state, and local funds are greater in the United States than in Canada, Germany, France, Japan, or Britain, measured both in absolute dollars per pupil and as a percentage of gross national product. While education spending in the United States rose some 40 percent in real dollars in the 1980s, academic performance in other advanced industrialized countries constantly outpaced that in the United States (*The Economist*, 1989b).

Newly elected President Bush thus decided to emphasize sweeping education reform for several reasons. First, the extent of the problem was both well documented and at a near-crisis level. Second, an opportunity existed to unlink the federal leadership role in education from the provision of significant new sums of money to the nation's school districts. Such an unlinking would dramatically redefine the federal role in public education and might actually allow Bush to become known as "the education president." Third, educational reform had been a traditional Democratic issue. Bush's education proposals thus were made partially in order to get the administration out in front of congressional Democrats, whose party had always been strong advocates of an increased federal role in education. And last, Bush does seem to be genuinely concerned about the state of public education in the United States. In his first State of the Union address on January 31, 1989, he stated:

So tonight, I'm proposing the following initiatives: the beginning of a $500 million program to reward America's best schools, "merit schools"; the creation of special Presidential awards for the best teachers in every State; . . . the establishment of a new program of National Science Scholars, . . . the expanded use of magnet schools; . . . and a new program to encourage "alternative certification," which will let talented people from all fields teach in our classrooms. (Bush, 1989, 179)

This bold attempt to seize the education policy agenda partially worked. Reactions to the president's remarks on education were guardedly positive, with education groups lauding the vision that Bush had articulated but wondering where the funds would come from to finance such a venture. The National Governors Association, in its February 1989 national meeting, endorsed the president's education goals with a statement that "America's educational performance must be second to none in the 21st century. A new standard for an educated citizenry is required" (Donohue, 1990, 343).

The Bush administration's first budget proposals on education further developed the theme of unlinking the federal leadership role from sources of funding. Some 10 percent of the total pages in the proposed fiscal 1990 budget were devoted to new education proposals: financial rewards for schools that improve academic performance, awards for good teachers, experimentation with additional methods of teacher certification, and so on. However, proposed spending on these programs—$440 million for fiscal 1990—represented some $200 million less than the Reagan administration had proposed in its last budget (*The Economist*, 1989b). Thus, as early as its first several months in office, the Bush administration had developed its major theme on education policy: The federal role would not be one of dramatically increased funding for new education programs. Instead, the administration would concentrate on demonstration projects and changing organizational structures (partially through the use of the introduction of market forces into public education).

In September 1989, Bush and administration officials met with the nation's governors in an "education summit" at the University of Virginia. The statement issued by the summit recognized that education was a joint federal-state partnership but that this partnership currently exhibited excessive rigidity on the part of both partners. Administration conferees agreed to examine federal regulations that might be overly restrictive and to introduce legislation in Congress that "would provide state and local recipients greater flexibility in the use of federal funds, in return for firm commitments to improved levels of education and skill training" (U.S. Department of Education, 1991, 76). A joint federal-state-private panel, the National Education Goals Panel, chaired by Colorado Governor Roy Romer, was established to develop baseline measures of the goals the summit had set and to monitor progress toward accomplishing those goals.

Bush administration efforts on education reform appeared to be on track until the president himself seemed to lose interest in the subject as a result of the tumultuous events in the Soviet Union and Eastern Europe, which dominated the international stage in the second half of 1989. Without consistent presidential attention to education, the effort to reform the nation's schools was left to Education Secretary Lauro Cavazos (and later to his successor, Lamar Alexander) and to Congress. It was not until 1991 that the president's attention shifted back to education policy.

Secretary Cavazos was simply not up to the task of spearheading a major education reform effort. His forced resignation in December 1990 was ostensibly over his department's abortive attempt to lift federal funding from colleges that administered minority-only scholarship programs. Looming larger in Cavazos' resignation than the controversy and embarrassment this issue caused the president was the generally lackluster performance of the Department of Education in the administration's first two years in office (*Time*, 1990). In seeking someone who could exercise leadership over education reform, Bush nominated former Tennessee governor and president of the University of Tennessee Lamar Alexander to succeed Cavazos. As governor, Alexander had proposed the Better Schools Program, which included merit pay for teachers, increased science, math, and computer instruction, and tougher educational standards—all components of the Bush's national education proposals. Bush's choice of Alexander was widely hailed by education policy analysts.

The absence of leadership within the administration, the press of events in Eastern Europe, and the Iraqi invasion of Kuwait allowed congressional Democrats to respond to the president's education proposals with little executive branch rebuttal. In February 1990, the Senate passed legislation authorizing $414 million in expenditures on new education programs. Since the Bush administration had budgeted for only a 2 percent increase in education funding and inflation was projected to run at a 4 percent rate in fiscal 1991, Senator Brock Adams (D-Wash.) warned his colleagues: "If we are to fund this . . . new initiative, we are going to have to cut other education programs to do it" (Zuckman, 1990a, 389). In March, the House Subcommittee on Elementary, Secondary, and Vocational Education, in a straight partisan vote, postponed a vote on the House version of the education bill the Senate had already passed. The bill under consideration by the subcommittee was a "series of compromises" (Zuckman, 1990b, 753) between Representative Augustus Hawkins (D-Calif.), chairman of both the full Education and Labor Committee and its Elementary, Secondary, and Vocational Subcommittee, and Representative Bill Goodling (R-Pa.), its ranking Republican member. Partisan debate on this bill involved disagreements over Adams' warning to the Senate: Should innovative but untried education programs be subsidized out of money that would have gone to support proven programs fully?

Congressional action through 1990 on education bills involved disputes over whether the president or Congress would get credit for the innovations as well as over the absolute level of funding for education and the mix of new and old programs. On the next to last day of the 101st Congress, the House of Representatives finally passed an omnibus education authorization. This bill carried some $800 million in spending authorizations and included provisions for some of Bush's education proposals: cash awards for excellent teachers and schools, math and science scholarships, and alternative methods for teacher certification. The bill went to the Senate for final approval on the last day of the session. During debate on the bill, conservative Republican senators used procedural delaying tactics to block its passage. According to one source, "Bush did not make even a telephone call to save [the bill]" (Zuckman, 1991, 983). Thus, the 101st Congress ended its session without taking action on Bush's education proposals, as a result of both partisan wrangling between Democrats and Republicans, and conservative Republican senators' discontent with the administration's willingness to compromise with the Democrats on education legislation (Zuckman, 1990c).

On April 18, 1991, President Bush made his most dramatic attempt yet at "grabbing the education initiative from congressional Democrats" (Zuckman, 1991, 983) by announcing a six-part education plan that encompassed many of the proposals that had emerged from the 1989 education summit and on which Congress had been working since that time. Bush's motivations in reannouncing this program with a great deal of fanfare were simple. Neither house of Congress had plans to work on elementary and secondary education in the 102nd Congress (which was to be devoted to the subject of higher education). By directing public attention to the issue of elementary and secondary education, Bush forced Congress to work on his policy agenda. Both houses of Congress responded, the Senate Labor Committee taking up legislation on literacy and the House allowing Labor and Education Committee Chairman William Ford (D-Mich.) to offer an amendment to the budget resolution that would increase education spending by $400 million.

The latest Bush education plan involves voluntary national standards and testing accompanied by parental choice in where their children attend school. Some $200 million of the total $690 million proposal would be devoted to financial incentives that would assist state and local governments in the development of school choice programs. An additional proposal is to establish a series of new schools with private funds. The New American Schools Development Corporation was incorporated in July 1991 and charged with soliciting $200 million from private enterprise to fund research and development of a series of non-traditional schools. Thomas Kean, former Republican governor of New Jersey and president of Drake University, was named the chairman of the corporation, with W. Frank Blount of AT&T Company as its chief executive officer. The creation of the corporation was announced with a promise of $30 million in corporate funds (*Wall Street Journal*, July 9, 1991). When research on what these non-traditional schools should be doing is complete, Bush will then ask Congress to authorize $535 million to fund the schools, creating one in each congressional district (Zuckman, 1991).

Reactions to Bush's education goals have been predictably mixed. Democratic members of Congress, looking at the 9.3 percent increase in the Department of Education's budget that Bush had proposed in his fiscal 1992 budget, wondered publicly how the president thought his ambitious education goals could be accomplished on so little money. At one point, Representative William Natcher (D-Ky.), chairman of the Education Subcommittee of the House Appropriations Committee, said to acting Secretary of Education Ted Sanders: "You've been in education for too long to believe in this budget. So we're going to bring you a good one." (DeLoughery, 1991, A23). Senator Edward Kennedy (D-Mass.) called the proposals "very constructive" (Reynolds, 1991, 13) but agreed with Representative Richard Gephardt (D-Mo.) that many of the proposals were of Democratic origin.

More scathing reactions came from some education policy analysts. For example, Gordon Davies, director of the State Council of Higher Education for Virginia, wrote: "The 'bold educational reform' recently proposed by President George Bush is a scam and won't work. . . . Schools have become a convenient scapegoat for the nation's ills" (Davies, 1991, A44). National Education Association (NEA) president Keith Geiger agreed with Davies' assessment that it is society rather than the schools that is to blame for poor academic achievement. At his keynote speech to the NEA national convention in July 1991, he said: "I can guarantee our fellow citizens that schools are improving. It's childhoods that are not." (*New York Times*, 1991, A–8).

The Bush education proposals have also been criticized for what they leave out. In his April 1991 package, Bush did not propose new programs for getting children ready for school. Programs designed to do this include prenatal care, child nutrition and immunization, and good preschools. Writing in *The National Journal*, Rochelle Stanfield observed that Bush has talked generally about readiness for school, "but has all but ignored the subject in the education agenda he announced on April 18" (Stanfield, 1991, 1044). The successful Head Start program serves as a convenient model for getting children ready for school, but this program is administered by the Department of Health and Human Services rather than the Department of Education and may not be viewed by the president as an education program. Secretary of Education Alexander has been quoted as saying that Bush thinks Head Start is very important and pointed out that funding for the program has increased by $700 million over the last few years. But as Stanfield (1991, 1044) writes, "All that translates into is a place for one of three poor children, up from one out of five."

CONCLUSIONS: GEORGE BUSH AND DOMESTIC POLICY

Evaluating a president before he has completed a third year in office is, in a sense, unfair to him. The record is not yet complete. Our assessment therefore should be treated as a preliminary one that is based on the record established thus far and our attempt to extrapolate from it.

From our perspective, Bush has not been an effective domestic leader. In general, we concur with Burt Solomon's grading of Bush's record as a "C", a "gentleman's C" (Solomon, 1991). His leadership style in these areas of policy has been reactive and short-term in its focus. There is no broader, articulated vision of the kind of America he would like to leave behind. In fairness to him, his political philosophy and approach to the presidency does not incline him to articulate one. Yet even in the domestic policy areas Bush claims to see as critical, there has been little personal involvement or follow-through from which a domestic vision could be developed. In the areas of drugs and education, Bush has focused on goal setting, but without effective implementation, those goals will not be achieved. His international record clearly indicates an understanding of this policy-making necessity, but his domestic one does not. He also has apparently not created a sense of his goals in the mind of the public. A recent national poll found that only 7 percent of the parents interviewed could identify even one of Bush's education goals and only one in four knew he had such goals (*The Daily Reflector*, 1991).

In some respects, Bush has been a lucky president. The major issues with which he has had to deal have been international in nature and have played to his strengths and experience. Moreover, the Democrats in Congress have been sufficiently disorganized and divided that they have not been able to offer effective domestic counter measures to Bush's more modest proposals. They also lack the necessary votes from supporting Republicans to override Bush's vetoes. Bush has played this situation capably in terms of preventing the Democrats from legislatively coming together. He has bargained hard and generally been able to stake out the public high ground, forcing the Democrats to deal with the nuts-and-bolts difficulties of forging legislation. This situation, however, seems to have ended as of late 1991. The economy has not improved as Bush had hoped, and the questions with which we began this chapter are being asked more pointedly than ever.

Ironically, Bush's international successes, and the benefits he has reaped from foreign events with which he had little to do, are now partially responsible for his domestic political problems. As we have stated, we think Bush has had a very limited domestic agenda and, as long as he had foreign affairs to balance him out, he and his supporters could make a case for giving domestic affairs a lower priority. However, once the domestic arena became more pressing, his successes and self-proclaimed leadership capabilities in the international arena create an expectation that the same kind of leadership can and will be forthcoming at home. The convergence of interests, experience, skills, and events that we noted earlier is no longer occurring. Similarly, the political tactics that Bush has used against the Democrats have been effective in blocking them, but they will be considerably less effective now that he needs the Democrats to address domestic issues if he does try to do so through legislation. He will need their support now. That moves him squarely into the domestic arena, where his limited domestic vision will make him much more politically and programmatically vulnerable.

REFERENCES

Biskupic, Joan. 1989. "Bush's Anti-Drug Campaign Emphasizes Enforcement." *Congressional Quarterly Weekly Review* (September 9): 2312–15.

Bush, George. 1991. "Remarks at the University of Michigan Commencement." *Weekly Compilation of Presidential Documents* (May 13): 563–66.

———. 1989. "Address Before a Joint Session of the Congress." *Weekly Compilation of Presidential Documents* (February 9): 177–83.

Congressional Quarterly. 1989. *President Bush: The Challenge Ahead.* Washington, D.C.: CQ Press.

The Daily Reflector. (Greenville, N.C.). 1991. "Most Parents Are Unaware of Bush's Education Goals." (November 12): 2.

Davies, Gordon. 1991. "The President's 'Bold Educational Reform' Is a Scam." *The Chronicle of Higher Education* (May 15): A–44.

DeLoughery, Thomas. 1991. "Democrats on House Panel Criticize Bush's Education Budget for 1992." *The Chronicle of Higher Education* (March 13): A–23.

Donohue, John W. 1990. "En Route with an 'Education President': Notes and Quotes." *America* (April 7): 342–59.

The Economist. 1989a. "Doing Without Money." (February 25): 25.

———. 1989b. "Willingly to School." (October 7): 25–26.

———. 1988. "Drugs: No Surrender Yet." (May 21): 26–27.

Felton, John. 1989. "Bush Turns to Military Aid to Stanch Narcotics Flow." *Congressional Quarterly Weekly Review* (September 9): 2322–25.

Guess, George, and Paul Farnham. 1989. *Cases in Public Policy Analysis.* New York: Longman.

Lauter, David, and William R. Long. 1990. "Bush Proclaims 'Anti-Drug Cartel.' " *Los Angeles Times* (February 16): A1.

Lieber, James. 1986. "Coping with Cocaine." *Atlantic* (January): 39–48.

Mackey-Kallis, Susan. 1989. "George Bush's National Drug Address: Considering the Role of the Public in Policy Debate." Unpublished manuscript.

McDaniel, Ann, and Evan Thomas. 1991. "Bush's No-Risk Policy." *Newsweek* (June 24): 20.

Moore, W. John. 1991. "Rethinking Drugs." *National Journal* (February 2): 267–71.

The New York Times. 1991. "Teachers' Union Assails Bush's School Strategy." (July 5): A–8.

Reynolds, Larry. 1991. "Bush's Education Reform Proposal Gets a Critical Look from Congress." *Personnel* (July): 13.

Rose, Richard. 1991. "Evaluating the Presidency: A Problem in Two Dimensions— Positive and Normative." Unpublished manuscript.

Sanders, Alain. 1990. "Who's in Charge Here?" *Time* (December 31): 16.

Solomon, Burt. 1991. "Grading Bush." *National Journal* (June 8): 1331–35.

———. 1990. "It Takes More than a Bully Pulpit to Wage a National War on Drugs." *National Journal* (January 13): 82–83.

Stanfield, Rochelle. 1991. "Shirking Job 1." *National Journal* (May 4): 1044–48.

Sundquist, James L. 1988. "The New Era of Coalition Government in the United States." *Political Science Quarterly* 103: 613–35.

Thurber, James A., ed. 1991. *Divided Government: Cooperation and Conflict Between the President and Congress.* Washington, D.C.: CQ Press.

Time. 1990. "A Losing Battle." (December 3): 44–48.

U.S. Department of Education. 1991. *America 2000.* Washington: Government Printing Office.

Wall Street Journal. 1991. "Education Group Raises $30 Million, Seeks More." (July 9): A–18.

Zuckman, Jill. 1991. "Elbowing Democrats Aside, Bush Unveils School Plan." *Congressional Quarterly Weekly Report* (April 20): 983–86.

———. 1990a. "Senate Passes Much-Revised Bush Schools Initiative." *Congressional Quarterly Weekly Report* (February 10): 389–91.

———. 1990b. "Democrats Reject Compromise, Block Bush Education Plan." *Congressional Quarterly Weekly Report* (March 10): 753.

———. 1990c. "GOP Senators Block Passage of Bush School Initiatives." *Congressional Quarterly Weekly Report* (November 3): 3752.

Chapter 10

Is Prudence a Policy? George Bush and the World

Daniel P. Franklin and Robert Shepard

In the three years that George Bush has been president, the international system has undergone an extraordinary series of changes. Most striking, of course, has been the end of the Cold War and the break-up of the Soviet Union. The relationship that for nearly half a century served as the core organizing element in world politics has not only been transformed, but has nearly vanished. In its place we have witnessed the creation of a new international system that is at once more secure, but at the same time more unstructured and unpredictable.

The collapse of the Soviet Union has dramatically altered every aspect of world politics and, thus, U.S. foreign policy. With the demise of the Soviet threat, America's military allies in Western Europe and Japan are effectively no longer dependent on the United States. Relations among the major powers have increasingly involved economic issues rather than security matters, a change that has significantly altered the relative power of the world's leading states. Japan appears ever more poised to become a major player in world politics, while China, viewed by the United States only ten years ago as a key balancer to the Soviets, has seen its relevance to the international community decline rapidly. Third World conflicts, once seen as crucial in determining the fate of the planet, are far less important today.

George Bush has devoted the greater part of his energy in the presidency to foreign affairs issues. He has made little secret of his preference for the challenges of international relations to those of domestic policy. His tenure in office has been marked by two epic international events: the disintegration of the Soviet empire and the multilateral effort to evict Iraq from Kuwait. Both events have led to increased U.S. stature in the world, and both have shown the president to have an excellent talent for guiding the United States through complex situations. Bush proved himself masterful at encouraging the spread of democracy in Eastern Europe and in the states that once composed the Soviet Union without unduly antagonizing the Kremlin, the new Eastern European governments, or America's traditional allies. And in the Persian Gulf war he demonstrated a remarkable talent for coalition-building as well as the ability to manage a complex military operation.

Despite these formidable successes, Bush has yet to develop a clear-cut strategy for dealing with the new international order. He has yet to articulate what sort of order would be amenable to the United States or what U.S. interests will be in the post-Cold War era. Instead, competence, management, and stability have been the hallmarks of the president's foreign policy. What strategic vision exists appears to be informed by an admixture of a traditional *realpolitik* view of the world and a predilection to continue the policies of the Reagan administration.

This does not suggest that his foreign policy has been flawed in any fundamental way. Indeed, *realpolitikers* would argue that policy succeeds despite convictions or the presence of a coherent ideology (Morgenthau, 1967).[1] What it does indicate, however, is that Bush has yet to seize on a direction, or an ordering principle, comparable to the containment policy that guided the United States since World War II and now seems in need of replacement.

BUSH'S WORLD-VIEW

Despite his long experience in foreign affairs, Bush's view of the world remains somewhat murky. Unlike Ronald Reagan, who stated his foreign policy goals in a blunt and forthright manner throughout his presidency, Bush has always resisted setting forth a substantive plan for dealing with the world. Where Reagan emphasized the destruction of communism and the installation of democracy on a global scale, Bush tended to emphasize rationality in the foreign policy-making process and the attainment of specific objectives.

If a clear, overriding strategy is hard to pinpoint, it is nonetheless possible to delineate some of the administration's tendencies. Its most striking characteristic has been its essential continuation of the policies of the late Reagan years. While the strident rhetoric of the Reagan years has disappeared and the faces of the principal foreign policy makers have changed, Bush's general stances remain markedly similar to those of his predecessor. Like Reagan, Bush has continued to view relations with America's major Western European allies and Japan as the cornerstone of U.S. foreign policy. Reagan's efforts to upgrade relations with Canada and Mexico have not only been continued but enhanced.

In style, too, continuity is evident. Neither president has been shy about using military force when deemed necessary. Both presidents have viewed a strong defense as a cornerstone of an effective foreign policy. Furthermore, despite the growing importance of international economic issues, both have tended to view international power primarily in military terms. Finally, like Reagan, Bush has seen international capitalism as the key tool in helping to spread democracy and bring the world a true Pax Americana.

Where Bush differs from Reagan, it is more the result of a modification in the international environment than a fundamental shift in philosophy. The most significant change came in U.S. relations with the Soviet Union. Even before its demise, Bush ceased to view the Soviet Union as the arch-enemy of the United States and the major threat to world peace, but rather as a withered military giant seemingly unable to deal with its own domestic problems. Bush handled the Soviet Union delicately: While closely consulting Moscow on all major issues and refraining from harsh criticism, he cautiously refrained from granting the Soviet Union full admission to the Western community.

Another important change has been in policy toward the Third World. Reagan's confrontational approach to left-wing Third World governments—a policy that was given a strong ideological basis in the so-called Reagan Doctrine—has lost its relevance in the wake of Western victories. Of the four states toward which the Reagan Doctrine was applied, only Cambodia remains under the rule of a communist government, and that conflict has been relegated to obscurity. Interest in the Afghan rebellion faded fast when Moscow decided to withdraw its forces. In Nicaragua, Violetta Chammoro's electoral defeat of the Sandanistas resolved that nation's conflict in a manner favorable to the United States, causing a decline in U.S. interest. Finally, with the May 1991 agreement between Jonas Savimbi and the Angolan government, U.S. intervention in Angola appears to be coming to an end.

But in a world that is changing dramatically, a reliance on continuity does not indicate a clear policy toward new issues. It is in those situations in which the past does not dictate a clear alternative that Bush has carved his own path.

In dealing with major powers, the president has shown great flexibility. This has been especially evident in his dealings with the Soviet Union, and now, with Russia. In responding to the unfolding events in Eastern Europe and the Soviet Union, Bush has shown himself capable of managing a policy of remarkable sophistication, carefully nurturing the relationship on a personal level while pursuing traditional U.S. security interests. While he resisted the temptation to interfere in the domestic politics of the Soviet Union and the states of Eastern Europe, he was not shy about prodding the Soviets on questions of arms control and human rights. And when the opportunities came to take action on disarmament, Bush moved promptly and decisively in initiating unilateral and bilateral actions to reduce the U.S. and Soviet nuclear arsenals.

The same pragmatism has been evident in the president's handling of relations with the People's Republic of China (PRC). Despite the bloody suppression of thousands of pro-democracy demonstrators at Tiananmen Square, the president stuck closely to his belief that good relations with the PRC remained important to the United States (Scalapino, 1990).[2] Within six months of the massacre, National Security Adviser Brent Scowcroft journeyed to Beijing to assert to the Chinese leadership that the United States would not diminish its relationship, and in the spring of 1991, Bush defeated congressional attempts to impose sanctions on trade with Beijing. While Bush's policy has come under heavy fire from the press and Congress, he has made it clear that long-term security and economic considerations, rather than the short-term behavior of the Chinese government, should guide American policy (Stanfield, 1989).[3]

With lesser powers, however, Bush has shown himself to be more ready to resort to condemnation and, ultimately, military action. In the two situations in which he has used force, in Panama and Iraq, Bush apparently decided that America's overwhelming might could bring about results quicker and more successfully than protracted negotiations or the imposition of a containment policy. In both instances, Bush appears to have determined at an early point on the military option, and he went forth with his decision in a forceful and unrelenting manner.

If there is a problem with this sort of decisive action, it has been that Bush, in the heat of the moment, has failed to consider fully the consequences of his actions in terms of America's long-term interests. Whatever the immediate success of the Gulf operation, the benefits to the United States remain somewhat unclear. While the administration has demonstrated great shrewdness and persistence in initiating peace negotiations between Israel and its neighbors, the Middle East remains one of the world's most dangerous regions. Iran and Syria remain powerful and unpredictable forces in the region; Lebanon remains in Syrian hands; and the reconstruction of Saddam Hussein's regime in Iraq has begun at an accelerated pace. For all the progress that the administration has made, it remains questionable whether U.S. involvement can genuinely achieve benefits for the United States or the nations in the region.

Perhaps Bush's foreign policy to date can be best characterized by its reactive quality. While he has taken the initiative in specific situations, such as in the Persian Gulf and Panama, those actions have been taken in response to crises in which some U.S. action was dictated by the circumstances. The larger vision remains obscure.

It could be argued that the lack of a vision in the Bush foreign policy may not be a liability, and may, to an extent, even be an asset. The collapse of the Soviet empire during Bush's first term in office certainly defied the predictions of most scholars and analysts. Had the president elucidated a clear-cut idea of where the United States was headed, that policy undoubtedly would have been scrapped immediately. For the moment, this improvisatory policy appears pragmatic and successful. But in the future, Bush may well be viewed as a president who missed the opportunity to create a new U.S. policy at a transitional period in history.

DOMESTIC POLITICS AND BUSH'S FOREIGN POLICY

While Bush was elected by an overwhelming majority, his freedom of action was heavily constrained by the fact that Congress remained in the hands of the Democrats. In addition, public awareness and support for the Republican domestic political agenda was relatively shallow.[4] It was quite unlikely that Bush would be able to translate, as Ronald Reagan had done in 1981, his electoral victory into a legislative honeymoon. Despite the new president's tremendous personal popularity, the initial experience of the Bush presidency was more like that of a second honeymoon, the mutual affection was there but the ardor was largely absent. It seemed as if the Bush administration was a continuation of business as usual.[5]

There were, however, subtle but important differences in the organization and style of the new president's White House office. Gone were the ideological purists who guided the Reagan foreign policy to the brink of disaster in order to aid the Contras. (To a certain extent, the shift in the ideological orientation of the president's staff had begun under Reagan in the aftermath of the Iran-Contra affair.) Replacing the Reagan "old guard" was a cadre of insiders—generally well-trained, highly experienced, and relatively colorless. They fit well and were, in fact, a reflection of their boss (DeFrank and McDaniel, 1990).

Gone also was the Reagan internal decision-making structure. Bush lent an active, knowledgeable, and experienced hand to foreign policy decision making. Even so, just as Reagan's limitations were reflected in the disorganization of his foreign policy, Bush's limitations were reflected in the organization of his foreign policy. The president's "hands-on" involvement and his ideological predilections lent their own strengths and weaknesses to his foreign policy.[6]

While Bush had the background and a seeming proclivity for foreign affairs issues, his activity in this area was also a result of political calculation. Without the congressional support so necessary to implement his domestic agenda, Bush, like many of his predecessors in comparable situations, directed the power of his presidency along the path of least resistance. Because the president can operate largely unchallenged in this realm, it became the logical arena to focus his energies.

Furthermore, because the president lacked the congressional support to guide his program through the legislative process, he tended to adopt a rather broad reading of the Constitution and the inherent powers of the presidency. Time and again the president would make expansive claims to powers of the presidency under the Constitution. Time and again he would be rebuffed in domestic affairs (Alston, 1990). However, in international affairs he enjoyed considerably more success.[7]

In his policy toward Panama and his conduct of affairs leading up to the invasion, the president took bold moves to commit U.S. forces without much regard for congressional sensitivities. Neither was there much protest in Congress to the extent that the problems of Panama and the Noriega regime, being out of the bailiwick of members of Congress, were left to the president's discretion.[8] When Bush finally decided to consult congressional leaders, he (like his predecessors) did so in a manner "consistent with" rather than "pursuant to" the War Powers Resolution, well after the fact of the invasion.[9] After the invasion was launched, in the late evening of December 20, 1989, congressional leaders were informed that Operation Just Cause was already in progress. In the euphoria of an easy victory over Panamanian defense forces, the president's failure to properly consult Congress meant little.

Further evidence of Bush's constitutional philosophy can be found in the administration's return to a traditional policy of restraint of the press during military actions. That policy had been eased during the Vietnam War and was reimposed under Reagan during the invasion of Grenada. Only much later were non-official accounts of the invasion leaked to the press that suggested that civilian casualties were much higher than originally claimed by the U.S. Army.

Consequently, it was not surprising that Bush, when he decided to send a large contingent of U.S. forces to the Persian Gulf following Iraq's invasion of Kuwait, chose to do so without consulting Congress. Bush's determination to exclude Congress from policy was further illustrated by his November 8, 1990, announcement that U.S. troop strength in the region would be doubled. The announcement came one day after the midterm elections, at a time when Congress was out of session.

Even though the president eventually did ask for congressional authorization for the use of force, by the time Congress considered the president's proposal, it was presented with limited options. U.S. troops were already deployed and in the process of being positioned for offensive action. Had the president chosen to ask for congressional authorization before the November 8 decision, the outcome might have been very different. However, the president presented Congress with a *fait accompli*—a level of commitment that was attained completely pursuant to presidential discretion. This, perhaps, was the most extreme example of the president's attitude toward and exercise of the powers inherent in the presidency.

Throughout the war, the administration maintained heavy censorship of the press and even went so far as to refuse to cooperate with congressional investigations. When, in early February 1991, Chairman Leon Panetta of the House Budget Committee asked administration officials from the departments of State and Defense to testify as to the costs of the war, those officials were conspicuously absent. Later, when the president proposed a plan for the expenditure of contributions made by U.S. allies to the coalition effort, Bush suggested that the contributed funds be fed into an account that would be under the complete control of the Secretary of Defense, subject to the review of the Office of Management and Budget (the president's budgetary arm). The Senate eventually rejected this proposal, with members from both sides of the aisle arguing that such a procedure violated Congress' constitutional authority to make appropriations (U.S. Congress, 1991). The administration proposal, however, was part of a clear pattern on the part of the president to assert the inherent powers of his office.

While Bush seemed to have a distinct view of the powers and responsibilities of the president under the Constitution, gone from his administration was the heavy ideological baggage of the Reagan presidency. Consequently, Bush has been under steady pressure from the Republican right almost from the moment he took office (Holmes, 1991). Several months prior to the Gulf victory, in the aftermath of the failure of the budget summit agreement, rumor had it that conservatives were planning to run a presidential candidate in the 1992 Republican primaries to the right of President Bush. The president, it seemed, was insufficiently doctrinaire for many on the Republican right. This was particularly true after the president so easily acceded in October 1990 to a tax increase and sacrificed most of his proposed capital-gains tax cut. While the president's spectacular rise in popularity in the aftermath of the Gulf War seemed to preempt any prospects for an opposition candidate from the Republican Party (not to mention the Democratic Party), there was still grumbling in some circles on the right concerning the president's ideological "purity" and commitment.

THE PRESIDENT AND HIS ADVISERS

Certainly, in foreign policy, the president's small circle of advisers represented the moderate wing of the Republican Party. In fact, much of the president's senior advisory staff was transferred from the Ford rather than the Reagan administration. For example, National Security Adviser Brent Scowcroft is a protégé of Ford's Secretary of State, Henry Kissinger. The major exception, Secretary of State James Baker, had always been a close personal friend and associate of George Bush rather than Ronald Reagan. It was as if the president skipped an ideological generation in the development of the Republican Party in his selection of foreign policy advisers. Furthermore, the fast-fading threat of Soviet communism reinforced Bush's personal tendency to eschew ideology in his conduct of policy. Gone were Reagan's pronouncements of the Soviet Union as the "evil empire," to be replaced by cold, hard decision making guided by the perceived national interest (Konracke, 1989; Thomas and McDaniel, 1991).

The Bush administration, however, was not beyond using the rhetoric of human rights. When the president ordered the invasion of Panama, he argued that he did so in order to install the duly elected government of Enrique Endara. This was the justification for the invasion, despite the fact that the President is earlier reported to have told the National Security Council after a Panamanian coup failed to overturn the Noriega regime: "Amateur hour is over. [Noriega will] overstep some day and [I] want [you] to be ready" (Moore, 1991, A9). When Noriega's drug dealing and erratic behavior became an embarrassment to the administration and a threat to the Panama Canal, the President felt compelled to act.

In making the same kind of human rights argument in regard to the restoration of Kuwaiti sovereignty, however, the administration may have painted itself into a corner. The protection of human rights in Kuwait became associated with a very limited goal. If all the United States intended to do, and if all the United Nations was willing to sanction, was the liberation of Kuwait, then the administration would have a difficult time justifying attacks on Iraq's industrial infrastructure and a military policy aimed at the removal of Saddam Hussein. When U.S. and coalition forces had Iraqi forces on the run, it was very difficult for the administration to justify the continuation of hostilities. In the end, the president decided to call a halt to military activities (an action that in the opinion of General Schwarzkopf was premature) and to thereby allow Saddam Hussein to maintain the wherewithal to remain in power. The administration, which had never shown an enormous amount of concern for the rights of the Kurds or the Shiites in Southern Iraq, then attempted to do what it had failed to do militarily by encouraging internal opposition against Hussein. When that insurrection failed, only after some very spirited prodding from domestic critics did the administration decide to intervene on behalf of the Kurds. This was clearly a human rights policy that was adopted under duress.

The fact that the stated purpose of the war reflected little more than the short-term and limited goal of freeing Kuwait reflected a central characteristic of the Bush foreign policy—the emphasis on tactics over strategy. In part, this emphasis is a function of the lack of ideology. It also arises from the administration's style of decision making, one that fosters a reactive, short-term rather than long-term, strategic approach to policy making. If Bob Woodward's account of the decision-making process in the White House is to be believed, the process by which decisions are made in the Bush presidency is vulnerable to the problems identified by Irving Janis' concept of "groupthink" (Janis, 1982).

The president has a very close personal relationship with Secretary of State

James Baker and his other high-level foreign policy advisers. That is, it has been said, part of George Bush's style. This relationship is so close and closed that there is some indication that the decision-making process itself may foreclose certain options (Solomon, 1990a). For example, Paul Wolfowitz, Undersecretary of Defense for Policy, is quoted by Woodward as saying, "There was little or no process where alternatives and implications were written down so they could be systematically weighed and argued" (Johnson, 1991, A9).

In one example of the exclusion of dissent, Chairman of the Joint Chiefs of Staff Colin Powell, who was apparently an early opponent of the use of armed intervention, was excluded from the consideration of some key decisions. Among the discussions from which he was excluded was the president's ultimate decision not to allow the Iraqi invasion to stand. Powell learned of the president's decision from a television news broadcast (Woodward, 1991). Banishing of dissent is another common manifestation of a flawed decision making structure (Janis, 1982).

Furthermore, Bush's penchant for conducting personal diplomacy may bias his conception of U.S. interests.

Certainly, personal antipathy between leaders can hurt. U.S.-Israeli relations, for instance, have suffered because Bush and Secretary of State James A. Baker III dislike Yitzhak Shamir, the sullen prime minister who Bush thinks deceived the White House last year. (Solomon, 1990a, 2986)

Similarly, the fact that Bush has a much closer relationship with former Soviet President Mikhail Gorbachev than with Russian President Boris Yeltsin may have been at work in the delay of U.S. recognition of the independence of the Baltic states and the muted U.S. response to the Soviet coup in the summer of 1991.

Finally, there is every indication that the president tends to contaminate the decision-making process by announcing his policy preference at the beginning of the process. Janis points out that should the president express his opinion, dissenters will be very reluctant to express their true preference. This is particularly the case if the dissenting view is to be received with hostility by a closed, homogenous decision-making group surrounding the President. Here, again, the Panama decision is illustrative. There was very little discussion of whether or not U.S. foreign policy would be well served by the removal of Manuel Noriega or the outcome of that decision because the president made it very clear that intervention was his policy preference. The Persian Gulf decision was revealing in that sense as well. It is apparent that Bush favored intervention very early on when he made it clear that he intended to go beyond the defense of Saudi Arabia (Woodward, 1991).[10]

No structure will guarantee that correct decisions will be made. It is an empirical question as to what point unanimity and a lack of vigorous dissent are detrimental to the decision-making process. The fact that the president as of this writing has enjoyed a major success in the two major military interventions he has undertaken indicates that he has good political instincts and a feel for the execution of military operations. However, the lack of long-term planning at the presidential level indicates that Bush does not encourage a type of analysis of his decisions that might point up long-term negative consequences. Whether this lack of structure for encouraging strategic planning will have a detrimental effect on the Bush legacy remains to be seen.

CONCLUSION

The substance as well as the nature of world politics has changed. The ideological factor that played such a huge role in shaping world politics since the end of World War II has disappeared. International economic issues have largely taken precedence over security issues. As Henry Kissinger and Cyrus Vance noted: "The U.S. political leadership in the world cannot be sustained if confidence in the American economy continues to be determined by substantial trade and budget deficits" (Kissinger and Vance, 1988, 910).

New problems of dire consequences to the planet must be dealt with: the global environment, the internationalization of labor, the intense competition between the world's leading economies, and the persistent inability of most of the world's population to escape poverty. For the United States itself, a new set of problems has emerged: the influx of drugs, the constant inflow of immigrants from Third World states, and the seeming inability of U.S. industry to compete with foreign producers.

Making sense of this new world order, identifying U.S. foreign policy goals, and developing a strategy for dealing with the post-Cold War order remain the principal challenge of the Bush administration. There remain enduring, long-term foreign problems facing the United States that Bush must address: What is the administration's vision of how the United States ought to be positioned in the world? What is the administration's vision of a world order conducive to U.S. interests? How has it gone about structuring the world? And how much flexibility does it have in bringing about such a vision?

It is on these questions that Bush ultimately will be judged. So far, neither he nor the public, press, or foreign policy scholars have pointed a clear path. But with the baseline of containment—from which U.S. foreign policy has been measured for the past forty years—no longer intact, it is the president's task to establish a new one.

NOTES

1. "History shows no exact and necessary correlation between the quality of motives and the quality of foreign policy" (Morgenthau, 1967, 6).

2. Robert Scalapino notes that the administration's best argument against cutting ties with China has essentially been that no irrevocable steps should be taken because of the fluid political situation in China and the possibility that change can occur swiftly. Scalapino argues for the administration's position, claiming that "a struggle over power and policy lies ahead. . . . In the long term, . . . a compatible, supportive Sino-American relationship has an innate logic that cannot easily be vitiated" (Scalapino, 1990, 94–96).

3. The president did impose an array of economic sanctions on the Chinese in the immediate aftermath of Tiananmen Square. However, he was back a little more than a year later to ask Congress to extend most-favored-nation trading status to the Chinese. In defense of his request, the president said:

I concluded that it is in our best interest, in the interest of the Chinese people, to continue China's trade status. Not to do so would hurt the United States. Trade would drop, dramatically hurting exporters, consumers, and investors. China buys about $6 billion a year of American aircraft and wheat and chemicals, lumber, and other products. Lose this market and we lose American jobs. (White House News Conference, May 24, 1990. In *Congressional Quarterly Weekly Report*, 1990, 1684)

4. For example, in March 1991, despite the fact that Bush enjoyed an approval rating of 89 percent in the aftermath of the war in the Persian Gulf, a *Washington Post*-ABC News poll found that only 22 percent of those surveyed had any idea of where the Bush administration planned to lead the nation.

5. Stephen Skowronek discusses regime changes in American politics and the presidency. It could well be argued, according to that theory, that Ronald Reagan presided over a regime change. That would make Bush responsible for regime "maintenance." It would be difficult in terms of timing, then, for the new president to effect a significant directional change in policy (Skowronek, 1990). [Editors' note: for a different view, see Chapter 1.]

6. " 'The President runs foreign policy,' a senior aide said, sometimes delving so deeply that State Department bureaucrats refer to him as, say, the China desk officer" (Solomon, 1990b, 1647).

7. For example, Bush made various claims to a pocket veto power whenever Congress recesses for more than three days, the power to withhold from Congress information concerning covert activities, and the power to refuse to enforce laws the president deems unconstitutional. In fact, the president's lawyers attempted to make a case for the existence of a presidential line-item veto within the provisions of the Constitution (Alston, 1990).

8. The War Powers Resolution requires that

The President in every possible instance shall consult with Congress before introducing United States Armed Forces into hostilities or into situations where imminent involvement in hostilities is clearly indicated by the circumstances. (50 U.S.C. 1542, 1982)

9. In 1983, a congressional committee investigating the matter of "proper" consultation in the meaning of the War Powers Resolution argued that congressional consultation was adequate only if such discussions took place in advance of decisions being made (U.S. Congress, 1983).

10. According to Woodward (1991), Bush ordered the CIA to begin planning the overthrow of Saddam Hussein as early as August 3, the day after the invasion. By

the middle of August, Bush signed a top-secret intelligence "finding" that while the CIA could not violate the ban on assassination, Iraqi dissidents could be recruited to remove Hussein from power.

REFERENCES

Alston, Chuck. 1990. "Bush Crusades on Many Fronts to Retake President's Turf." *Congressional Quarterly Weekly Report* 48 (February 3): 291–95.

Congressional Quarterly Weekly Report. 1990. 24 May, p. 1684.

DeFrank, Thomas, and Ann McDaniel. 1990. "Point Men." *Newsweek* 115 (January 29): 32–34.

Holmes, Kim R. 1991. "In Search of a Strategy: Bush's Professional but Rudderless Foreign Policy." *Policy Review* 55 (Winter 1991): 72–75.

Janis, Irving. 1982. *Groupthink: Psychological Studies of Policy Decision*, 2nd edn. New York: Houghton Mifflin.

Johnson, Haynes. 1991. "Book Says Powell Favored Containment." *The Washington Post* (May 2): A9.

Kissinger, Henry, and Cyrus Vance. "Bipartisan Objectives on American Foreign Policy." *Foreign Affairs* 67 (Summer 1988): 910.

Kondracke, Morton M. 1989. "Blind Men's Bluff." *New Republic* 200 (March 6): 20–23.

Moore, Molly. 1991. "U.S. Sought Premise for Using Military in Panama: Months Before 1989 Invasion, Bush was Waiting for Noriega to Overstep, Book Reports." *Washington Post* (May 9): A9.

Morgenthau, Hans. 1967. *Politics Among Nations*, 4th edn. New York: Alfred Knopf.

Scalapino, Robert. 1990. "Asia and the United States." *Foreign Affairs: America and the World 1989/90* 69, no. 1: 89–115.

Skowronek, Stephen. 1990. "Presidential Leadership in Political Time." In *The Presidency and the Political System*, 3rd edn. Edited by Michael Nelson. Washington: CQ Press, pp. 117–61.

Solomon, Burt. 1990a. "Bush's Passion for Friendship Abets His Diplomatic Policy." *National Journal* December 8: 2986–97.

———. 1990b. "In Bush's Image." *National Journal* July 7: 1642–47.

Stanfield, Rochelle. 1989. "Muted Response." *National Journal* (July): 1719.

Thomas, Evan, and Ann McDaniel. 1991. "Bush's United Front." *Newsweek* 117 (March 4): 49.

U.S. Congress. 1991. U.S. Senate, Senate Appropriations Committee. *Hearings of the Senate Appropriations Committee: Supplemental Appropriation for Operation Desert Storm.* February 26.

———. 1983. U.S. House of Representatives, Foreign Affairs Committee. *Strengthening Executive-Legislative Consultation on Foreign Policy.* Congress and Foreign Policy Series 8 (October).

Washington Post ABC-News. 1991. "Bush Popularity Surges with Gulf Victory." March 6: A1.

Woodward, Bob. 1991. *The Commanders.* New York: Simon and Schuster.

Chapter 11

Kinder, Gentler? George Bush and Civil Rights

AUGUSTUS J. JONES, JR.

Each president receives a variety of opportunities to shape the development and enforcement of civil rights policies. As chief executive, he must take care that the laws are faithfully executed and can thus determine whether civil rights laws will be forcefully implemented or weakly enforced. Moreover, the president serves as chief legislator. Through his various messages to Congress and to the nation (for example, in his State of the Union address), he sets the nation's agenda. He proposes legislation and through his veto power can dispense with legislation passed by the Congress. A president who proposes that steps be taken to protect the victims of bias can certainly help engender equality. In contrast, a president who opposes measures to protect bias victims may delay equality.

The president's appointment powers also afford him the chance to affect civil rights causes. He possesses the power to appoint cabinet officials, agency directors, and federal judges who are responsible for interpreting and enforcing civil rights laws. In making such appointments, the president can select persons who are either supportive or non-supportive of anti-discrimination measures. A president who selects federal officials who are sympathetic to civil rights interests may facilitate the implementation of civil rights policies. By contrast, a chief executive who appoints federal officials unsympathetic to those measures may inhibit the administration of civil rights policies.

The president's public pronouncements may also influence the nation's views about civil rights. As the leader of the nation and as the political leader who receives the greatest press attention, his words and deeds may influence public opinion on vital issues, including civil rights. For example, a president who calls for racial equality and takes forceful steps to bring this about may promote a political environment conducive for civil rights advancement. By contrast, a chief executive who does not endorse anti-discrimination measures and/or takes steps to hinder the adoption of implementation of these measures may make it difficult to carry out civil rights laws.

This chapter investigates how President Bush has used his vast powers to shape the development and enforcement of civil rights policies. In particular, it considers whether the president has displayed leadership in the civil rights field on such issues as school desegregation, affirmative action, equal employment opportunity, and voting rights. In making this assessment, I will focus on whether the president's rhetoric matches his record. In addition, an effort will be made to determine whether his policy stands are consistent with those espoused by groups representing blacks' policy interests, including the National Association for the Advancement of Colored People, the Congressional Black Caucus, and the Leadership Conference on Civil Rights.

Focusing on Bush's leadership in the civil rights field is appropriate for many reasons, but only one need be cited here: This issue is essentially unexplored territory. There have been studies centering on other presidents' civil rights policies (Jones, 1982), but there appears to be no study that systematically assesses the Bush administration's posture toward civil rights. Part of the explanation for this is that scholars may have decided to postpone studying Bush's record because the jury is still out. While it may seem premature to make any judgment on the president's record, doing so fills a gap in the literature and affords me the opportunity to illuminate whether Bush's performance documents his claim that he cares greatly about civil rights.

A KINDER, GENTLER REAGAN?

In January 1989, George Bush succeeded President Ronald Reagan, whom he had served as vice president for eight years. Bush assumed the presidency when the federal deficit exceeded $200 billion, when taxpayers were asked to pay $100 billion to bail out the savings and loans industry, and when black Americans' trust in the outgoing administration was particularly low. This lack of trust was due to the fact that civil rights groups were continually at odds with the Reagan administration's civil rights policies. Indeed, the National Association for the Advancement of Colored People (NAACP), the Urban League, and the Congressional Black Caucus had sharply criticized the Reagan administration's unsuccessful efforts to: (1) grant tax exemptions to racially segregated schools; (2) encourage municipalities to abrogate the use of race-conscious hiring and promotion schemes; (3) convince the federal courts to stop using busing as a tool to eliminate racially segregated schools; (4) sway the courts to strictly interpret the Voting Rights Act of 1965; and (5) persuade the courts to read civil rights statutes (Title IX) narrowly.

While these efforts proved unsuccessful, the attempt to change policies that civil rights groups considered essential for facilitating racial equality resulted in bad feelings between the civil rights community and the Reagan-Bush administration. Reagan seemed to aggravate matters when, in one of his last interviews with the *New York Times*, he asserted that civil rights leaders were exaggerating the degree of racism in the United States for their personal gain (1989a, A1). In an apparent effort to end the feuding and to promote healing, Bush came to office calling for a "kinder, gentler" nation. The new president seemed to clarify what he meant when he told the United Negro College Fund in March 1989 that he was ready to use his office to heal the nation. Said Bush:

Most Americans, I am convinced, believe that the national government can be an instrument of healing. There are times when government must step in where others fear to tread. I share that belief, and I will act on it. (*Public Papers of the President, 1989*, 202)

Bush's statements were welcomed by the civil rights community because they suggested that the new president was interested in better relations between the White House and civil rights organizations.

This was not the first time that Bush had reached out to the black community or had spelled out his vision of the federal government's role in civil rights. During the first three months of his administration, Bush used several public addresses to signal that he was interested in improving ties with the black community. In an address to a joint session of Congress in February 1989, the president let it be known that he shared civil rights leaders' views that discrimination existed and that he intended to use his leverage to attack the remaining barriers of bigotry. The president stated:

I believe in a society that is free from discrimination and bigotry of any kind. And I will work to knock down the barriers left by past discrimination and to build a more tolerant society that will stop such barriers from ever being built again. (*Public Papers of the President, 1989*, 75)

Overall, black Americans and civil rights leaders were pleased with Bush's positive remarks, yet they cautioned that the new administration would be judged by deeds as well as by words. Still, Bush's supportive statements were warmly greeted in the black community. His approval rating among blacks reached 60 percent, a level Reagan had never achieved. But veteran civil rights observers were cautious. They noted that despite the president's positive rhetoric, Bush had long maintained an ambivalent attitude toward civil rights.

As a student at Yale, Bush chaired a committee to support the United Negro College fund, and as vice president he gave financial support to this fund. In addition, Bush's support for civil rights was seen in 1968 when, as a U.S. congressman from Texas, he voted for the Federal Fair Housing Act despite opposition from his conservative constituency in Houston. But Bush's ambivalence toward civil rights was displayed when, as a candidate for a U.S. Senate seat in Texas, he opposed the omnibus Civil Rights Act of 1964. This celebrated and far-reaching law was drafted to prohibit egregious discrimination against blacks in education, employment, and public accommodations. Further, Bush seemed to display non-support for civil rights in 1988 when, in the midst of the presidential campaign, he observed that he favored Reagan's veto of the 1988 Civil Rights Act designed to overturn the Supreme Court case of *Grove City College v. Bell* (1984). In this case, the Supreme Court limited the reach of Title IX of the Education Amendment of 1972, which bans sex discrimination. Critics of the decision, including women, blacks, the disabled, Republicans and Democrats, all charged that to allow the Supreme Court's decision to stand could make it difficult to advance the cause of equality for all Americans. The critics managed to persuade both houses of Congress to override Reagan's veto. Asked why he backed the president's veto, the vice president asserted that he had been loyal to the president for eight years and now was not the time to become disloyal. Still, Bush indicated that he favored civil rights.

Civil rights leaders greeted his proclamation with skepticism. Their suspicion flowed from the 1988 Bush campaign commercials that focused on Willie Horton, a black criminal who had raped a white woman while on furlough from a Massachusetts state penitentiary. Bush's media consultants found the Horton ad an effective device for attacking Democratic nominee Michael Dukakis, the governor of Massachusetts, although black leaders and Democratic Party representatives accused the Republican campaign of appealing to whites' racist fears of blacks. Bush tried to assuage the concerns of black community leaders by promising in his inaugural address to work toward realizing Martin Luther King's dream of racial equality in America. Although comforted by the president's words, civil rights leaders indicated that words alone were not enough: They expected the White House to act in defense of civil rights.

WORDS AND DEEDS: THE BUSH RECORD IN CIVIL RIGHTS POLICY

School Desegregation

George Bush's wavering support for school desegregation was reflected in two actions by the administration in the area of higher education: one, in a case before the Supreme Court: the second, in a proposal to ban race-based scholarships in colleges and universities.

In the case of *Ayers v. Mabus* (1991), the Supreme Court was asked to determine whether a state had met its legal obligation to desegregate its public colleges by ending race-specific entrance requirements. Civil rights groups and Justice Department officials in the Bush administration concurred that the state of Mississippi had to do more than ban racial discrimination in predominantly white colleges' admission decisions. They maintained that the state also should take steps to attract more minority students to attend predominantly white colleges and universities. However, civil rights leaders and the Justice Department were at odds over whether Mississippi had to provide black colleges with extra funds to make up for past discrimination. Civil rights groups contended that Mississippi should provide black colleges with extra funding because the state historically had engaged in systematic discrimination against blacks and, through this funding, it could make up for this discrimination.

The Department of Justice initially disagreed with this contention. It argued that additional dollars to black colleges could merely perpetuate discrimination. Justice Department officials reasoned that more funds to black colleges would lead simply to the duplication of programs at black and white universities, and this would result in separate and equal institutions. After making this argument before the Supreme Court, intensive lobbying by civil rights groups convinced the president to change this particular position. Bush ordered Solicitor General Kenneth Starr to change course and support the view that Mississippi should be forced to provide extra funding to black colleges and universities to compensate for past discrimination. In October 1991, the Justice Department filed a new brief that reflected this shift.

A second incident raised further questions about the president's position on civil rights. It involved an administration proposal to prohibit colleges and universities from awarding scholarships based on race. On December 12, 1990, Michael E. Williams, assistant secretary for civil rights in the Department of Education, asserted that race-exclusive scholarships discriminated against other students and violated Title VI of the Civil Rights Act of 1964, which prohibits discrimination on the basis of race, color, and national origin. Williams went on to assert that colleges and universities that did not adhere to the new policy stood to lose federal funding.

Williams' proposal stimulated forceful reaction. Critics observed that it would reverse more than 20 years of government policy to support minority enrollment in higher education. Robert H. Atwell, president of the American Council on Education, attacked the plan as "a giant step backward for minority students" (Zuckman, 1990, 4143). Similarly, Benjamin Hooks, executive director of the NAACP, called the administration's proposal a crude and blatant attempt to seriously cripple the well-intended efforts of a number of colleges and universities to provide good educational opportunities.

In the face of such reaction, the White House attempted to distance itself from Williams' comments. Press Secretary Marlin Fitzwater claimed that the president had learned of the proposal only when he read about it in the newspaper. It was clear that the administration had been stung by the affair and the president was not willing to take on civil rights leaders and the higher education community.

Voting Rights

A 1989 report of the Citizens Commission on Civil Rights pointed out that disenfranchising devices such as racial gerrymandering of election districts, discriminatory multimember districts, at-large elections, and majority vote requirements all had the effect of undercutting minority voter strength. As George Bush assumed the presidency, he faced a challenge: Would he take the lead and seek to reduce or eliminate these barriers to minority participation?

The evidence strongly suggests that the president, and particularly his subordinates in the Justice Department, took the initiative to eliminate those factors that prevent minorities from full participation in the political process. For example, the Bush Justice Department went to court on several occasions in Texas, Georgia, and Louisiana to stop these states from using measures that had the effect of diluting minority voting clout. In addition, in 1990, the administration joined forces with minority voters in the case of *Chishom v. Roemer* (1990). In that case, minority voters in Louisiana challenged the system for selecting the seven justices of the state supreme court, which had never had a black member. The Justice Department sided with the plaintiffs, and the Supreme Court ultimately enforced their position that the Voting Rights Act applied to judicial elections.

Civil rights groups were pleased with the Bush administration's help and the Supreme Court ruling, noting that this decision allowed an opportunity to integrate the judiciary. In endorsing this interpretation of the Voting Rights Act, Bush's behavior was consistent with that of most of his predecessors, but in sharp contrast with the view of the Reagan administration. In this area of civil rights, Bush appeared to be kinder and gentler than his former boss.

Affirmative Action

On assuming the presidency, Bush indicated support for affirmative action. In remarks at a meeting with the Commission on Civil Rights, he stated:

We must see that the affirmative action is not reduced to some empty slogan and that this principle of striking down all barriers to advancement has real, living meaning to all Americans. We will leave nothing to chance and no stone unturned as we work to advance America's civil rights agenda. (*Public Papers of the President, 1990,* 675)

While the president seemed to back these comments by appointing blacks to prominent positions in the government—General Colin Powell as chairman of the Joint Chiefs of Staff, Louis Sullivan as Health and Human Services Secretary—Bush also made statements that suggested he was not a steady defender of affirmative action. He indicated as much when addressing the Urban League in 1989, noting that he and the League were not always in agreement on the issue. Similarly, while stating his commitment to equal opportunity, Bush stressed that he was opposed to quotas and unfair hiring practices. In 1990 and 1991, he made it clear that he opposed civil rights measures he believed would lead to racial quotas.

Where has the Bush administration actually stood on the issue of affirmative action? Three incidents help illuminate the record: one in the courts, one a legislative battle, and one an administrative initiative.

First, in the case of *Metro Broadcasting v. F.C.C.* (1990), Solicitor General Kenneth Starr filed a brief in the Supreme Court that was viewed as a clear signal that the administration was not firmly committed to affirmative action. In this case, the Solicitor General maintained that it was constitutionally impermissible for the Federal Communications Commission to use race in awarding broadcasting licenses to promote diversity. While the court rejected Starr's view by a five to four vote, the fact that the administration was on record against federal race-conscious programs was viewed by civil rights groups as proof that civil rights were not a top priority at the White House.

Second, Bush battled with Congress over civil rights bills in 1990 and 1991. Although he ultimately endorsed the view favoring affirmative action, his efforts convinced many civil rights leaders that the president was not a strong supporter of their cause. To understand this perception, it seems appropriate to offer some background material on the 1990 and 1991 civil rights measures.

In 1989, the Supreme Court handed down six cases that were widely viewed as limiting the reach of anti-discrimination statutes. The case of *Wards Cove Packing Co. v. Antonio* (1989) was seen as making it more difficult under Title VII of the Civil Rights Act of 1964 for minorities and women to combat employment discrimination. Title VII bars employment discrimination on the basis of race, color, gender, religion, or national origin. In its first interpretation of Title VII, in *Griggs v. Duke Power Co.* (1971), the Supreme Court unanimously ruled that Title VII prohibits the use of employment practices that operate to exclude blacks if the practices are not related to job performance. Indeed, the court ruled here that when employers adopted job requirements or followed practices that had the effect of discriminating against minorities, the onus was on the employer to justify the necessity of such practices. However, in its 1989 opinion in *Wards Cove,* the

Supreme Court, by a five to four vote, shifted the burden to employees, who must now prove that challenged practices are in fact not necessary.

Civil rights groups and attorneys representing them stressed that the *Wards Cove* ruling placed a heavy burden on minorities and women to prove discrimination. They petitioned Congress to overturn the ruling in this and other cases. Responding to this petition, Congress drafted legislation that would make it clear that the Supreme Court was right in the *Griggs* case but wrong in the *Wards Cove* case.

The president vetoed the first attempt by Congress to overturn *Wards Cove*. He objected that the bill would require quotas in pursuit of affirmative action goals. In 1991, however, political circumstances had changed. First, Bush was under increasing pressure to demonstrate support for civil rights. In August, the Senate hearings on the nomination of Clarence Thomas to the Supreme Court featured a highly publicized fight over the issue of the nominee's alleged sexual harassment of his former subordinate, Anita Hill. Moreover, the November political season featured a gubernatorial election in Louisiana, with former Ku Klux Klan leader David Duke running under the Republican Party banner, despite disclaimers from Bush and the Republican Party organization that Duke was no Republican. Second, the president faced the threat of Congress breaking his record of not having any vetoes overridden. In consequence, he acquiesced and signed the Civil Rights Bill of 1991. The signing, however, created a third incident that raised questions about the president's view of civil rights.

In November, as the occasion of the signing of the new law neared, a draft presidential directive to accompany the bill was made public. The order would require the termination of twenty-five years of government affirmative action and set-aside programs. When the proposed change was leaked to the press and a few Republicans, many Democrats and virtually all civil rights groups objected to it on the grounds that it undermined the nation's commitment to equality. Bush sought to quell criticism by reaffirming support for affirmative action. But his statement did no such thing. While Republicans took the president at his word that he favored affirmative action and that the proposed order was conceived by a handful of aides without his consent, Democrats and civil rights groups were not so generous. They accused the president and his aides of consciously engaging in racial politics. They charged that in floating a proposal to ban race-based or gender-based programs or quotas on the very day that he was to sign a major civil rights bill, the president was deliberately appealing to middle-class white resentments by repeatedly raising the specter of quotas and preferences that provide special treatment for minorities.

Overall, this incident demonstrates once again Bush's ambivalence toward civil rights in general and affirmative action in particular. In this regard, Bush's stand on affirmative action differed from that of many of his predecessors. Presidents Johnson, Carter, and Nixon were stronger champions of affirmative action than George Bush. For example, in 1965, Johnson issued Executive Order 11246, urging federal contractors to develop an affirmative action program. It is this particular order that the Bush administration contemplated revising and possibly revoking.

Nixon developed the "Philadelphia Plan," a scheme that required labor unions and federal contractors to adopt "goals and timetables" for hiring more minorities. Carter supported the affirmative action orders and plans proposed by Presidents Johnson and Nixon. In addition, more blacks, women, and Hispanics were appointed to the federal courts during the Carter administration than in all previous administrations. Finally, Carter's Department of Justice consistently supported affirmative action in court.

Bush has certainly been more supportive of affirmative action than Ronald Reagan. Unlike Reagan, Bush has stated that he favors affirmative action. Moreover, in contrast to the Reagan Justice Department, the Bush administration has not actively and openly encouraged municipalities to abandon their affirmative action programs.

Bush's ambivalence toward affirmative action may stem from the fact that polls show that most Americans, particularly middle-class and blue-collar voters, oppose these programs because they are perceived as benefiting only blacks. The president appears to be trying to assuage both minority voters and his core constituency.

PEOPLE MAKE POLICY: THE RECORD OF BUSH APPOINTMENTS

The president's appointment power also affords him the opportunity to affect the enforcement and implementation of civil rights policy. In this regard, Bush's appointments to key administrative and judicial posts have also been quite mixed. On several occasions, his appointees have been actively supportive of civil rights, but not all have been so.

Bush's selection of Arthur Fletcher as chairman of the Civil Rights Commission was viewed as a sign of support for civil rights. Fletcher, a former Assistant Labor Secretary in the Nixon administration, was someone whom the president asserted would fight bigotry with every weapon at his disposal. Civil rights leaders agreed, noting that, unlike Reagan appointees to similar positions, Fletcher was a longtime civil rights veteran who favored activist remedies—affirmative action, school desegregation—to end racial discrimination.

Similarly, Bush's selection of Louis Sullivan, a distinguished black physician and president of Morehouse Medical School, as Secretary of the Department of Health and Human Services was looked on as a sign of his support for civil rights. Responding to the nomination, civil rights groups praised Bush and, particularly, Sullivan, noting that the nominee's record as president of the medical college and his membership in various civil rights organizations revealed that he was committed to educational advancement and social justice for all Americans.

In stark contrast, Bush's efforts to appoint William Lucas, a black attorney, former sheriff, and unsuccessful Republican candidate for the governor of Michigan, as Assistant Attorney General for Civil Rights was perceived as a sign of soft support for civil rights. In nominating Lucas, Bush indicated that he nominated him because he was qualified to do the job and was solidly committed to civil rights enforcement. Civil Rights groups and their supporters disagreed with the president. They charged that Lucas was not qualified to head the Civil Rights Division of the Justice Department. They maintained that the post to which Lucas was being nominated was one responsible for shaping the civil rights litigation program and advising the president and other governmental agencies on civil rights matters. These duties, they maintained, required a nominee who possessed a solid background in federal litigation, civil rights, and constitutional law. Lucas possessed little or no experience in these areas. The Senate Judiciary Committee seemed to agree with the critics when they refused to recommend him for confirmation to the full Senate. Civil rights groups charged that Bush's selection of a decent but unqualified minority male to serve as Assistant Attorney General for Civil Rights suggested that the president was not strongly committed to the development and forceful execution of civil rights policies.

Similarly, Bush's selection of David Souter, the former Attorney General and state supreme court judge from New Hampshire, was viewed as a sign of presidential unconcern for civil rights. While little was known about Souter overall, what was known about his views on civil rights was not comforting. As Attorney General, Souter had filed opinions non-supportive of civil rights. While on the state high court, he wrote an opinion indicating that the state did not have to honor the federal government's request that New Hampshire submit data outlining the racial composition of the state's workforce. In another case, he defended the use of electoral schemes that deny minorities the right to vote.

Bush's nomination of Clarence Thomas, a conservative black federal appellate court judge, to serve as the second black on the U.S. Supreme Court was viewed as a very mixed signal in the area of civil rights. Some groups, including the National Urban League, took no position on the Thomas nomination but hinted that the president's decision to elevate Thomas from the Court of Appeals was positive. Black conservatives observed that in selecting Thomas, Bush was ensuring black representation on the highest court. They pointed out that the retirement of Thurgood Marshall, a black liberal, left open the possibility that there would be no minority member of the Supreme Court. By appointing Thomas, the president opened the way for the new justice to champion black policy preferences because he had grown up in the segregated South.

Nevertheless, there were others, including the NAACP, the largest civil rights organization, who charged that Bush's selection of Thomas was a sign of only weak support for civil rights. They noted that Thomas, as chairman of the Equal Employment Opportunity Commission, had opposed measures—busing for school desegregation and affirmative action—that had proven effective in combating discrimination. Given this record, the NAACP stated that it opposed Thomas's nomination because he was not supportive of minority policy goals.

Compared with the appointments of his predecessors in office, President Bush's record falls somewhere in the middle. Some presidents, such as Lyndon Johnson, demonstrated strong support for civil rights. Johnson named Thurgood Marshall, a distinguished NAACP lawyer, to be the first black Supreme Court justice; he made Robert Weaver the first black Cabinet member as Secretary of Housing and Urban Development. Similarly, Carter's appointments to key posts were viewed favorably by civil rights groups. Carter put more women, blacks, and Hispanics on the judiciary than any other president. He appointed Patricia Harris as Secretary of Health, Education, and Welfare; he named Drew Days, an experienced civil rights attorney, Assistant Attorney General for Civil Rights; he selected Wade McCree as the Solicitor General of the United States; and he chose Eleanor Holmes Norton, a distinguished black attorney, to chair the Equal Employment Opportunity Commission.

Ford's appointment of William Coleman, a distinguished civil rights attorney, as the first black Secretary of Transportation was viewed as a signal of support for civil rights. His selection of moderate John Paul Stevens to replace liberal Associate Justice William O. Douglas on the U.S. Supreme Court was perceived as a sign of support for civil rights, particularly given Stevens' moderate civil rights record as an appellate court judge.

In contrast to Johnson, Carter, and Ford, Nixon's and Reagan's appointments—or attempted appointments—to key civil rights posts were not viewed as signaling support for civil rights. For example, Nixon's unsuccessful efforts to place conservative jurists Clement Haynesworth and G. Harrold Carswell on the U.S. Supreme Court were not favored by civil rights interests. Haynesworth was rejected by the Senate because of the appearance of ethical improprieties and because, as a federal appellate judge, he approved measures that would have facilitated resegregation of schools and hospitals. Similarly, Carswell was rejected by the Senate because of his civil rights record. In particular, Carswell gave a speech in 1948 in which he declared his firm belief in white supremacy (*Congressional Quarterly Almanac*, 1970, 155) and he and his wife sold a lot with the proviso that it could be occupied only by white people. Not surprisingly, civil rights groups charged that Carswell's nomination signaled Nixon's hostile view toward civil rights.

Although unsuccessful in securing Haynesworth and Carswell's confirmation, Nixon was successful in elevating conservative Justice Department lawyer William Rehnquist to the U.S. Supreme Court. A brilliant lawyer from Arizona, Rehnquist was opposed by civil rights groups because in 1964 he had written a document opposing the public accommodation section to the omnibus Civil Rights Act of 1964 (*Congressional Quarterly Almanac*, 1971, 853) and stated: "We [Americans] are no more dedicated to an integrated society than we are to a segregated society. We are dedicated, to a free society in which each man is accorded the maximum amount of freedom of choice in his individual activities."

These documents and statements by Rehnquist prompted Roy Wilkins, then the executive director of the NAACP, to state that "Rehnquist's philosophy was dangerous for black citizens" (*Congressional Quarterly Almanac*, 1971, 852). Despite Wilkins' objections, the Senate confirmed Rehnquist.

Like Nixon, Reagan was regarded as non-supportive of civil rights. Reagan's decisions to elevate conservative Rehnquist to Chief Justice and appoint Antonin Scalia as an Associate Justice of the Supreme Court were not perceived as in civil rights interests. Both Rehnquist and Scalia opposed affirmative action and busing for school desegregation, two remedies heartily endorsed by civil rights groups.

Reagan's decisions to nominate black conservative Clarence Pendleton to chair the Civil Rights Committee and Clarence Thomas to lead the Equal Employment Opportunity Commission were also viewed as evidence of non-support for civil rights. Both Pendleton and Thomas vigorously opposed measures backed by civil rights groups such as busing and affirmative action. That these men rejected such measures was viewed by civil rights groups as proof that they did not care about civil rights.

Finally, Reagan's unsuccessful efforts to elevate Brad Reynolds, Assistant Attorney General for Civil Rights and a noted conservative, to the post of Associate Attorney General was also perceived as a sign of non-support for civil rights. As Assistant Attorney General, Reynolds urged local communities to oppose busing for school desegregation. He even argued (unsuccessfully) before the Supreme Court that it would be constitutionally permissible for the federal government to grant tax-exempt status to racially segregated schools. Reynolds had also sought to make it more difficult for minorities to prove discrimination under the provisions of the Voting Rights Act of 1965 by proposing that they prove discriminatory intent and effect, another proposal rejected by the Supreme Court. Not surprisingly, Reagan's nomination of Reynolds to the number two position in the Justice Department was opposed by civil rights groups. The Senate rejected Reynolds partly on the basis of his views on affirmative action and partly because Senate members were "troubled by conflict between Reynolds' testimony and information provided by other witnesses and documents from his own department" (*Congressional Quarterly Almanac*, 1985, 221).

CONCLUSION

Has President Bush been a kinder and gentler president than Reagan in the area of civil rights? The evidence reveals that in some instances Bush has followed in Reagan's footsteps, but in others, he has gone his own way. For example, where Reagan suggested that civil rights leaders were exaggerating the scope and depth of racism in the United States for their personal gain, Bush has often adopted the language and repeated the goals of the civil rights movement. He has emphasized that racial, ethnic, gender, and religious bigotry exist and the American people ought to take steps to eliminate it, not tomorrow but right now.

Unlike Reagan's Justice Department, which actively encouraged communities to do away with busing and affirmative action programs, the Bush administration has not taken the initiative in prodding communities to drop either. However, the Bush administration has backed communities or groups who want to end busing or affirmative action plans, although it has not led the way in encouraging communities to take these steps.

Like Reagan, who vetoed the Civil Rights Bill of 1984, aimed at overturning a Supreme Court decision that narrowly construed a civil rights law, Bush in 1990 vetoed a civil rights bill that was designed to overturn several Supreme Court decisions. But Bush also ultimately signed a bill that he had once denounced as a "quota bill," after congressional leaders agreed to make some cosmetic changes in the legislation. His White House drafted an executive order that would have nullified much existing federal affirmative policy, but in the face of criticism, the president killed the proposal.

While Bush's nominees have not always been the choices of civil rights leaders, nevertheless the president has made key appointments that won praise (or at least acquiescence) from the civil rights community. In at least one important case, it is not yet clear what the selection of Clarence Thomas for the Supreme Court will mean for civil rights.

How are we to account for this record of ambivalence? A large part of the answer lies in the political environment of civil rights in the United States and the president's response to it. Blacks and whites have displayed widely different views on the issue: When asked whether they believed that black and white Americans receive essentially the same treatment in this country, 63 percent of whites said yes, but only 37 percent of blacks agreed (*Gallup Opinion Index*, 1990). This discrepancy is reflected in divergent policy positions as well. White middle-class voters, the president's core constituency, tend to regard affirmative action programs as giving unnecessary preference to one group in society. Black voters, only 20 percent of whom supported Bush in 1988, tend to regard affirmative action plans as essential to redressing wrongs they perceive are still being committed.

Bush has attempted to walk a tightrope between these views. He has seen his office as one dedicated to serving all the people, hence his vocal support of civil rights and various actions in that direction. But his personal political interests require him to attend to his base vote. Therefore, he has taken several steps to distance himself from the agenda of civil rights leaders. This effort to be all things to all constituencies has left an uncertain record.

The jury is still out on whether George Bush has exercised leadership in the area of civil rights, because his presidency is not yet finished. But we can say tentatively that, on balance, he has been kinder and gentler than Ronald Reagan. That does not mean, however, that he has used the White House to consistently advance the cause of civil rights in the United States.

REFERENCES

Amaker, Norman. 1988. *Civil Rights and the Reagan Administration*. Washington: Urban Institute.
Ayers v. Mabus. 1991. 90–6558.
Biskupic, Joan. 1991a. "Deal on Civil Rights Measure Stymied by Quota Issue." *Congressional Quarterly Almanac 1990*. Washington: Congressional Quarterly, p. 2225.
———. 1991b. "House Joins in the Standoff Over Civil Rights Measure." *Congressional Quarterly Almanac 1990*. Washington: Congressional Quarterly, p. 2517.
"Bush Caught in Contradiction over Job-Bias Remedy." 1990. *Congressional Quarterly Weekly Report* (April 21): 1196.
Chishom v. Roemer. 1990. 90–787.
Congressional Quarterly Almanac. 1970, 1971, 1985, 1989, 1990. Washington: Congressional Quarterly.
Gallup Opinion Index. 1990. New York: Gallup Organization.
Griggs v. Duke Power Co. 1971. 401 U.S. 424.
Grove City College v. Bell. 1984. 465 U.S. 555.
Jones, Augustus J. 1982. *Law, Bureaucracy, and Politics: The Implementation of the Civil Rights Act of 1964*. Lanham, Md.: University Press of America.
Martin v. Wilks. 1989. 109 S. Ct. 2180.
Metro Broadcasting, Inc. v. F.C.C. 1990. 110 S. Ct. 2997.
New York Times. 1990. (March 23): A20.
———. 1989a. (January 12): A1.
———. 1989b. (January 14): A8.
———. 1989c. (June 28): A1.
Patterson v. McClean Credit Union. 1989. 109 S. Ct. 2363.
"President Vetoes Civil Rights Bill." 1990. *Nation's Cities Weekly* (October 29): 5.
Public Papers of the Presidents: George Bush, 1990, vol. 1. Washington: Government Printing Office.
Public Papers of the Presidents: George Bush, 1989, vol. 1. Washington: Government Printing Office.
———, vol. 2. Washington: Government Printing Office.
Wards Cove Packing Co. v. Antonio. 1989. 109 S. Ct. 2115.
Zuckman, Jill. 1990. "Minority Scholarship Fracas Raises a Sensitive Issue." *Congressional Quarterly Weekly Report* (December 15): 4143.

PART 5

INTO THE TWENTY-FIRST CENTURY

Chapter 12

Presidential Power and Accountability after Reagan

NORMAN C. THOMAS

Following the Nixon presidency and Watergate, scholars devoted extensive attention to the abuse of presidential power and the problem of making the office accountable (Hardin, 1974; Sorensen, 1975; Thomas, 1978; Sundquist, 1981). Congress took several steps to strengthen the accountability of the president within the institutional framework established by the Constitution. Among the more important of these were: the War Powers Resolution of 1973; the Budget and Impoundment Control Act of 1974; the Hughes-Ryan Act of 1974, which was amended by the Intelligence Oversight Act of 1980; and increased use of the legislative veto.

The conduct of the Reagan and Bush presidencies, with their consistent emphasis on strong foreign policy leadership and the reassertion of presidential prerogatives, the U.S. military operations in Panama in 1989, the Persian Gulf war of 1990–91, and persistent questions about the Iran-Contra affair all suggest the need to assess the status of presidential accountability. Some old issues of presidential accountability have re-emerged, and new ones have arisen.[1] Several of these issues, most notably, congressional insistence on sharing the power to commit military forces to combat, have remained unresolved to this point in the Bush administration. In addition the Supreme Court has affected some separation-of-powers aspects of accountability in its decisions in *Immigration and Naturalization Service v. Chada* (462 U.S. 919 [1983]), *Bowsher v. Synar* (478 U.S. 714 [1986]), and *Morrison v. Olson* (487 U.S. 654 [1988]).

This chapter examines these and other developments during the Reagan and Bush years from the perspective of presidential accountability. Its fundamental assumption is that although the U.S. constitutional system requires effective use of presidential power, as Neustadt (1990) argues, experience has demonstrated repeatedly the need to guard against the abuse of that power, as Corwin (1957) and Pious (1979) caution. In analyzing recent developments in presidential accountability, the chapter addresses four questions: To what extent have measures taken in the post-Watergate era to strengthen accountability proved effective? What accounts for the failures among those measures? What new accountability problems have arisen since then? What does the future portend for accountability?

THE CONCEPT OF ACCOUNTABILITY

Accountability is of fundamental importance in democratic theory. It means that public officials are answerable for the discharge of their duties or their conduct. The *Dictionary of American Government and Politics* defines accountability as "the extent to which one must answer to higher authority— legal or organizational—for one's actions in society at large or within one's particular organizational position" (Shafritz, 1988, 4). Accountability poses three questions: To whom are officials accountable? What are the permissible limits of their conduct? Through what means are they called to account?[2] Democracies hold government officials accountable through periodic elections and through structural arrangements within government.

The U.S. Constitution does not rely exclusively on political accountability. As Madison remarked in *Federalist No. 51*, while elections provide the "primary check on government," power will be divided among the three branches, "ambition will be made to counteract ambition," and certain "auxiliary precautions" will keep officials within constitutional limits. The Constitution seeks institutional accountability through a government of "separated institutions sharing powers" (Neustadt, 1990, 29).

However, political and institutional means of achieving presidential accountability often work at cross purposes (Rockman, 1986, 152; Seligman and Covington, 1989, 150–51). If presidents are to be held responsible to the electorate, which judges them on the basis of performance, they need ample powers and resources to meet the voters' expectations. But if the public and Congress distrust "fully autonomous presidential behavior," restraints on the exercise of presidential power are necessary (Seligman and Covington, 1989, 151). Primary reliance on political accountability suggests a high level of presidential discretion, while resort to institutional accountability implies extensive restrictions and constraints on the president's freedom of action. The tension between the two means of achieving accountability is unavoidable. Both cannot be maximized simultaneously, and trade-offs must be made (Seligman and Covington, 1989, 151). Developments during the past decade have highlighted and intensified this dilemma.

INSTITUTIONAL ACCOUNTABILITY

The post-Watergate/post-Vietnam efforts to make presidents more accountable were primarily structural. They involved curbs on the exercise of presidential power and mandatory sharing of certain powers with Congress. Controversy over certain enhanced institutional accountability measures, most notably the War Powers Resolution, continued through the Reagan and into the Bush presidencies. In addition, the attempt of Congress in the 1974 Budget Act to assert parity with the presidency with respect to fiscal policy has succeeded only in restricting impoundments. Neither Congress nor the president has been able to bring the federal budget under control, as manifested in the failure of the Gramm-Rudman-Hollings Act of 1985. But the most pressing recent issues regarding presidential accountability have emerged from the Iran-Contra affair.

The War Powers Resolution

The War Powers Resolution (WPR), passed over Richard Nixon's veto on November 7, 1973, sought to ensure that Congress would be involved in any decision to commit U.S. armed forces to potential hostilities.[3] The resolution provides that the president may deploy armed forces into situations of potential or actual combat only pursuant to a declaration of war, statutory authorization, or a national emergency created by an attack on the nation or the armed forces. The WPR urges that the president consult with Congress "in every possible instance" prior to committing U.S. forces abroad, and it requires regular consultation after commitment. It also requires a written report to Congress within forty-eight hours of a commitment and termination of the commitment within sixty days unless Congress declares war or authorizes continuation. The president may extend the commitment for thirty additional days by certifying to Congress that unavoidable military conditions require continued use of the troops for their safety.

Originally, the WPR provided that Congress could at any time order the disengagement of U.S. forces by passage of a concurrent resolution. Such resolutions are not subject to presidential veto. However, the Supreme Court's 1983 decision in *INS v. Chada*, invalidating the legislative veto, rendered this provision inoperative. Later that year, Congress substituted a joint resolution for the concurrent resolution. The effectiveness of the amended procedure is highly questionable, as a joint resolution is subject to presidential veto which, of course, can only be overriden by a two-thirds vote in each house.

Presidents have submitted twenty-four reports under the WPR since its passage (Collier, 1991, 10–12). In only one of these, the rescue of the *Mayaguez* in 1975, did the president trigger the 60-day clock. Gerald Ford submitted four reports, Jimmy Carter one, Ronald Reagan fourteen, and George Bush five. Beginning with Nixon, all presidents have maintained that the WPR is unconstitutional, imprudent, and unnecessary. In their reports, they have been careful to avoid any acknowledgement of the resolution's constitutionality (Katzmann, 1990, 53). By not activating the trigger mechanism, by stating that they were reporting in a manner "consistent with the War Powers Resolution," and by defining consultation as merely the act of informing, they have kept Congress off-balance and circumvented the intent of the WPR. While the position of the executive with respect to the WPR has been consistent over time, Congress has been unable to articulate a "unitary position or statement of institutional interest" (Katzmann, 1990, 55). Neither has it been willing to challenge the president by triggering the 60-day clock.[4]

The actions of Bush in the Panamanian invasion in December 1989 are typical of presidential conduct with respect to the WPR (Cohen, 1989, 3120). A few hours prior to the invasion, he informed key congressional leaders of the imminent action. Three days later, he reported by letter to House Speaker Thomas Foley and Senate President Pro Tempore Robert Byrd that U.S. forces had been sent into action. In his letter, which carefully avoided activating the trigger mechanism, he stated the reasons for the actions, which he claimed were "consistent with the War Powers Resolution."

In the case of the Persian Gulf war of 1990–91, Bush operated in a similar manner (Prober, 1990, 192–93). On August 8, 1990, prior to initiating the deployment of forces to the Persian Gulf in response to Iraq's August 2 invasion of Kuwait, he notified key congressional leaders of the planned deployment. A day later, he reported the deployment by letter to the Speaker and the President Pro Tempore. In addition to stating that the report was "consistent with the War Powers Resolution," he stated that involvement in hostilities was "not imminent," thus avoiding triggering the time clock.

In spite of the massive and rapid military build-up during the next several months, the exchange of verbal threats between the United States and Iraq, and the adoption of a resolution by the United Nations imposing a deadline for Iraq to withdraw from Kuwait, neither Bush nor Congress started the clock. In fact, the president consistently maintained that he had the authority to force Iraq out of Kuwait without congressional approval. However, on January 8, 1991, one week prior to the UN-imposed deadline, Bush formally asked Congress to approve a joint resolution authorizing the use of force. On January 12, Congress did so, by votes of 52 to 47 in the Senate and 250 to 183 in the House (Doherty, 1991, 65). In signing the resolution, Bush reasserted his positions with respect to the unconstitutionality of the WPR and the president's constitutional authority to use the armed forces to defend the interests of the United States (Prober, 1990, 194). The resolution authorizing the use of force in the Persian Gulf was widely recognized as the functional equivalent of a declaration of war (Biskupic, 1991, 70). Whether or not the president's January 8 request constituted a weakening of his position is an open question.

Most commentary on the War Powers Resolution has tended to be negative.[5] There is a "growing consensus" that it "has not worked as Congress envisioned" (Katzmann, 1990, 35). Presidents have not tried to make the law workable by invoking its provisions; neither have they consulted Congress in "any meaningful manner" (Hillebrecht, 1990, 511). Indeed, they have deliberately sought to circumvent it so as to avoid any restrictions on their substantial freedom of action. Moreover, Congress has been unwilling to assert its institutional prerogatives by challenging presidential non-responsiveness to the resolution, and the courts have been unwilling to intercede until it does so.[6] Glennon aptly summarized the effectiveness of the WPR: "Whatever congressional intent underlay the War Powers Resolution, any expectation that its procedures would actually lead to collective Legislative-Executive judgment in the war-making process was mistaken" (1990, 102–3). Presidential evasion, congressional acquiescence, and judicial deference and tolerance have combined to accomplish this (Koh, 1988, 1291–1316).

Some commentators argue that poor drafting has contributed to the failure of the WPR to meet the expectations of its framers (Koh, 1988, p. 1299; Franck, 1989, 768). Glennon maintains that the resolution should be made more precise by: (1) defining the nature of "hostilities"; (2) specifying precisely whom the president is to consult, when, and under what circumstances; and (3) clarifying the reporting requirement (1990, 113–15). But Glennon, Koh, and Ely recognize that the WPR will not work as intended unless Congress asserts itself—an unlikely development. Glennon, Koh, and Franck also argue that judicial reluctance to intervene is misplaced and erroneous.

Can anything be said in defense of the WPR? Congress certainly is aware of its deficiencies, as is evidenced by extensive hearings on it and frequent proposals for its amendment. If the resolution is fatally flawed and revision is not possible, why has it not been repealed? The answer may be that Congress has found the WPR to be quite useful for its purposes. The WPR "allows Congress the luxury of being politically comfortable with its decisions regarding a military action while providing a convenient forum for criticizing the President" (Prober, 1990, 222). Depending on public opinion, Congress can either use the resolution to end a military operation when the public opposes it strongly or criticize the president for not observing the requirements of the WPR when popular attitudes are supportive or mixed. In either case, Congress cannot lose (Prober, 223–26, 229).

According to this perspective, the WPR does impose a brake on presidential war-making in that presidents have been forced to take it into consideration and to recognize the possibility, however distant, of possible congressional action. The WPR is a constant reminder to the president that he does not make national security policy alone and that Congress claims constitutional authority to share in the crucial decision to lead the nation into war. The WPR has enhanced the institutional accountability of the president, "albeit symbolically rather than operationally" (Thomas, 1978, 421).

The Iran-Contra Affair

The Iran-Contra affair raised important issues with respect to presidential accountability: (1) the ability of Congress to direct foreign policy through denial of appropriations and its ability to oversee covert operations; (2) the capacity of Congress to ensure that the president receives broad-ranging advice; (3) the adequacy of a national security policy process that allows the conduct of sensitive covert operations by National Security Council (NSC) staff; and (4) the appropriate responses for a Congress confronted by a president who pursues policies that are foolish and of questionable legality. These questions remain largely unanswered.

For a while, the Iran-Contra affair appeared to threaten the survival of the Reagan presidency (Cannon, 1991, 703–5). It continues to present problems to Bush as ongoing legal proceedings against some of its participants have resulted in new revelations of Bush's knowledge of the affair.[7] The details of the affair are complex and widely available (Draper, 1991; Mayer and McManus, 1988; Cohen and Mitchell, 1988). This analysis will be limited to the major aspects of the affair that raise issues of presidential accountability.

First, and most important, is the assumption of an operational role by the National Security Adviser and the NSC staff. This problem extends back to the Nixon administration, when Henry Kissinger conducted secret negotiations, bypassing the State Department, with the government of the People's Republic of China, leading to the president's historic 1972 visit. In the Iran-Contra affair, the operational role was more extensive and sustained. It involved, *inter alia*, covert operations (which the presidential staff was not equipped to perform, as events revealed) that had been prohibited by Congress in the Boland Amendment of 1984. The participants were two National Security Advisers, retired Marine Lt. Col. Robert McFarlane and his successor, Vice Admiral John Poindexter, Marine Lt. Col. Oliver North, assistant deputy director for political-military affairs on the NSC staff, and members of his unit. Both McFarlane and Poindexter were well aware of Reagan's intense desire to maintain the Nicaraguan Contra insurgency and to secure the release of the Mideast hostages. On their own initiative, they used North and his staff to give effect to those presidential desires. The result was what Draper has described as government by a "junta-like cabal" operating within the White House (1991, 579), which acted in the president's name, although it is unclear whether he approved or knew of their efforts.

North's highly questionable operations were the fulcrum on which the affair pivoted. He actively coordinated the raising of money from third parties (both private individuals and foreign governments) to provide support for the Contras. Money raised by government officials or received by the government becomes public funds and cannot be spent unless appropriated for purposes approved by law (Stith, 1988). To raise funds and channel them to the Contras, North availed of the services of private individuals, such as fund-raiser Carl (Spitz) Channell, retired U.S. Air Force Major General Richard Secord and his partner Albert Hakim (a naturalized Iranian-American), and Manauacher Ghorbanifar, a shadowy Iranian businessman. These men were accountable to no one but North, who had little leverage to apply to them.

Also of great consequence for accountability was the secret presidential pursuit of a policy (the release of hostages held in Lebanon) through means (arms sales to Iran) that directly contravened explicit policies of the U.S. government (no negotiations with terrorists and no arms to Iran). Although Reagan made a finding on January 17, 1986, that relieved him of the obligation to inform Congress, the State Department continued to pressure other governments not to engage in arms sales to Iran and the government publicly voiced its unwillingness to negotiate with the persons who had seized a TWA airliner in Beirut in July of that year. Not only was Congress uninformed about the hostage negotiations; so were certain key operating units of the government.

A related development was Reagan's exclusion of Secretary of State George Shultz and Secretary of Defense Caspar Weinberger from any information or decisions involving arms sales to Iran after they voiced strong objections to the initiative in early 1986. Neither was informed that the policy was moving ahead. A major high-risk, national security operation proceeded without their knowledge or participation.

The key event in the affair was the diversion of some of the substantial profits (North and Secord overcharged Iran for the weapons it received) from the Iranian arms sales to support the Contras. This joined the two operations, which North previously had been running independently of each other. Poindexter approved of the diversion but decided not to inform the president, so as to provide him with "plausible deniability" to shield him from domestic criticism (Draper, 1991, 560). However, the purpose of deniability in covert operations is to mask them from other governments. The consequences when it is applied within the U.S. government are profound: It makes those conducting the operation accountable to no one. As Draper so eloquently puts it:

Since accountability is a basic principle of the American political system, deniability cannot be applied to the highest elected American officials in the executive branch and Congress without nullifying accountability. This perversion of deniability, therefore, strikes at the very foundation of the American constitutional order. (1991, 561–62)

The mechanisms employed to inquire into the Iran-Contra affair, to affix responsibility, and bring any law-breakers to justice—the Tower Commission appointed by Reagan, the joint congressional investigation conducted by the Committees on Intelligence, and the appointment of a special counsel—produced mixed results. The Tower Commission concentrated heavily on the national security policy process and found it to be flawed, primarily because of excessive informality. It placed primary blame on Reagan's detached management style. The report paid little attention to the substance of the actions taken on behalf of the president and made several recommendations designed to enhance the integrity of the process and define more clearly the responsibilities of the National Security Assistant (Tower, Muskie, and Scowcroft, 1987, 94–99). But it did not suggest fundamental changes to the process.

The congressional investigation focused narrowly on possible instances of criminal misconduct. The counsel that it hired to assist it were criminal lawyers. The central questions were: What happened? How much did the participants (especially the president) know, and when did they know it?

While the committee uncovered a substantial amount of information, it did not find evidence of impeachable conduct by the president. Its major recommendation was that the Intelligence Oversight Act of 1980 be amended so as to remove the president's discretion over the timing of reports to Congress of covert operations (Malbin, 1989, 385). Only the Senate passed the recommendation.

On November 26, 1986, Attorney General Edwin Meese took steps to initiate the appointment, by the Special Division (a three-judge panel) of the Court of Appeals of the District of Columbia, of a special counsel to investigate the Iran-Contra affair. Meese initially opposed the appointment, but pressure from Congress and the media became irresistible. On December 19, the panel named Lawrence Walsh, a lawyer and former diplomat who had served in the Eisenhower and Nixon administrations. Eventually, Walsh brought indictments against McFarlane, Poindexter, North, Secord, Hakim, Channell, fund-raiser Richard Miller, and CIA officer Joseph Fernandez. All were either convicted or pleaded guilty to various offenses.[8] Federal appeals courts have reversed the felony convictions of both North and Poindexter, and no further prosecution is likely. Walsh has complained that congressional immunity granted to North and Poindexter impeded his ability to prosecute them.

The Independent Counsel Act, passed in 1978 as part of the Ethics in Government Act, creates a separate criminal justice system for persons holding high office. (In the Iran-Contra affair it also applied to private persons carrying out important activities for the government.) The Supreme Court upheld the constitutionality of the statute, which had been challenged on the grounds of the separation of powers, in *Morrison v. Olson*. The manifest intent of the independent counsel device is to ensure that powerful individuals do not escape punishment for crimes because of their closeness to the incumbent administration. In the Iran-Contra case, two of the key officials were prosecuted, but none was punished. Moreover, there is no evidence that anyone involved in the affair was deterred by fear of prosecution. Bickering and negotiating between Walsh and the congressional investigating committee may have impeded the operations of each. The independent counsel appears to be necessary to the establishment of accountability, but its effects are entirely a posteriori.

What, then, are the implications of the Iran-Contra affair for presidential accountability? The answer first requires an understanding of its causes. In summary form, these include: Reagan's management style and state of mind; the actions of key national security policy officials; and the failure of congressional safeguards in the national security policy system to operate in a timely fashion.

There is little disagreement among students of Iran-Contra that primary responsibility for the affair rests with Reagan. Whether his conduct was that of a knave or a fool is, however, a matter of some dispute. The Tower Commission report faulted his detached style of management, which delegated extensive authority to his national security advisers and placed extremely heavy responsibility on them (Tower, Muskie, and Scowcroft, 1987, 79–80). Most certainly, Reagan failed to monitor the exercise of discretion by his advisers. His lack of curiosity and interest compounded the problem.

In addition to his detached delegator style, Reagan acted with a reduced sense of political accountability following his overwhelming reelection victory (Cannon, 1991, 593). Operating with diminished political instincts, he stubbornly pursued his Contra policy and the release of the hostages in spite of strong advice to the contrary from Secretary of State Shultz and Secretary of Defense Weinberger (Cannon, 1991, 631).

However, Reagan's key national security advisers, including Shultz and Weinberger, did little to save the president from himself. The chief of staff, Donald Regan, lacked the political experience and sensitivity of his predecessor, James Baker III, and aides such as Michael Deaver and Edwin Meese, who were aware of the danger of allowing Reagan to indulge his predilections (p. 593–94).[9] National Security Advisers McFarlane and Poindexter failed to provide objective advice based on experience, because each felt unsure of his relationship to the president (pp. 596–98, 623–26). Poindexter's isolated, almost hermetic administrative style allowed North to fully control the Iranian side of the affair. Although Reagan gained responsiveness and secrecy by relying on the NSC staff, he sacrificed the expertise, technical judgment, and institutional support that the State and Defense departmental bureaucracies could provide (Koh, 1988, 1296).

Congressional attitudes and actions (or inaction) also helped to set the stage for Iran-Contra. The on-off-on again position of Congress on Contra funding created an atmosphere of uncertainty and frustration. Procedural gamesmanship, as in the Boland Amendment, eroded "comity" between Congress and the president (Malbin, 1989, 388–90). Once it enacted the Boland Amendment, Congress exercised little oversight of its implementation (Draper, 1991, 596). Moreover, in the past, Congress had tolerated both presidential evasion of reporting requirements for covert actions and the assumption of operational roles by presidential staff. Finally, a substantial congressional majority had little stomach for challenging a popular president's domination of national security policy and even less desire to find evidence of criminal misconduct that would justify impeachment proceedings. There were strong reasons for the NSC staff to assume that it enjoyed a wide latitude for its actions.

The implications of Iran-Contra for presidential accountability depend on one's evaluation of the effectiveness of the national security policy system and the safeguards in it. Draper concludes that "with few exceptions, the safeguards in the system failed to operate" (1991, 596). But he recommends only that the three branches of government assume their constitutional responsibilities. Koh shares the view that the system failed and makes extensive recommendations for legislation to curb free-wheeling executive initiatives and to involve the courts (1988, 1323–38). He recognizes that prospects for enactment of such sweeping legislation are problematic, but he argues that the attempt "will at least focus national attention on the right questions" (p. 1338). It should be noted that to date, Congress has not passed any significant legislation in response to the Iran-Contra affair. Crabb and Mulcahy also believe that Iran-Contra reveals major failings in the search for accountability, but they place responsibility for correction on future presidents who, presumably, will have learned its lessons (1991, 185–87).

In contrast, others find little wrong with the national security process. The principal recommendation of the Tower Commission was that "no substantive change be made in . . . the structure and operation of the NSC system" (Tower, Muskie, and Scowcroft, 1987, 94). Malbin finds no fault with the process but maintains that it can be made to work better if both the president and Congress more aggressively defend their institutional interests (1989, 389–91). Treverton believes that "the process is about the best we can do" (1990, 108). He argues that presidents bent on doing something stupid "will find someone, somewhere to do it" (p. 92). The lesson that he draws from Iran-Contra is that there are limits to the extent that procedural safeguards can guarantee against unwise presidential actions.

The Budget Deficit

One of the major post-Watergate actions that Congress took to increase presidential accountability was the Budget and Impoundment Control Act, generally known as the 1974 Budget Act. Prompted by congressional confrontations with President Nixon over massive impoundments, the legislation sought to establish balanced congressional-presidential control over budgeting, which the legislators believed had shifted strongly in favor of the executive. It attempted to accomplish this by requiring Congress to adopt annual budget resolutions that would set aggregate spending limits and provide meaningful debate on spending priorities (Fisher, 1985, 239). To assist Congress in its new budgetary procedures, the statute created budget committees in each house and established a Congressional Budget Office to provide it with an independent source of professional economic analysis and advice. The Budget Act also placed controls on impoundments by making them subject to a one-house legislative veto.

The 1974 Budget Act erred in its assumption that Congress and the president would behave after its passage as they had before (Fisher, 1985, 240–41). Although the process that the statute established was neutral, its permissiveness enabled both Congress and the president to pursue their own political and policy objectives through it. Congress saw in the budget resolutions the opportunity to be generous by voting high ceilings. It also used the concept of the "current services budget" to shelter favored programs from budget cuts, while entitlements, to which the Budget Act gave preferred status, were not restricted until 1980. Presidents submitted budgets that were less realistic and based on assumptions favorable to their policies (Devins, 1990, 1001). In 1981, President Reagan used the reconciliation feature of the Budget Act to reduce entitlements and domestic spending.[10] After that incident, however, Congress paid little heed to Reagan's budgets, which were greeted as "dead on arrival." Following passage of the Budget Act, Congress increasingly ignored the deadlines and passed major appropriations bills in omnibus continuing resolutions, which also contained extensive legislative provisions. The result of the 1974 Budget Act has been a confused process in which it is difficult to hold either presidents or Congress accountable (Fisher, 1987, 206).

During the 1980s, federal budget deficits soared to unprecedented levels, although Schick attributes the budget crisis to three factors: a bias toward growth resulting from the indexation of benefits, tax expenditures, and credit assistance; mandatory spending, including entitlements and interest; and public and official unwillingness to raise taxes to match the spending increases (Schick, 1990, Chaps. 2–5). By the end of 1985, it had become apparent that the congressional budget process could not handle massive deficits. Without holding committee hearings or debate in the House, Congress passed the Balanced and Deficit Reduction Act of 1985 (known as Gramm-Rudman-Hollings, or GRH). GRH established a series of deficit reduction targets over a five-year period ending in 1991. If in any year the deficit did not come within $10 billion of the target, an automatic spending reduction would be imposed and the funds would be "sequestered" in the Treasury.[11]

In passing GRH, Congress apparently assumed that President Reagan was so opposed to reductions in defense spending that he would accept increased taxes to avoid a sequester. In signing the bill, the president apparently assumed that Congress would prefer to cut domestic spending before it would accept a sequester. Both were wrong, and the fiscal standoff continued. When GRH threatened to cause pain, its targets were revised and moved ahead in time. The October 1990 budget summit between President Bush and congressional leaders transformed GRH by adopting new rules involving appropriations caps and pay-as-you-go restrictions on entitlements. However, it then exempted the consequences of "technical adjustments," such as mistakes in revenue estimates, and held itself (and the president) "harmless" for developments beyond its control, such as the costs of the Persian Gulf war and the savings and loan bailout (Hager, 1991, 232–37). The effect of the changes enacted in the 1990 budget deal has been to shift the focus of the budget process, as established in GRH, from deficit reduction "to limiting spending and guaranteeing that the baseline level of revenues is collected" (Collender, 1991, 19).

Assessments of GRH are strongly negative but vary somewhat in content. Wildavsky charges Congress with abdicating its most fundamental power—that of controlling the purse strings—and replacing it with a statutory formula. This symbolizes its failure to make hard choices (1988, 236). He does not place any of the blame on the executive. Devins sees GRH as a combination of reliance on an automatic mechanism and a delegation of responsibility to the president (1990, 1003). Schick notes that while there have been some reductions in the deficit, GRH has primarily served both Congress and the president as "a means of hiding the deficit and running away from responsibility for it" (1990, 205). Haas argues that GRH reveals that "no law can force America's leaders to do what they don't want to do" (1990, 2194). Like Schick, he feels that the law has encouraged the practice of deceit in government.

The attempts by Congress since 1974 to tilt the balance in fiscal policy in its direction have succeeded, but at the cost of diminished presidential responsibility. Impoundments are a dead letter, omnibus spending bills have diluted the impact of the presidential veto, and the president's budget has been transformed from "an authoritative policy into a legislative gambit" (Schick, 1990, 214). Neither the president nor Congress offers realistic economic forecasts based on honest assumptions. Congress has evaded its responsibilities by circumventing some of the procedures that it has established to protect itself from presidential aggrandizement and from its own weaknesses. Nevertheless, efforts should be made to restore presidential budget clout. Schick suggests some—emphasis on spending authority as well as outlays, multiyear budgeting, budgeting for entitlements, tighter rules for the use of baselines, and better interbranch cooperation—but argues that "nonbudgetary factors, such as erosion of confidence in the government, political and policy frictions between the two branches, and overloading the government" are primarily responsible for the crisis in budgeting (1990, 219–23).

To summarize, congressional efforts following Vietnam and Watergate to strengthen the institutional accountability of the president in the critical areas of the war power, covert operations, and fiscal policy have not filled the expectations held for them. A substantial majority of commentators conclude that measures such as the War Powers Resolution, the Hughes-Ryan Act of 1974, the Intelligence Oversight Act of 1980, the 1974 Budget Act, and the Gramm-Rudman-Hollings Act of 1985 have been failures and call for new legislation to curb presidential discretion. In particular, they question the effectiveness of framework statutes, such as the WPR and GRH.[12] Such devices attempt to subject presidents to congressional will while at the same time allowing legislators to avoid making hard choices. Other analysts, however, argue that the system of institutional constraints on the president has worked as well as can be expected and that there is no way to provide by law safeguards against stubborn presidents bent on pursuing wrong-headed policies.

POLITICAL ACCOUNTABILITY

Even if one concedes, for the sake of argument, that institutional accountability has failed, has political accountability been satisfactory? After all, it is Madison's "primary check" on government. Here as well, assessments are mixed.

One of the most striking developments in twentieth-century U.S. politics has been the establishment of a direct link between presidents and the people. This linkage, which has resulted primarily from extended and extensive presidential nomination and election campaigns, serves as the basis on which modern presidents claim a mandate to govern the country. However tenuous the assertion of a mandate may be, the president is uniquely able to claim it as the only representative of the entire nation. The price that the president pays for the mandate is often very steep—exaggerated expectations of performance that lead him to make ever-increasing claims that he is acting in the name and on the authority of the people. It is they who will determine, in their approval ratings and ultimately, at the next election, the appropriateness of his policy goals and the legitimacy of his methods of achieving them. Consequently, Congress and the federal courts had best tread lightly before moving to overturn the president's judgment and actions.

This plebiscitary presidency places enormous popular demands and expectations on the president. Presidents have had to develop new strategies to cope with the pressures of the office. These have included "going public" (Kernell, 1986), the "administrative presidency" (Nathan, 1983), and "centralization" of power in the presidency and "politicization" of the White House (Moe, 1985). Use of these strategies intensified under Reagan (Pika and Thomas, 1990). Such developments may appear necessary given the difficult contexts in which modern presidents find themselves, but they raise serious questions about the system of accountability established in the Constitution. What checks remain, for example, on the exercise of presidential power if Congress is ignored or bypassed? The answer, as phrased by Dahl, is that the presidency has become "an office that is the very embodiment of the kind of executive the Framers, so far as we can discern their intentions, strove to avoid" (Dahl, 1990, 369).

Moreover, the decline of institutional restraints (Elkin, 1991) has not been balanced by the rise of effective political restraints, such as party government (Lowi, 1985, 157). Indeed, the party responsibiiity model seems to have lost the limited effectiveness that it once had in U.S. politics (Sundquist, 1988–89). The plebiscitary presidency has also weakened political accountability. Even though the presidency and presidential elections have been increasingly democratized, democracy has not been strengthened, as deliberation and understanding of public issues have suffered (Dahl, 1990, 370–71).

Not all reaction to the plebiscitary presidency is negative. Rockman cogently argues that presidential accountability stems ultimately from popular sovereignty (1986, 152–54). When presidents have a mandate, things get done; when they do not (which is most of the time), stalemate results. In either case, politics are salient. The president's ability to bargain depends on his popular support, and his opportunities to lead derive from the political context in which he must operate. The plebiscitary presidency is a reality that is not necessarily good or bad. It can neither guarantee wise leadership nor produce desirable policy outcomes. As Rockman sees it, we might as well accept it for what it is: a fairly effective but limited form of democratic accountability that currently appears quite acceptable to the American people.

Somewhat similarly, Jones (1991) argues that we should not worry unduly about the policy stalemate that has resulted from the condition of divided government that has prevailed for much of the time since 1955. We need to recognize that party government is a will-o'-the-wisp and be more realistic by adopting a "diffused responsibility perspective by which separated institutions compete for power, seeking to take credit and avoid blame" (p. 156). The president's role is to certify the agenda to Congress, which then sets priorities. Meanwhile, the two branches hold on to their respective institutions, neither being willing to take the risks to capture the other one (p. 165). Positive accomplishments will require both "bipartisan and inter-institutional cooperation."

Whether the means of holding presidents politically accountable are satisfactory depends, then, on the eye of the beholder. From one perspective, U.S. politics has degenerated into a form of populistic democracy dominated by an elected ruler whose effectiveness depends on his ability to satisfy the masses of voters. Under such conditions, constitutional restraints have largely gone by the boards and political parties do little to mediate the relationship between the president and his people. Alternatively, the modern plebiscitary presidency can be regarded as democratic accountability in action. That governmental stalemate results from the decisions of the electorate and is the usual state of affairs is not particularly worrisome. One suspects that the critics of the plebiscitary presidency have somewhat overstated their case, while those who seek to reassure us of its benign consequences are a bit too complacent.

THE BUSH PRESIDENCY AND ACCOUNTABILITY

Three years into the Bush presidency, no major issues affecting presidential accountability, such as Watergate or Iran-Contra have arisen. However, several developments have had significance for both institutional and political accountability.

The most important of these in the area of institutional accountability involve war powers, the budget process, and Bush's use of the veto. Bush has maintained the posture that his predecessors established regarding the WPR, most notably in the crucial cases of Panama and the Persian Gulf war. Consultation with Congress has been limited to perfunctory notification, great care has been taken to avoid activating the 60-day time clock, and the president has acknowledged the existence of the WPR but refused to accept its constitutionality. The importance of the WPR was solidified when Bush requested and received congressional authorization to initiate military action against Iraq. However, neither the executive nor Congress has been willing to submit its interpretation of the WPR to judicial review.

Changes in the budget process that were made in the October 1990 budget summit agreement between the Bush administration and congressional leaders have had mixed effects on accountability. On the one hand, the agreement raised the GRH deficit maximums and provided that the maximums may be revised at any time (previously, they have been fixed) to reflect changes in the economic forecast in the budget message and technical changes. The agreement also relieved both the president and Congress of responsibility for any increases in the deficit due to events beyond their control (Collender, 1991, 20–26). In fiscal 1991, these included the costs of the Persian Gulf war, increased costs of the savings and loan bailout, and a recession. This has provided greater adaptability to changing conditions but reduced pressures for controlling the deficit. On the other hand, the imposition of pay-as-you-go restrictions on revenues and mandatory spending programs has reduced the flexibility of fiscal policy and enhanced budgetary restraints.[13] In late 1991, as economic conditions deteriorated, pressures mounted on the president and congressional leaders to void or modify the summit agreement to permit the enactment of measures to counter the recession. In negotiating the agreement, neither the administration nor Congress appears to have anticipated that a severe recession was imminent. The new budget process rules that they thought would ease the Gramm-Rudman-Hollings constraints tightened them instead. The fiscal stalemate that has paralyzed the government since 1982 continues and cannot be broken without a joint effort by the president and Congress. Until now, neither has been willing to sacrifice its political and institutional interests to do so. Both are responsible, but neither has been held accountable.

Stalemate also characterizes relations between Bush and Congress with respect to domestic policy. In the absence of a positive domestic legislative program on the part of the administration, congressional Democrats seized the initiative and offered proposals of their own, almost all of which Bush vetoed. Congress was unable to override any of the twenty-four vetoes Bush cast during his first three years in office. More than any modern president, Bush has used the veto to work his will with Congress. Depending on one's political orientation, this stalemate can be viewed either as an example of institutional accountability working as the framers of the Constitution intended or as a deadlock under which it is impossible to hold anyone accountable.

If the effectiveness of institutional accountability during the Bush administration appears debatable, has political accountability functioned more satisfactorily? Apparently, it has. Bush was elected to preserve the gains of the "Reagan Revolution." For the first two and one-half years, he did so. No major domestic legislation was enacted, judicious use of military force strengthened national security, significant progress was made toward nuclear disarmament, and the "evil empire" that was international communism based in the Soviet Union collapsed. Bush provided the nation with "competent Reaganism" (Deibel, 1991, 3). His approval ratings reflect this performance. From an initial low of 51 percent, they rose to 70 percent by June 1989 and reached 80 percent in January 1990. Although they dropped to 54 percent in October and November 1990, in reaction to his battle with Congress over the 1991 budget and concerns about prospective military action in the Persian Gulf, they reached a historic high of 89 percent following the decisive victory in the Gulf War. After declining slightly during the summer of 1991, they fell sharply to 47 percent late in the year as the recession worsened.

The drop in his approval ratings induced Bush to try to find a way to stimulate the economy and to meet mounting criticism over the lack of a domestic policy. With the approach of his re-election campaign, he turned the focus of his attention from foreign policy, where it had been concentrated since he took office, to economic and domestic policy. Political accountability, through the polls and an impending election, appeared to be working after a fashion. Although the polls gave precise measurements of Bush's popular support, his administration's policy responses were tentative and their prospective impact on immediate problems and conditions was uncertain and distant. It was unlikely that policies adopted in early 1992 could take effect in time to influence the outcome of the election.

CONCLUSION

This review suggests that both institutional and political means of ensuring presidential accountability are flawed and have substantial limitations, but that both are necessary. At the same time, it shows that there is a conflict between the values that underlie each system of accountability. On the one hand, it appears that to the extent that the president is subjected to strict constraints by Congress and the courts, his ability to act in response to popular opinion and his election mandate (when he can lay claim to one) is diminished. On the other hand, strategies to free the president from institutional restraints so that he can more effectively respond to the public and unrestrained presidential pursuit of policies perceived to satisfy popular demand seem to render constitutional checks and balances ineffectual.

The U.S. political system faces two challenges with respect to presidential accountability. The first is to resolve the tension between institutional and political accountability. The defects and limitations of each make this task imperative. Is it really the case that every initiative to establish cooperation between the president and Congress necessarily diminishes the former's capacity to respond to the people? Congress is an elective legislature, and it, too, has responsibilities to the public. It has constitutional prerogatives, as does the president. Political considerations must always be evaluated within the framework of the Constitution, which requires "balanced institutional participation and power sharing" (Koh, 1990, 153). Surely, implementation of Madison's design in *Federalist No. 51* is not beyond our capabilities (Hamilton, Madison, and Jay).

The developments surveyed above suggest that all is not lost with respect to the interbranch comity required for institutional accountability to be effective. By and large, recent presidents have been sensitive to the authority of Congress over national security and its power of the purse. The WPR is a constraint over presidential deployment of the armed forces. Even though the NSC staff did run amok while seeking to serve a disengaged president, Congress, a special counsel, and the courts applied *a posteriori* sanctions, and the national security policy process appears to have been corrected. As for the budget crisis, neither Republican presidents, Democratic majorities in Congress, nor the American people appear disposed to end it any time soon. While this may have grave long-range consequences for the country, constitutional and statutory devices are not likely to bring an end to the large structural deficits that have plagued the economy since 1982. That can only happen if the public lets its leaders know that it will support the painful steps necessary to do so. Blaming Congress for a lack of will and the president for the lack of leadership ignores the dependence of both on the popular mood. When that mood shifts, and it could do so with courageous bipartisan leadership, the system of political accountability will produce an end to the fiscal stalemate that has paralyzed the government.

The second challenge appears less daunting but may be more difficult to meet. It entails adjusting expectations held for both the institutional and political systems of accountability while continuing to adapt them to changing political conditions. Current expectations held for both systems are unrealistic. It is not possible to design institutional constraints that will coerce sound judgment by presidents, or members of Congress, for that matter. Neither should we expect presidents to meet all of the demands made on them by the public or hold them solely accountable for the condition of the nation. Recognition of human fallibility should be factored into the values undergirding each system of accountability.

At the same time, there are good reasons for continuing to examine ways to improve both systems. Constitutional amendments, such as those requiring a balanced budget or authorizing an item veto, need to be considered and debated if for no other reason than to increase awareness of the defects of existing arrangements. And statutory improvements in the WPR, the Independent Counsel Act, the 1974 Budget Act, and GRH deserve serious study and possible enactment. On the political side, continued modification of the presidential nomination system seems certain as the parties search for a more satisfactory balance between democracy and elite leadership. The perennial quest for campaign finance laws that reduce the influence of special interests and strengthen the responsiveness of elected officials exemplify continuing efforts to strengthen accountability.

Presidential accountability after the Reagan era continues to pose a problem for U.S. politics. The effectiveness of some of the institutional devices adopted in the aftermath of Vietnam and Watergate have been tested and found lacking, although not without value. Few, if any, of them are likely to be discarded, and perfecting amendments or some sort may well be enacted. Although events since 1974 have given rise to doubts about the effectiveness of the separation-of-powers system and its accompanying checks and balances, there is no sign of a strong movement to revise the Constitution or to add structural amendments. More serious questions have been raised regarding the consequences of a plebiscitary presidency for the accountability of the incumbent. Here again, no sweeping reforms appear imminent. Most of us realize the unlikelihood of such developments, but we continue to search for possible improvements.

NOTES

1. The author of the most extensive study of the Iran-Contra affair insists that the correct term is "affairs," as there were two different lines of policy being pursued (Draper, 1991, 3). Moreover, the attempt to provide support to the opponents of

Nicaragua's revolutionary Sandinista regime—the Contras—preceded the effort to free U.S. hostages in Lebanon by selling arms to the fundamentalist Islamic regime in Iran. The two affairs came together rather late in the game, when Lt. Col. Oliver North, a member of the National Security Council staff who was managing each undertaking, decided to divert profits from the Iranian arms sales to support the Contras. However, I will use conventional terminology and refer to a single affair, as both were operated as projects of the NSC staff and managed by North.

2. The most comprehensive discussion of presidential accountability is Rockman's (1986). Starting with the sample definition of "being answerable," he explores the legal, institutional, political, and moral sources of accountability and its a priori and a posteriori forms. The problem of accountability is "how to give adequate discretion to be able effectively to carry out responsibilities while providing some means to check clearly unacceptable conduct" (Rockman, 1986, 152).

3. P.L. 93–148. This summary of the provisions of the resolution follows that in my 1978 article (Thomas, 420).

4. Congress did trigger the 60-day-clock in 1983, in legislation involving the multinational force in Lebanon, but at the same time it authorized U.S. participation in the force for eighteen months. This was done after an agreement was reached with the White House (Katzmann, 1990, 66).

5. See, for example, Ely (1988), Franck (1989), Glennon (1990), Hillebrecht (1990), and Katzmann (1990).

6. The most important cases are *Lowry v. Reagan*, 676 F. Supp. 333 (D.D.C. 1987) and *Dellums v. Bush*, 752 F. Supp. 1141 (D.D.C. 1990). In *Lowry*, the court rejected the request of 110 members of Congress that it issue a declaration that President Reagan was required to file reports under the WPR concerning two incidents in the Persian Gulf. In July 1987, a reflagged Kuwaiti tanker sailing with a U.S. naval escort struck a mine, and in September of that year, the Navy attacked an Iranian minelayer. The court held that it could not act because Congress had not acted on the issue (Lavy, 1988, 851). In *Dellums*, the court rejected the request of forty-five Democratic members of Congress that it enjoin President Bush from conducting military operations in the Persian Gulf without a declaration of war by Congress. The court held that the issue was not ripe for decision since a majority of Congress had not sought relief and the executive had not committed itself to a course of action that made war imminent (Clark, 1991, 676–79). Because a constitutional impasse had not been reached, judicial intervention was inappropriate. However, the Dellums court did assert its willingness to make a decision should the two branches arrive at one (Clark, 1991, 683).

7. According to Draper, "Bush brought trouble on himself by denying too much about what he knew, if not about what he did" (1991, 573). Draper notes that according to Poindexter's testimony before the congressional investigation, Bush was usually present at the national security adviser's daily briefings of the president.

8. In July 1991, Alan Fiers, who directed the CIA's covert operations in Latin America, pleaded guilty to charges initiated by Walsh of lying to Congress about the diversion of funds from the Iran arms sales to the Contras. Fiers' admissions raised doubts about the accuracy of the testimony in the 1987 investigation of his CIA superior, Claire George, and that of Elliott Abrams, Assistant Secretary of State for Inter-American Affairs. In addition, it caused the Senate Intelligence Committee to

delay hearings on Bush's nomination of Robert Gates, who was deputy director of the CIA in 1985–86, to direct the intelligence agency (Layco, 1991).

9. A senior Reagan administration official, who served in various posts from 1981 until 1989, told me in a conversation in August 1987 that, in his opinion, Iran-Contra "never would have happened with Jim Baker in the White House."

10. Reconciliation entails passage of an omnibus bill directing tax-writing and appropriations committees to make budgetary savings that will preserve the aggregate spending limit set in the budget resolution.

11. Initially, the Comptroller General was to determine if the targets had not been met. Upon notification by the Comptroller General, the president must issue the sequestration order. In 1986, the Supreme Court, in *Bowsher v. Synar* (478 U.S. 714), ruled that section of the statute invalid as a violation of the separation of powers. The court reasoned that because the Comptroller General is a legislative officer and not subject to removal by the president, he cannot perform what is an executive function. Congress subsequently authorized the director of the Office of Management and Budget to determine when the automatic reductions are required.

12. For a positive view of framework statutes, see Harold Hongju Koh, *The National Security Constitution: Sharing Power After the Iran-Contra Affair* (New Haven: Yale University Press, 1990), pp. 157–61, 206–7, 227–28.

13. Pay-as-you-go requires that increases in mandatory spending, primarily entitlements, be funded by revenue increases or reductions in other entitlements and that tax cuts be offset by corresponding tax increases or by reductions in entitlements.

REFERENCES

Biskupic, Joan. 1991. "Constitutional Questions Remain." *Congressional Quarterly Weekly Report* (January 12): 70.

Cannon, Lou. 1991. *President Reagan: The Role of a Lifetime*. New York: Simon & Schuster.

Clark, Scott D. 1991. "Questioning the Constitutional Distribution of War Powers in the Wake of the Iraqi Crisis and Operations Desert Shield/Storm." *Southern Illinois University Law Journal* 15:669–84.

Cohen, Richard E. 1989. "Marching Through the War Powers Act." *National Journal* (December 30): 3120.

Cohen, William S., and George J. Mitchell. 1988. *Men of Zeal: A Candid Inside Story of the Iran-Contra Hearings*. New York: Viking.

Collender, Stanley E. 1991. *The Guide to the Federal Budget: Fiscal 1992*, 10th edn. Washington: Urban Institute.

Collier, Ellen C. 1991. "War Powers Resolution: Presidential Compliance." *Congressional Research Service Issue Brief IB81050, May 24, 1991*. Washington: Congressional Research Service.

Corwin, Edward S. 1957. *The President: Office and Powers*, 4th edn. New York: New York University Press.

Crabb, Cecil V., and Kevin V. Mulcahy. 1991. *American National Security: A Presidential Perspective*. Pacific Grove, Calif.: Brooks/Cole.

Dahl, Robert A. 1990. "Myth of the Presidential Mandate." *Political Science Quarterly* 105: 355–72.

Damrosch, Lori Fisler. 1989. "Covert Operations." *The American Journal of International Law* 83: 795–805.

Deibel, Terry L. 1991. "Bush's Foreign Policy: Mastery and Inaction." *Foreign Policy* 84:3–23.

Devins, Neal. 1990. "Budget Reform and the Balance of Powers." *William and Mary Law Review* 31: 993–1020.

Doherty, Carroll, J. 1991. "Bush Is Given Authorization to Use Force Against Iraq." *Congressional Quarterly Weekly Report* (January 12): 65–70.

Draper, Theodore. 1991. *A Very Thin Line: The Iran-Contra Affairs.* New York: Hill & Wang.

Elkin, Steven L. 1991. "Contempt of Congress: The Iran-Contra Affair and the American Constitution." *Congress and the Presidency* 18:1–16.

Ely, John Hart. 1988. "Suppose Congress Wanted a War Powers Act that Worked." *Columbia Law Review* 88:1379–1421.

Fisher, Louis. 1987. *The Politics of Shared Power: Congress and the Executive,* 2nd edn. Washington: Congressional Quarterly Press.

———. 1985. *Constitutional Conflicts Between Congress and the President.* Princeton, N.J.: Princeton University Press.

Franck, Thomas M. 1989. "Rethinking War Powers: By Law or by 'Thaumaturgic Invocation?' " *The American Journal of International Law* 83:766–77.

Glennon, Michael J. 1990. *Constitutional Diplomacy.* Princeton, N.J.: Princeton University Press.

Haas, Lawrence J. 1990. "Pleading Poverty." *National Journal* (September 15): 2192–96.

Hager, George. 1991. "New Rules on Taxes, Spending May Mean Budget Standoff." *Congressional Quarterly Weekly Report* (January 26): 232–37.

Hamilton, Alexander, James Madison, and John Jay. 1960. *The Federalist Papers.* Edited by Clinton Rossiter. New York: Popular Library.

Hardin, Charles M. 1974. *Presidential Power and Accountability.* Chicago: University of Chicago Press.

Hillebrecht, John M. 1990. "Ensuring Affirmative Congressional Control Over the Use of Force: Two Proposals for Collective Decision Making." *Stanford Journal of International Law* 26: 509–48.

Jones, Charles O. 1991. "The Diffusion of Responsibility: An Alternative Perspective for National Policy Politics in the U.S." *Governance* 4:150–67.

Katzmann, Robert A. 1990. "War Powers: Toward a New Accommodation." In *A Question of Balance: The President, the Congress, and Foreign Policy.* Edited by Thomas E. Mann. Washington: Brookings Institution.

Kernell, Samuel. 1986. *Going Public: New Strategies of Presidential Leadership.* Washington: Congressional Quarterly Press.

Koh, Harold Hongju. 1990. *The National Security Constitution: Sharing Power After the Iran-Contra Affair.* New Haven, Conn.: Yale University Press.

———. 1988. "Why the President (Almost) Always Wins in Foreign Affairs: Lessons of the Iran-Contra Affair." *Yale Law Journal* 97: 1255–1342.

Lavy, Glen. 1988. "Constitutional Law: Judicial Restraint and the Law Powers Resolution—*Lowry v. Reagan,* 676 F. Supp. 333 (D.D.C. 1987)." *Harvard Journal of Law and Public Policy* 11:849–54.

Layco, Richard. 1991. "The Cover-Up Begins to Crack." *Time* (July 22): 14–16.

Lowi, Theodore J. 1985. *The Personal President: Power Invested Promise Unfulfilled.* Ithaca, N.Y.: Cornell University Press.

Malbin, Michael J. 1989. "Legislative-Executive Lessons From the Iran-Contra Affair." In *Congress Reconsidered*, 4th edn. Edited by Lawrence C. Dodd and Bruce I. Oppenheimer. Washington: Congressional Quarterly Press.

Mayer, Jane, and Doyle McManus. 1988. *Landslide: The Unmaking of the President 1984–1988.* Boston: Houghton Mifflin.

Moe, Terry M. 1985. "The Politicized Presidency." In *The New Direction in American Politics*. Edited by John E. Chubb and Paul E. Peterson. Washington: Brookings Institution.

Nathan, Richard P. 1983. *The Administrative Presidency.* New York: Wiley.

Neustadt, Richard E. 1990. *Presidential Power and the Modern Presidents: The Politics of Leadership from Roosevelt to Reagan.* New York: Free Press.

Pika, Joseph A., and Norman C. Thomas. 1990. "The President as Institution Builder: The Reagan Case." *Governance* 3: 438–56.

Pious, Richard M. 1979. *The American Presidency.* New York: Basic Books.

Prober, Joshua Lee. 1990. "Congress, the War Powers Resolution, and the Secret Political Life of 'a Dead Letter.' " *Journal of Law and Politics* 7: 177–229.

Rockman, Bert A. 1986. "The Modern Presidency and Theories of Accountability: Old Wine *and* Old Bottles." *Congress and the Presidency* 13:135–56.

Schick, Allen. 1990. *The Capacity to Budget.* Washington: Urban Institute Press.

Seligman, Lester G., and Cary R. Covington. 1989. *The Coalitional Presidency.* Chicago: Dorsey Press.

Shafritz, Jay M. 1988. *The Dorsey Dictionary of American Government and Politics.* Chicago: Dorsey Press.

Sorensen, Theodore R. 1975. *Watchmen in the Night: Presidential Accountability after Watergate.* Cambridge, Mass.: MIT Press.

Stith, Kate. 1988. "Congress' Power of the Purse." *Yale Law Journal* 97: 1343–96.

Sundquist, James L. 1988–89. "The New Era of Coalition Government in the United States." *Political Science Quarterly* 103: 613–36.

———. 1981. *The Decline and Resurgence of Congress.* Washington: Brookings Institution.

Thomas, Norman C. 1978. "Presidential Accountability Since Watergate." *Presidential Studies Quarterly* 8: 417–34.

Tower, John, Edmund Muskie, and Brent Scowcroft. 1987. *The Tower Commission Report.* New York: Bantam Books and Times Books.

Treverton, Gregory F. 1990. "Intelligence: Welcome to the American Government." In *A Question of Balance: The President, the Congress, and Foreign Policy*. Edited by Thomas E. Mann. Washington: Brookings Institution.

Wildavsky, Aaron. 1988. *The New Politics of the Budgetary Process.* Glenview, Ill.: Scott Foresman.

Conclusion

George Bush's years in office have revealed the opportunities and risks of presidential leadership in a time of dramatic changes. The president, fascinated by and caught up in the swirl of events surrounding the end of the Cold War and the collapse of Soviet-style communism, has seen the highs and lows of officeholding in a republic. At the close of the Persian Gulf war, his performance in office won the approval of an unprecedented 91 percent of the American people. He was hailed as a coalition-builder and resolute statesman both at home and abroad. Yet by the time the 1992 presidential election campaign began in earnest, he faced a serious challenge from within his own party and less than half of the public approved of his handling of his job. The man who once seemed to stand astride the globe had to beg for votes in New Hampshire.

What has Bush's conduct of the presidency shown us about leadership and the role of the chief executive in U.S. politics? The preceding chapters have examined these issues from a variety of perspectives, but we can discern certain general lessons. First, a president's putative leadership is closely related to the context in which he operates. In many ways, Bush had the qualities necessary for facing a time of rapid international change: He was well-versed in the mechanics and methods of diplomacy; he was not given to rashness in response to turmoil; and he had a sense of when to bend and when to stand firm. Yet this skillful player of the game of world affairs took far too long to adapt to changing domestic circumstances and seemed at times either ignorant of or isolated from the vicissitudes of the economy and national politics. Perhaps the president should have remembered the fate of Winston Churchill at the end of World War II, when a grateful British people turned the Tories out of office and brought in a Labor government in Churchill's very moment of triumph. Britain was ready to put war behind it; America in late 1991 and 1992 was ready to deal with problems at home.

Second, presidential leadership is as much response as initiative. Some students of leadership have tended to denigrate actions that they regard as mere reactions to changing events. Yet leadership is as much what a leader makes of the problems and opportunities he is presented as it is setting out to mold new situations. Franklin Roosevelt and Abraham Lincoln in their times responded to situations not of their own making. It was in the quality of their responses that these men won their reputations for leadership. However Bush's conduct of the presidency is ultimately judged, it cannot be dismissed as merely reactive. Bush took steps to deal with the circumstances he found, and assessments of his leadership or lack of it must evaluate the quality of his response to the collapse of the Soviet empire; to the problems of drugs and education; to the continuing issue of civil rights; to the state of his party and his coalition; to the Iraqi invasion of Kuwait; to the Democratic Congress; to the unraveling of the Soviet Union; to the sagging economy; to the challenge of declining U.S. competitiveness; and to a host of other problems. There is no simple dichotomy of initiative and reaction.

Third, just as each solution creates its own problems, so do each president's leadership efforts shape his own future environment and/or that of his successors. The conduct of Bush's presidency has left a legacy for a second term. If re-elected, the president will have to devote more time and energy to domestic matters, unless he decides to forget about his own public standing or the chances of a Republican victory in 1996. Next, he will have to provide some specificity to his concept of a "new world order," lest his internationalism be repudiated by resurgent isolationism in the nation. Furthermore, the president will have to consider how his actions will influence his party's chances for winning the White House again in 1996. He will have to pay attention to his relations with conservatives, with the Democratic Congress, and with state and local leaders; he will need to articulate a sense of direction for national policy, now that the Reagan-era economic expansion is over and world politics are in flux; and he must be attentive to the extent to which his policy choices in a second term will constrain a Republican nominee in the next election.

Perhaps more important is the legacy of Bush's tenure for future presidents. He has demonstrated that presidential dominance of foreign policy is not limited to Cold War conditions. His handling of the Persian Gulf crisis, especially in maneuvering Congress to support his plans with minimal legislative input, will serve as a precedent for future chief executives seeking to shape U.S. policy in the face of congressional resistance.

In domestic affairs, the president's limited agenda and relative inaction (until 1992) will put pressure on future incumbents to present a more balanced program. Concentrating too much on the domestic side or foreign side of government carries enormous risk: the president is in effect betting that all will remain well in the area he chooses to de-emphasize.

Beyond the substance of policy, there is leadership style. Bush has shown the adaptability of television for different modes of presidential communication. Whether in the Reagan/Carter/Nixon-style set speech, Bush's sound-bite-oriented news conferences, or some other approach, chief executives can find a way to use the now-universal medium of television to communicate their message. In retrospect, one wonders whether Jimmy Carter might have been more successful in his public communications if he had made fewer formal television addresses and conducted more Bush-style news conferences.

Another legacy that Bush will leave for his successors is a presidential office firmly ensconced in a post-modern phase of its institutional evolution. By his use of prerogative power (in foreign affairs, the veto, budget summits, and White House control over administrative rule-making), his approach to Congress, his use of appointments to advance his goals, his "MTV" style of public politics, and his determination to shape policy (whether by aggressive action or somewhat self-conscious inaction), this president has confirmed that the chief executive in the late twentieth century is different from the position that Richard Neustadt examined at mid-century. Bush's successors, of whatever party or ideology, will inherit an office that bears the marks of change over the past three decades.

Many of the preceding chapters have emphasized that Bush has given his own "twist" to his handling of the various aspects of his job—in his style of public rhetoric and communication, in his hierarchical approach to Congress, in his approach to various areas of policy, and in the tone he has attempted to set for U.S. government. This insight reveals the final lesson we can discern from our examination of leadership and the Bush presidency: Whatever his supporters and critics conclude about his performance, Bush has attempted to exercise presidential leadership *as he understands it*. This fact makes assessments of his leadership efforts all the more complex. In evaluating leadership, we noted in our introduction the need to consider both influence and ends. Now we must also add the president's own understanding of what leadership means.

Within his own view of his responsibilities and goals, Bush has been quite influential. As the preceding chapters reveal, that influence at times has been achieved through aggressive action (e.g., the Persian Gulf crisis), while in other areas (drugs and education, relations with the career bureaucracy), it has been through setting a tone. Another tactic, used especially with regard to Congress, has been for the president to enter battles only when he believed he could win. In areas in which Bush has not chosen to seek influence (e.g., federalism), there is a case to be made that "inaction and drift" (to use John Winkle's words) are the result of a conscious choice. Just as Camus observed that in not choosing, one makes a choice, so in presidential inaction there can be direction.

Even if Bush has been influential in the ways he has wanted to be, what about the ends and means of his influence? As the preceding chapters illustrate, the answer is a complex one. In the near term, it appears that the president has taken important steps to adapt U.S. foreign policy and the international system to a post-Cold War order. The work in this regard, however, is certainly unfinished and not without its difficulties. On the domestic side, the president has offered less leadership than the nation needed. But there is certainly no consensus on whether (as critics charge) he has abandoned domestic affairs or (as supporters argue) provided a period of consolidation after the changes of the Reagan era.

These arguments will not be settled here. Just as we cannot reduce our evaluations of chief executives to summary judgments of greatness, near-greatness, or whatever, so we cannot "paper over" disagreements about the best direction for national policy. The divergent views expressed in this book only suggest the array of conclusions that will be reached about George Bush as leader. Our work will not end the debate. We hope only that it will inform it.

Bibliography

Editor's Note: Because of the wide array of sources cited throughout the chapters of this book, we have selected a relatively short list of the most important ones for inclusion in this bibliography. What follows is a starting point for exploration of leadership and the Bush presidency. Individual chapter references point the way to further study.

Barilleaux, Ryan J. 1988. *The Post-Modern Presidency*. New York: Praeger.

Bush, George, with Victor Gold. 1987. *Looking Forward*. New York: Doubleday.

Campbell, Colin, and Bert Rockman, eds. 1991. *The Bush Presidency: First Appraisals*. Chatham, N.J.: Chatham House.

Ceasar, James, Glenn Thurow, Jeffrey Tulis, and J. Bessette. 1981. "The Rise of the Rhetorical Presidency." *Presidential Studies Quarterly* 11 (Spring): 233–51.

Edwards, George C., and Stephen J. Wayne. 1990. *Presidential Leadership*, rev. edn. New York: St. Martin's Press.

Greenstein, Fred. 1988. *Leadership and the Modern Presidency*. Cambridge, Mass.: Harvard University Press.

Hart, Roderick. 1987. *The Sound of Leadership: Presidential Communication in the Modern Age*. Chicago: University of Chicago Press.

Kellerman, Barbara. 1986. *Political Leadership: A Source Book*. Pittsburgh, Pa.: University of Pittsburgh Press.

Kellerman, Barbara, and Ryan J. Barilleaux. 1991. *The President as World Leader*. New York: St. Martin's Press.

Neustadt, Richard. 1990. *Presidential Power and the Modern Presidents*. New York: Free Press.

Pfiffner, James P. 1990. "Establishing the Bush Presidency." *Public Administration Review* (January/February): 64–72.

Rockman, Bert. 1985. *The Leadership Question*. New York: Praeger.

Skowronek, Stephen. 1990. "Presidential Leadership in Political Time." In *The Presidency and the Political System*, 3rd edn. Edited by Michael Nelson. Washington: CQ Press, pp. 117–62.

Stuckey, Mary. 1991. *The President as Interpreter-in-Chief*. Chatham, N.J.: Chatham House.

Woodward, Bob. 1991. *The Commanders*. New York: Simon & Schuster.

Index

About the Editors
and Contributors

FREDERICK J. ANTCZAK is an associate professor and chair of the department of rhetoric at the University of Iowa in Iowa City.

RYAN J. BARILLEAUX is an associate professor of political science at Miami University, Oxford, Ohio. He is the author of *The President and Foreign Affairs*, *The Post-Modern Presidency*, *The President as World Leader* (with Barbara Kellerman), and a number of articles on U.S. government and politics in *Congress and the Presidency*, *World Affairs*, and *Presidential Studies Quarterly*.

HAROLD F. BASS, Jr. is a professor of political science at Ouachita Baptist University in Arkadelphia, Ark. He is the author of several studies on presidents and U.S. political parties and was a contributor to *Congressional Quarterly's Guide to the Presidency*.

DANIEL P. FRANKLIN is an assistant professor of political science at Georgia State University in Atlanta. He was an APSA Congressional Fellow and is the author of *Extraordinary Measures: The Exercise of Prerogative Power in the United States*.

AUGUSTUS J. JONES, Jr. is an associate professor at Miami University, Oxford, Ohio. He was a fellow at the Brookings Institution and is the author of *Affirmative Talk, Affirmative Action*.

HENRY C. KENSKI is a professor of communication and political science at the University of Arizona. He is the author of *Attack Politics: Strategy and Defense* and *Saving the Hidden Treasure: The Evolution of Ground Water Policy*.

GARY LEE MALECHA is an associate professor of political science at Weber State University in Ogden, Utah. His work is on U.S. political thought, populism, and the policy sciences.

JANET M. MARTIN is an associate professor of political science at Bowdoin College in Brunswick, Maine. She was an APSA Congressional Fellow and is the author of *Legislative Triumph*.

MATTHEW C. MOEN is an associate professor of political science at the University of Maine, Orono. A former APSA Congressional, he is the author of *The Christian Right in Congress* and *The Transformation of the Christian Right*.

KENNETH T. PALMER is a professor of political science at the University of Maine, Orono. He is co-author of *The Changing Politics of Federal Grants* and author of *Reelecting the Governor* and *Maine Politics and Government*, as well as a contributor to *Publius* and the *Journal of Politics*.

DANIEL J. REAGAN is an assistant professor of political science at Ball State University in Muncie, Ind. He has written extensively on congressional and state legislative politics.

CARMINE SCAVO is an assistant professor of political science at East Carolina University in Greenville, N.C.

ROBERT SHEPARD formerly taught at the Johns Hopkins University in Baltimore, Md. His latest book is *Nigeria, Africa, and the United States*.

MARY E. STUCKEY is an assistant professor of political science at the University of Mississippi in Oxford. She is the author of *Getting into the Game: The Pre-Presidential Rhetoric of Ronald Reagan*, *Playing the Game: The Presidential Rhetoric of Ronald Reagan*, and *The President as Interpreter-in-Chief*.

NORMAN C. THOMAS is a professor of political science at the University of Cincinnati. A former president of the Presidency Research Group, he is the author of *The Presidency in Contemporary Context* and *The Presidency and Public Policy Making* (with George C. Edwards and Steven Shull).

ROBERT J. THOMPSON is an associate professor and chair of the department of political science at East Carolina University in Greenville, N.C.

He is the author of a number of studies of British and American politics. His current research focuses on presidential time management and advising.

JOHN W. WINKLE III is a professor of political science at the University of Mississippi in Oxford. A former chairman of the department of political science, he is the author of a number of studies of the politics of U.S. federalism.